CENTER FOR MIDDLE EASTERN STUDIES
HARVARD UNIVERSITY

CENTER FOR MIDDLE EASTERN STUDIES HARVARD UNIVERSITY

REFLECTIONS ON THE PAST, VISIONS FOR THE FUTURE

EDITED BY DON BABAI

FIFTIETH ANNIVERSARY VOLUME

Center for Middle Eastern Studies, Harvard University
Cambridge, Massachusetts 02138

Photography Credits: 3567405003354 8

Courtesy of *Bangkok Post:* 65 (top right)
Courtesy of Catherine Bateson: 63 (bottom right)
Courtesy of Eva Bellin: 123 (top right), 156
Courtesy of Leonard Binder: 64 (top left photos)
Courtesy of Richard Bulliet: 64 (bottom left photos)
Courtesy of Public Affairs Office, United States Central Command (CENTCOM):
    65 (top left)
Courtesy of Sarah Chayes: 65 (bottom left photos)
CMES Archives: xii (bottom right),13, 20, 27, 28, 29, 50 (top left), 51 (top), 74, 86, 87,
    88, 93 (bottom)
Harvard News Office: xii (bottom left), 16, 103
Harvard University Archives: xii (bottom left center, bottom right center), 1 (top right),
    6, 13, 20
Richard Johnson: 1 (bottom left), 31, 34, 41, 50 (bottom center), 51 (top right), 53,
    56, 76, 93 (center), 110, 116, 122–123 (background), 122 (top row, bottom left,
    bottom center left and bottom right), 123 (top row, bottom left, bottom center),
    124, 135, 139, 147, 152, 160, 164, 174, 181, 186
Courtesy of Salmaan Keshavjee: 111, 123 (bottom right), 190
Courtesy of Philip Khoury: 64 (top right photos)
Courtesy of Habib Ladjevardi: 51 (bottom right), 100
Courtesy of David Mack: 63 (top photos)
Courtesy of Surin Pitsuwan: 65 (top right center)
Ted Polumbaum (1965), courtesy of *Saudi Aramco World:* xii (all four photos in top
    row), xii–1 (background), 1 (top left), 4, 5, 7, 9, 11, 14, 63 (bottom left)
Courtesy of Eve Troutt Powell: 64 (bottom right photos)
Jonathan Ramljak: cover, 1 (bottom right), 42, 50 (top center, bottom right), 50–51
    (background), 51 (bottom left), 81, 93 (top), 99, 113, 115, 117, 122 (bottom
    center right), 168
Courtesy of Said Saffari: 65 (bottom right photos)

Book design and production: Christine Reynolds/Reynolds Design and Management,
    Waltham, Massachusetts
Scanning: Harvard Printing and Publications, Cambridge, Massachusetts
Printer: Recyled Papers, Inc., Boston, Massachusetts

To the alumni and friends of the Center

CONTENTS

PREFACE

N o organization—certainly not one as creative as Harvard . . . —should go more than a generation without reassessment and renewal." So declared Lawrence B. Summers in his address at the University's 352nd Commencement Day on June 6, 2003. Harvard's President was referring to some of the reasons behind the University's plans for the first major overhaul of its under-graduate curriculum in thirty years, but his remarks seem equally pertinent to Harvard's Center for Middle Eastern Studies (CMES), which marks its 50th year in 2004.

After two generations, the Center has embarked on its own process of "reassessment and renewal." As part of that process, the Center held several retreats in 2003 and 2004 to discuss its mission and to consider new directions and new initiatives for the years ahead. This volume is an outgrowth of that process. Its gen-esis lies in a request by Cemal Kafadar, Director of the Center from July 1, 1999, to June 30, 2004, to take the lead in the preparation of a publication that would coincide with a 50th anniversary com-memoration planned for October 2004. CMES, he felt, had a story to tell to the rest of the world, both inside and outside Harvard, and the approaching anniversary appeared to be an opportune occasion to tell it. The result is at once less and more than we orig-inally intended. The publication does not provide the detailed nar-rative of the history of the Center we had entertained initially. To do justice to the many facets of the Center's complex history, such a narrative would have required a separate and more elaborate monograph. However, the publication also contains an element we had not contemplated at the outset: a series of reflections on the state of Middle Eastern studies at Harvard and beyond.

The volume is divided into three Parts. Part I presents the highlights of the Center's history over the last five decades. It examines the major events and trends in the evolution of the Center, along with the forces that have helped to shape them. It also looks at the roles played at different junctures by influential directors, from William Langer and Hamilton Gibb to Roger

Owen and Cemal Kafadar. The treatment is selective rather than comprehensive and the exposition is more an interpretative essay than a standard history. No attempt was made was made to air-brush any aspect of the record of the Center. The analysis explores the Center's limitations as well its strengths, its failures as well as its successes. It goes without saying that this part remains very much of a personal statement and it does not reflect the views, official or otherwise, of the Center. I was granted full access to the Center's internal records and to confidential material in the Harvard Archives. I was also allowed free reign in structuring the essay, and the volume as a whole, and I was encouraged to present a candid account instead of an "infomercial." That not one of four directors who read the essay requested or suggested any editorial changes in controversial, potentially embarrassing, material for a jubilee publication is testimony to the openness the Center proclaims in its mission statement.

The second segment turns to various aspects of the Center's multifaceted activities today. It looks at the AM and PhD programs that are at the heart of the Center's teaching mandate, a mandate that is unique among area studies centers at Harvard insofar as CMES is the only one that is responsible for both research and teaching. The discussion also includes a brief profile of the Center's students and its alumni, whose ranks are replete with luminaries not only in teaching and research but also in such fields as business and diplomacy. In addition, this part features descriptions of the Center's major research projects, from the recording of interviews with political influentials in Iran under the Pahlavis to the compilation of the *shari'a* court records of Istanbul under the Ottomans. Other sections take up the Center's outreach program, the activities of visiting scholars and research associates, the seminars and conferences that are an essential ingredient of the intellectual life of the Center, and its scholarly publications. As with Part I, the chronicle stops at the end of June 30, 2004, and the material is current up to that date. I alone am responsible for all errors of fact or interpretation in both parts.

Part III consists of essays by individuals, for the most part members of the core faculty, who are intimately connected with the Center. They were asked to consider how the Center should redirect its intellectual and organizational energies in the years ahead. More specifically, they were asked to address two questions: What are we not doing now that we should be doing? And what are we doing now that we should not be doing or that we should be doing differently? The result is a set of illuminating reflections on how the Center in particular and Harvard at large might respond to the challenges in Middle Eastern studies that are likely to be faced in the coming decade. Beginning with an integrative essay by Steven Caton, the incoming director, each of the contributors advances a vision for the Center that embraces more inclusive forms of inquiry and a more inclusive notion of what constitutes the Middle East itself. The bulk of the essays are organized around different disciplines, covering both the humanities and the social sciences, and they offer different perspectives on what are the most pressing problems and the most promising opportunities in the field. Nevertheless, they contain substantial areas of convergence, especially as it concerns the need for interdisciplinary knowledge and collaborative ventures.

Projects like this volume are themselves typically collaborative ventures and this one is no exception. I owe a huge debt of gratitude to many people who have helped me to reconstruct different facets of the history of the Center. Of the numerous individuals within Harvard, I am specially thankful to Richard N. Frye, who was present at the creation, and who spent many hours patiently entertaining my questions. William Graham, Cemal Kafadar, Edward Keenan, Roy Mottahedeh, Roger Owen, and Nur Yalman, all former directors of CMES, generously shared their insights about the inner workings of the Center. Among others at Harvard today, I am grateful to Wolfhart Heinrichs and Gülru Necipoğlu. Cemal Kafadar and Steven Caton offered unwavering support during many critical moments. For individuals beyond Harvard, I am particularly thankful to a long and lively exchange with someone I have yet to meet, Richard Bulliet, one of our many distinguished alumni, whose recall of events, names, faces, places, and conversations he encountered more than a third of a century ago would astound even the most seasoned veterans of the Center. Among many others who shared their thoughts and memories about CMES, I extend my immense appreciation to Richard Antoun, Leonard Binder, Oleg Grabar, Ira Lapidus, Dennis Skiotis, and John Voll.

Of the team who worked on the project, it would be difficult to enumerate all the contributions of Jonathan Ramljak, whose formal title of Coordinator of Publications, Communications, and Graduate Studies barely hints at the many roles he has played in holding the Center together in recent years. Suffice it to say that

Jonathan was involved in every aspect of the publication, from content to design, from start to finish, and was a font of creative ideas throughout. Hannah-Louise Clark, an AM student, and Rafi Mottahedeh, a student at the University of Chicago, both offered superb research assistance. Others who helped with research for several sections of Part II are two doctoral candidates, Rachel Goshgarian and Cihan Yuksel-Muslu. Among other graduate students at CMES, we were lucky to have a talented photographer in Richard Johnson. Christine Reynolds designed and managed the production of the book with consummate skill and endured the many changes we inflicted on her with infinite patience and good cheer. Hope Steele, our copy editor, helped to smooth many of the rough edges.

Several other acknowledgments are in order. For help in navigating the labyrinths of the Harvard Archives, I thank Andrea B. Goldstein, along with Michelle Gachette and Barbara Meloni. For assistance in sharing material and ideas on the foundations, I am grateful to Bruce Byers, Director of Information Technology at the Social Science Research Council. Last but not least, a huge word of thanks to Barbara Henson, the Center's financial administrator and its walking and breathing institutional memory nonpareil.

We hope that this publication will be of interest not only to those who are curious about the Center for Middle Eastern Studies, but also to scholars and students who have a more general stake in the study of the Middle East and in the future prospects of the field. We think that some of the issues we have raised, particularly in the essays in Part III, are likely to be at the center of debate for a while to come as their relevance is not confined to this Center or to Harvard. Our hope, therefore, is that for all our readers, especially our alumni and our other friends to whom it is dedicated, this work will be seen as marking not the end of a chapter in our history but the beginning of a new one.

⟨ Don Babai
September 2004

Students in the Gibb Room
Widener Library, 1965

PART I

Fifty-Year Odyssey: A Historical Overview of CMES

Fifty-Year Odyssey:
A Historical Overview of CMES

by Don Babai

The Center for Middle Eastern Studies (CMES) was created in 1954 to advance the study of the Middle East at Harvard University. It was charged with a dual mission: first, to expand instruction in the languages, literatures, history, economics, politics, and culture of the Middle East, initially defined as the region stretching from the eastern Mediterranean to the frontiers of India; and second, to organize a program of interdisciplinary research, bridging the social sciences and the humanities, into all aspects of life in the Middle East, with special emphasis on the modern and contemporary periods. The Center soon established itself as the home base for Middle Eastern studies at Harvard, providing both a voice and a forum within the university community for the advancement of a broad range of scholarly activities focused on the Middle East. It became a primary source of intellectual and material support for academic programs dealing with the Middle East. It also became a magnet for scholars and students from different departments and schools who shared a common interest in the area.

The Founding of the Center

Like other parts of the changing landscape of Harvard in the early postwar years, CMES was born in that moment of extraordinary enthusiasm about the enterprise of furthering the pursuit of knowledge about the world beyond the borders of the United States. More than a few of its professors had dedicated themselves to the war effort by enlisting in fields such as intelligence that demanded specialized knowledge about regions and countries that had seldom been the object of serious inquiry. Those same professors would return to Harvard to take up the cause of "regional studies" or "area studies" and build the institutional infrastructure to support them. The Center's first director was William L. Langer, Coolidge Professor of History, who during the war had organized and directed the research and analysis branch of the Office of Strategic Services, the forerunner to the Central Intelligence Agency.

CMES had been preceded by the Russian Research Center, which in 1947 became the first regional studies center to be set up at Harvard, and by an embryonic program for East Asia, which would culminate in the Center for East Asian Studies. Now, the geopolitical importance of the Middle East in the struggle between the superpowers, along with the region's position in an increasingly oil-dependent world, seemed to demand a similar initiative for the study of the Middle East at Harvard. In a statement that would not have been out of place fifty years later, a 1952 memorandum calling for such a program declared, "Americans in general know almost nothing about the Middle East, despite a steadily increasing realization that an understanding of [its] problems is vital to us."[1] However, the pursuit of knowledge about the region was not treated as an end in itself. Rather, it was in terms of the strategic interests of the United States that the foremost rationale for a Middle Eastern studies center was framed. Such were the opening words of a proposal by the Committee on International and Regional Studies: "Our international commitment to counter the Soviet threat in the Middle East, the fundamental importance of Middle-eastern [sic] oil to our economy, and the continuing crisis in the area make it imperative that American universities turn their attention to this vitally important but hitherto relatively neglected region." What was needed, the proposal added, was a graduate program "designed both to train selected men for service in private industry and in government and at the same time to encourage scholarly basic research on the modern Middle East in the fields of economics, political science, anthropology, history, and social relations including social psychology."[2] Like many of the other considerations underlying the decision to establish the Center, the strategic imperative offers few clues about how CMES would evolve five decades, or even one decade, later. Nevertheless, in the environment of the Cold War, it proved instrumental in attracting support within Harvard for the proposal.

Two external and related developments provided an additional spur for the establishment of the Center. First, the foundations—beginning with Rockefeller and followed by Ford—expressed a strong interest in funding the study of the Middle East

Coolidge Professor of History William L. Langer, founder and first Director of CMES, 1954–1957.

at a select number of universities. However, this signal came with a warning, expressed most explicitly by the Rockefeller Foundation: the foundations were not interested in the kind of work produced by virtually all departments that went under the rubric of "Semitic Languages." Instead, they insisted, teaching and research on the Middle East would have to be infused with an explicitly modern and a social scientific thrust in order to warrant their support. Second, partly as a direct response to these and other calls for a sea-change in the study of the Middle East, several universities had already begun to venture in directions that emphasized the modern and contemporary. Michigan took the lead when it became the first university to set up a Middle East center structured outside a Semitic department and devoted primarily to the modern period. Princeton and Columbia also began moving to take up the challenge. Harvard was not about to be eclipsed.

The architects of the Center capitalized on the opportunities presented by these developments. Within Harvard, they were able to mobilize a powerful constituency who would support the launching of the project and also ensure that it would be sustained. The prime movers, internationalists through and through, were some of the most influential figures at Harvard in the 1950s. Aside from Langer, a solid pillar of the History Department who would soon become President of the American Historical Association, they included Edward S. Mason, Professor of Economics, Dean of the Littauer School of Public Administration (now the Kennedy School of Government), and President of the American Economics Association; William Y. Elliott and Merle Fainsod of the Government Department; and McGeorge Bundy, Dean of the Faculty of Arts and Sciences, who would preside over an explosive period of growth before leaving the University to become National Security Advisor in the Kennedy Administration. Assisting in the spadework for the Center was a young linguist and historian, Richard N. Frye, who, through such bodies as the American Council for Learned Societies and the Social Science Research Council, had already played a major role in the push for expanding and modernizing the study of the Middle East. Frye would become the first associate director of the CMES and in 1957 the occupant of the newly created Aga Khan Chair of Iranian at Harvard.

Harvard also seized upon the momentum to garner the financial resources for the undertaking. Although the University provided a modest amount of support, the bulk of the funds needed to launch the Center came from private companies and individual donors. By far the largest contributors were the oil companies, foremost among which was the Arabian American Oil Company (ARAMCO). From these same sources came commitments that would secure the Center's existence for five years. The belief that the Center was kept afloat by oil money would persist long after funding from that source had evaporated.

The Center was immediately confronted with a task more daunting than its founders had anticipated and compounded by the multiple missions with which it had been entrusted. Unlike the other area studies centers, CMES did not have the broad range of specialists to further its research program. The programs for the Soviet Union and East Asia both had established historians, economists, and political scientists in the various departments who were working on modern and contemporary issues. The field of the Middle East at Harvard in 1954, by contrast, had few counterparts. There were several endowed professorships in the Department of Semitic Languages and History, but the specialties were far removed from the interests of CMES. The Center's research program, therefore, had to be built from a thin base.

Richard N. Frye, Associate Director of CMES from 1954 to 1957, and Harvard's first Aga Khan Professor of Iranian.

Also unlike the other regional centers, which devoted their energies exclusively to research, CMES was given the responsibility for organizing a teaching program, especially for instruction in modern languages. The planners of CMES were aware that, given the multiplicity of languages to be taught and the variety of cultures to be studied, the Middle East represented the greatest diversity, and perhaps also the greatest difficulty, of any field of area study. Indeed, the original blueprint for CMES had contemplated a Middle East Research Center and an entirely separate teaching program. However, there was little confidence that such a program could be established in the Department of Semitic Languages and History. Consequently, the burden of both research and teaching was placed on CMES. Yet, the Center was not designed to offer any courses on its own. Nor did it have the final word on academic appointments; these decisions were, and remain, in the hands of individual departments. It was therefore only through the Semitic Department that CMES could hope to fulfill its teaching mandate, especially for languages such as modern Arabic, Persian, and Turkish. But the department showed little inclination at first in moving in the directions sought by the Center, let alone in

Exterior and interior of Dudley Hall, which housed the first headquarters of CMES.

bringing about the transformation advocated by the foundations. The department was closely tied to the Divinity School and its emphasis was on biblical studies. The few courses it offered in classical Arabic were taught as adjuncts to Hebrew.

Early Years: In Search of "Academic Amphibians"

The Center for Middle Eastern Studies began formal operation in September 1954, sharing floor space with the Russian Research Center in Dudley Hall, a resplendent Italianate structure occupied mainly by affluent undergraduates and hence known as one of Harvard's "Gold Coast" buildings.[3] While in its first year CMES had only six students, not all of whom would graduate, it already had in place the structure of its two degree programs: a two-year master's program, termed Middle Eastern Regional Studies, designed mainly for careers in government or business; and a joint program for the PhD, combining Middle Eastern studies with the conventional discipline of a department, which could include Anthropology, Economics, Government, History, or Semitic Languages and History. The Center also quickly drew the interest of a growing number of researchers, many of them from the Middle East, who were attracted by its offers of fellowships and by Harvard's exceptional library holdings on the field.

The immediate preoccupation of the Center was to find the people to run its programs. The support it enjoyed when it was established notwithstanding, neither success nor survival was assured. Communication among administrators in the University hierarchy more than once referred to CMES as an "experiment" even years after it had been created. Eleven out of the 53 courses listed in its 1954–55 course offerings were future promises inasmuch as they did not have instructors; many others were either tangentially related to the Middle East or taught by instructors with little or no background in the field. The Center, therefore, devoted much its energies to three tasks: (1) securing, through a combination of financial inducements and intellectual suasion, appointments and courses in departments that often were either indifferent or recalcitrant; (2) stimulating a body of innovative research that would pass muster within Harvard and beyond; and (3) raising the funds to accomplish its goals, thereby heeding Harvard's hallowed dictum of "every tub on its own bottom."

The number of faculty initially attached to the Center were four in number. Langer, the director, made no claims to being an expert on the Middle East, but the region did figure heavily in his work on imperialism and he devoted more than fleeting attention to its historical problems, leading him to speak about what he called "the clash of cultures"[4] decades before such terms became widespread. He also taught a course entitled "The Ottoman Empire and the Middle East since the Thirteenth Century," which became an introduction to the field for a generation of students. As Langer was simultaneously directing the Russian Research Center and chairing the Committee on Regional Studies,[5] the day-to-day running of the Center at its inception fell to Frye, the associate director, who also was the mainstay of instruction in Persian and Turkish, among other languages. The Center had also recruited another linguistics specialist, Charles Ferguson, who had headed the US State Department's Arabic School in Beirut and would now offer one of the first courses in modern Arabic at Harvard. The fourth member of the team was Derwood Lockard, an anthropologist with an extensive background in intelligence in the Middle East. Lockard would remain long after the others had left, serving as associate director in charge of administration until 1972.

Sir Hamilton Gibb, Jewett Professor of Arabic, University Professor, and from 1957 to 1966 Director of CMES.

The turning point for the Center came in 1955 when Sir Hamilton Gibb resigned his position as Laudian Professor of Arabic at Oxford University to come to Harvard. Gibb was appointed Jewett Professor of Arabic and also University Professor, the highest honor Harvard can bestow on one of its faculty members, and formally assumed the directorship of the Center in 1957. In the ten years he spent at Harvard he built CMES into one of the world's leading Middle Eastern centers. With a distinguished publication record that includes such magisterial works as *Mohammedanism* and *Islamic Society and the West*, and that spanned subjects as diverse as Arabic philology and Arab unity, Gibb had already gained an Olympian reputation long before coming to Harvard. It even found expression in such sobriquets, occasionally echoed in the press, as "the leading Arabist in the West" and "the last of the Orientalists." That reputation, coupled with the equally Olympian presence Gibb commanded, helped in many ways as he committed himself to expanding and deepening teaching and research on the Middle East at Harvard. Under his stewardship, the fledgling Center saw its position solidified and its stature enhanced.

Gibb personally attracted the four sets of actors that mattered most to the Center: students, faculty, administrators, and donors. Students flocked to his classes, and his courses on Islamic history and Islamic institutions soon became the stuff of legend. Some of the graduate students who spent time at the Center and studied with him did not get a joint degree from CMES. Hanna Batatu was one such student. A few, notable among them Malcolm H. Kerr, did not even get a degree from Harvard. Gibb had a presence not only at CMES but also in the History Department and the Department of Near Eastern Languages and Literatures,[6] the successor to the Semitic Department. He was an active member of the Committee on Middle Eastern Studies and the Committee on Regional Studies. In addition, he had cultivated a personal connection with President M. Pusey. These relationships helped to secure appointments, and, with a lesser degree of success, promotions in the field. Among the appointees were George Makdisi, who became Professor of Arabic; George Kirk in History and Government; and Albert Julius Meyer ("A.J."), who became Lecturer in Economics and a long-time associate director of the Center.

With donors, the name Sir Hamilton Gibb seemed to work magic. Money flowed to the Center from both individuals and corporations. Gibb excelled at playing the funding game with the foundations, in particular. He moved swiftly to forge links with senior officials at Rockefeller and Ford, who, in turn, turned to him as a source of ideas for developing not only Middle Eastern studies but area studies in general. These efforts produced tangible results before the end of the decade. In 1957, CMES received a $300,000, five-year grant from the Ford Foundation for instruction, fellowships, research, travel, and general operating expenses. A memorandum at Ford recommending the grant argued that the Center had already "demonstrated its value and promise." It went on to insist, "The national interest requires the additional training and research on Middle Eastern affairs which the Harvard program provides."[7] Lesser amounts were also secured that year from Rockefeller and Carnegie. In 1959, Rockefeller gave Harvard $500,000 outright to be used for any purpose related to Middle Eastern studies, including the endowment of CMES. The climax came in 1960 when, as part of a $5.6 million grant to Harvard for "non-Western and other international studies," Ford awarded $500,000 for partial funding of two chairs in Middle Eastern studies and an additional $450,000 to CMES for faculty research, student fellowships, and a discretional miscellany ranging from travel support to secretarial assistance.

Gibb's imprint on the Center and on Middle Eastern studies at Harvard at large would be felt for decades. It is evident in at least two concrete respects. First, there is the generation of students who have become some of the leading lights in the field. They have included Leonard Binder, Carl Brown, Richard Bulliet, Ira Lapidus, and Roy Mottahedeh, the latter a dominant presence at CMES for almost the last twenty years. Secondly, it is evident in the Center's preponderant emphasis in much of its existence on history and the humanities. No direct cause-effect attribution can be claimed here. Gibb's goals for the Center, like the methods he used to pursue them, were quite complex. He was not interested in replicating the orientalist tradition at Oxford even though it had served him very well. If anything, it was out of a desire to escape the confines of Orientalism, particularly of the variety institutionalized in European academia, that he was drawn to Harvard. In the fullest statement of his vision for area studies, he offered a paean to multidisciplinary and interdisciplinary work. Regional studies centers, he insisted, should strive to "breed a new kind of academic amphibian, the scholar whose habitat is in one medium but who is fully at home in another."[8] He welcomed the opportunities he found at Harvard for building bridges across faculties and disciplines, a refreshing contrast to Oxford's "jealous rigidity of Faculty and School lines (that) inhibited any attempt to cross them."[9] He encouraged his own students to seek not only depth but also breadth. He insisted that without the insights offered by the social sciences the orientalist's comprehension "must remain circumscribed and his interpretation correspondingly defective."[10] The collaboration with departments such as Economics and Government, especially through the organization of joint doctoral programs, he pronounced "the most significant contribution of the Center to academic life, both in Harvard itself and eventually in other American universities."[11] Nevertheless, the overriding emphasis remained on classical scholarship and classical training, with history and language at the core.

Gibb was by no means averse to modern or contemporary themes. Yet, even when it came to communicating with the foundations, he defined his preferred priority for a modern research program at a center like CMES "the investigation of the antecedents of the actual present-day problems." Such a program would need to focus on the study of the evolution of Middle Eastern societies from the beginning of the nineteenth century. Contemporary social and problems could then be explored "in

Derwood Lockard, Associate Director of CMES, 1954–1972.

terms of this evolution."[12] In practice, Gibb was quick to warn, such preferences could not be translated into rigid rules and he did not apply any such rules to research at CMES. As the many titles in economics and politics suggest, the research output of CMES in its first decade was more wide-ranging than in any other subsequent period in the history of the Center.

By the end of its tenth year, CMES had undergone a level of expansion and development that surpassed most initial expectations. It was no longer an experiment. It could claim twenty members among its core faculty. The erstwhile hostilities between the Center and the former Semitic Department had dissipated. The Department of Near Eastern Languages and Literatures had begun to seriously embrace the teaching of languages such as Arabic and Turkish, which were vital to students at CMES. A change in leadership in that department helped. Money helped, too: only a year after it was passed, CMES became one of the first centers to receive funding under Title VI of the 1958 National Defense Education Act, which provides support for language instruction and other area studies programs. The funds allowed CMES to underwrite a substantial expansion and improvement in language training. By the end of the 1963–64 academic year, the Center had produced thirteen PhDs with joint degrees in no less than five disciplines. It had also conferred seventy-four MA degrees. However, the infelicitously labeled "terminal AM program" turned out to be not so terminal, as more than one-half of AM recipients chose to do further graduate work, confounding the original assumption that most of them would head directly for careers in government and business. The Center was equally surprised by the large number of undergraduates it attracted: undergraduate enrollment in courses and the selection of senior theses on the Middle East both showed marked increases.

The Center's research program also was thriving. It had appointed sixty-five research fellows and associates, some supported by grants from Rockefeller and Ford. Among them were Edmund Asfour, Khodadad Farmanfarmaian, Benjamin Halpern, Kemal Karpat, Firuz Kazemzadeh, Walter Laqueur, Ragaei El-Mallakh, and Yusif Sayigh. CMES had already put out an impressive number of works in two sets of publications: a Harvard Middle Eastern Studies series, consisting of books subsidized by the Center and published by Harvard University Press; and a Harvard Middle Eastern Monographs series, devoted to more specialized works published by the Center and distributed by

Harvard University Press. The Center's visiting scholars program brought to Harvard prominent scholars in the Middle East, including Fuat Köprülü from Turkey and Seyed Fakhr ud-Din Shadman from Iran. The Center's visiting committees, which perform an oversight function on behalf of the Board of Overseers of Harvard, were no less distinguished: Ralph Bunche, Kermit Roosevelt, Carl Pforzheimer, and John Goelet were among the early members. The Center had become a prime mover behind the rapid build-up of the University Library's Middle East collections. And the Center's finances were on a solid footing: by 1964 it had raised more than $5 million, about $3 million of which went into its endowment.

CMES appeared to have fulfilled all the essential rites of passage. But not all was well.

Professor George Makdisi, the mainstay of Arabic instruction at Harvard in the 1960s.

From Crisis to Crisis

A massive stroke that struck Gibb at the Harvard Faculty Club on the evening of February 21, 1964, ushered in the beginning of a long crisis for Harvard's Center for Middle Eastern Studies. Gibb had already served notice that he would be retiring to Oxford at the end of the academic year. However, as the search for a successor had come to naught, in December 1963 the Harvard President and Fellows, the University's governing body, had voted to "recall [Sir Hamilton] to active service" for another two years. The exceptional arrangement called for Gibb to reside in Oxford, but to return to Cambridge for two month-long visits, one in the early fall and another in the early spring, each year.[13] The next six years were an interregnum. Gibb held the title of director even as he remained across the ocean and even as his health continued to deteriorate. Unlike Gibb, his first two successors—David David Landes (1966–68), Professor of History, and Peter Elder (1968–70), Professor of Greek and Latin and Dean of the Graduate Schools of Arts and Sciences (GSAS)—did reside in Cambridge, but they showed little interest in running the Center, let alone in exercising leadership. Only rarely did they visit the Center and, therefore, the pattern of absentee directorships continued, masked in part by the continuity in day-to-day operations provided by one associate director, Lockard, and by the fundraising feats of another, A.J. Meyer. In the apparent absence of anyone both able and willing to pick up the mantle, CMES found itself in a precarious position. Speculation that the Center might fold was common both within and outside the University.

The main void left by Gibb was less administrative than intellectual. As a University Professor, Gibb had not been part of a departmental mainstream. While he had taught History Department courses, his links with that department were tenuous and episodic.[14] Hence, the Center did not have the critical History Department anchor that other regional studies directors, for example Edwin Reischauer and John Fairbank of East Asian Studies, had given their centers, or that Langer had offered CMES on its founding. The consequences became immediately apparent and would persist for at least another two decades. Different Middle Eastern historians, classical and modern, senior and junior, found themselves deprived of the support Gibb had given them and, in fairly quick succession, all were pronounced to be unacceptable by the History Department. Many of them went on to stellar careers elsewhere. But their departure robbed the Center of a coherent program in one of its most important fields. The low point came in the 1966–67 academic year when CMES decided it had no choice but to temporarily suspend the joint doctoral program with the History Department.[15] The Center resorted with growing frequency to the stopgap measure of securing visiting professorial appointments. The visitors included some of the most distinguished figures in the field: Marshall Hodgson, Albert Hourani, André Raymond, Ann Lambton, and Walid Khalidi. Yet none of them was a substitute for a permanent instructor who could offer the continuity needed by colleagues and, perhaps even more so, by doctoral students.

The absence of a permanent appointment in Middle Eastern history, a matter that had not been one of Gibb's overriding preoccupations, became the most glaring deficit of CMES and Middle Eastern studies at Harvard at large. At different points, the History Department wooed several prominent scholars—including Hourani, Claude Cahen, Bernard Lewis, and Gustave Von Grunebaum—for such a position, which simultaneously would also have given the Center the director it sought. For a variety of reasons, most commonly because the offers were turned down, none of these prospective appointments materialized.

The Center found itself on a firmer footing with the next three directors: Muhsin Mahdi (1970–73, 1976–81), an authority on Islamic intellectual history and philosophy, who succeeded Gibb as Jewett Professor of Arabic; Nur Yalman (1973–76),

Professor of Social Anthropology who had been director of the University of Chicago's Center for Middle Eastern Studies; and Edward L. Keenan (1981–83), an early product of the CMES-History PhD program who became a specialist in Russian history and who ran the Center while also serving as Dean of GSAS. CMES in this period achieved a measure of stability that contrasted markedly with the immediate post-Gibb era. The Center did succeed in undertaking several important initiatives, but there was no escaping the reality that the exuberant expansion of its early years had ended.

Edward L. Keenan, Professor of History, CMES Director from 1981 to 1983, and twice acting director (1986–87, 1994–95).

Student interest in Middle Eastern studies remained high. The AM program continued to attract a large number of qualified students each year. Enrollment in the PhD program, on the other hand, declined by 1980 to almost half the level of the 1960s, partly due to a tightening of the academic market. In the 1970s, support from CMES contributed to considerable improvements in language training, an area to which the Center from the outset had attached immense importance, so much so that initially students were expected to devote fully one-half of their course work to languages.[16] By the middle of the decade, CMES had achieved one of the objectives it had sought for Arabic: instruction from the elementary to advanced levels was divided into the modern and classical tracks to reflect the different interests of students in the contemporary and medieval fields. CMES also began to devote serious attention to undergraduate education. Between 1978 and 1980, CMES-based faculty introduced four new courses to the Core Curriculum that attracted enrollments not seen in more than a decade. They included Mahdi's "Modern Middle Eastern Civilization" and "The Civilization of Islam," which was co-taught by Oleg Grabar, William Graham, Mahdi, Abdelhamid Sabra, and Wheeler Thackston. In 1978–79, the Center began sponsoring jointly with the Law School a year-long Islamic Law Colloquium. An indicator of both institutions' growing interest in the Islamic legal field, the colloquium brought to the University leading scholars such as Noel Coulson, Majid Khadduri, Abraham Udovitch, and Ann Mayer. CMES and the Law School took this collaboration a step further in the 1980s by instituting a joint degree program in Law and Middle Eastern Studies.

Also during this period, the Center initiated a program of outreach to the general public. The outreach program (now the CMES Outreach Center) was formally launched in 1974 and had as its initial mainstay a Teaching Resource Center that offered

A.J. Meyer, beginning in 1955 Lecturer in Economics, later also Professor of Middle Eastern Studies, and Associate Director of CMES until 1983.

pre-collegiate institutions a variety of services, including annual workshops and educational material on the Middle East. The program soon broadened its scope to include the community at large, fielding daily requests from across New England for information about the Middle East and the Muslim world and assisting educational or cultural groups in organizing activities related to the Middle East. Yet another initiative that began in this phase was the Iranian Oral History Project. An ambitious endeavor launched at the Center in 1981 and directed by Habib Ladjevardi, the project has opened a window on Iran's turbulent past by recording the recollections of individuals who played a central role in the political decisions and events of that country under the Pahlavis.

For many, the highlight of CMES from the late 1960s to the early 1980s was the work of Meyer, commonly known as "A.J." A.J., who had the seemingly improbable title of "Professor of Middle Eastern Studies,"[17] did not attain a position above that of lecturer in the Department of Economics. Yet it was in that position and in that department that he taught Middle Eastern economics to a generation of students at Harvard and the Greater Boston area. Largely through him, CMES served as the focal point as well as the primary catalyst for teaching and research in the energy field at Harvard. A seminar on the economics of Middle East oil that he began with Morris Adelman of MIT in the mid-1960s expanded a decade later into the famed Energy Seminar, offered jointly by the Economics Department and the Harvard Business School. It brought to Cambridge a stream of dignitaries such as Sheikh Ahmed Zaki Yamani, Saudi minister of petroleum and natural resources. A.J. set up an Energy Library that became Harvard's largest collection of material on oil in the Middle East. He testified regularly before Congress on American oil policy and the Middle East. Simultaneously, he undertook corporate fundraising, an area in which he had no peer at the Center, expanding the list of CMES corporate supporters from the original five firms to thirty-two. He also engaged in extensive consulting and advisory work in many countries of the Middle East, among them Saudi Arabia, where for many years he, in tandem with Harvard's John Dunlop and MIT's Everett Hagen, assisted the government in formulating its economic development plans. Further afield, he led the Center on its first serious foray into North Africa with one of its more ambitious ventures in interdisciplinary collaboration: a large-scale research project, sponsored jointly by CMES, the School of Public Health, and the School of Education, to measure the impact of health and education investments in Tunisia. All along, A.J. continued to forge links with scholars in the Middle East and was instrumental in bringing many students from the region to Harvard. In addition, he functioned as a one-man placement bureau for CMES graduates intent on careers in business and government.

For the Center, A.J. represented perhaps the height of its engagement with the Middle East, especially in the Arab world, in its fifty-year history. Through him, the Center acquired multiple constituencies, many of which it shed after his death in 1983.

While CMES managed to arrest its downward slide, the 1970s and early 1980s proved to be a difficult period. Maintaining the breadth and quality of its teaching program was an ongoing struggle. The problems of recruitment for senior positions remained intractable. The Center was beset by financial difficulties as funds from traditional sources began to diminish. Funding from foundations such as Ford and Rockefeller, who had given the entire field a solid boost, declined precipitously as their priorities shifted to domestic issues such as poverty and violence. Government support, through such vehicles as National Defense Language Fellowships, continued, albeit generally at steady or reduced levels. Expressions of disappointment with Middle Eastern studies in the United States, and with area studies in general, became more commonplace. As yet, they did not escalate into the wholesale assault on the discipline that would be seen two decades later. As one of the pioneers and leaders of the field, however, CMES could not remain immune from them.

CMES entered the 1980s with a pervasive sentiment—echoed by faculty, students, administrators, visiting committees, and outside observers—that it lacked the dynamism of its early years. In the words of one faculty member who has been intimately involved in the Center, "After Gibb's stroke we were lost for twenty years. None of the directors who followed him had their heart in it."[18] Emblematic of the altered fortunes of the Center was the fact that it had shrunk in perhaps the most literal sense: from more than two floors in the late 1960s, the space the CMES headquarters occupied in Coolidge Hall was reduced by the early 1980s to two-thirds of a single floor as a result of the encroachments of more powerful institutions, especially the Center for International Affairs (now the Weatherhead Center).

Nevertheless, CMES seemed poised to turn the corner in the mid-1980s. In 1983, the position of director was taken over by the

Nadav Safran, the Murray A. Albertson Professor of Middle Eastern Studies, Government Department, and Director of CMES from 1983 to 1986.

Government Department's Nadav Safran, Murray A. Albertson Professor of Middle Eastern Studies and an alumnus of the CMES joint degree program with that department. As a social scientist in what had been largely a succession of historians as directors, Safran at once made known his intention to steer the Center toward new directions in both the academic and policy worlds. In his first two years, he launched a flurry of initiatives that suggested to many that the Center had begun to move out of its long period of dormancy. These years saw a substantial expansion in course offerings and research activity at CMES. The Center announced the launching of a Moroccan Studies Program, which was to serve as the basis for expanding the study of the entire Maghrib at Harvard. It rejuvenated the Forum, its weekly seminar series, by bringing over prominent speakers from near and afar. Safran developed a five-year plan for the development of the Center with special emphasis on the modern and contemporary periods in both teaching and research on the Middle East. The plan envisaged a vigorous push by CMES for an undergraduate major in Middle Eastern studies at Harvard. The Center was to explore the creation of a joint program on the political economy of the Middle East with the Kennedy School. It would strengthen its links with the Economics and Government departments. There was to be a seminar on "The Middle East: Critical Decisions Reconsidered" that would bring in not only scholars but also senior policymakers who would look at historic decisions affecting American policy and behavior in the Middle East. There would be conferences on such themes as "Water, Land, and People in the Middle East" that would examine from inter-disciplinary perspectives specific issues vital to the region.

To colleagues and administrators alike, Safran proclaimed the need for CMES to become more relevant within the Harvard community and in Washington, DC. Two decades after the departure of Gibb, the Center once again had an ambitious and resourceful leader determined to leave a lasting imprint.

What appeared to be an auspicious beginning came to an abrupt halt in early October 1985 when Harvard awoke to the news, widely believed to have been leaked, that Safran had accepted secret funding from the Central Intelligence Agency to run a conference on Islamic fundamentalism. Within days, the campus paper, *The Harvard Crimson*, revealed another embarrassing piece of news: Safran also had received a six-figure sum from the CIA to complete research for a book on Saudi Arabia and had given the agency the right of of pre-publication review and approval. The conference was held as planned, but about half of the expected participants stayed away. By then, the disclosures had made headlines around the world and triggered a full-blown scandal that plunged the Center into the most severe crisis in its fifty-year history.[19] Harvard's official inquiry into the matter led to a report by FAS Dean A. Michael Spence that took Safran to task for failing to apprise the dean of the conference contract as required by University policy; for failing to channel the contract through the University, which would normally receive a portion of the funds to cover overhead expenses; and for failing to heed the CMES Executive Committee's advice to inform the conference participants of the source of funding.[20] The Spence Report put most of the blame for the handling of the book contract on the Harvard administration itself, acknowledging that Safran had consulted as early as 1981 with University officials, and had even submitted the full text to them, but had never received a response.[21]

The cautious approach and measured tone of the report was not matched by others. The period from the fall of 1985 through the spring of 1986 witnessed a furor at Harvard and elsewhere over the episode. Faculty, alumni, and others aired opposing positions, often in unusually acerbic language, through a barrage of letters and op-ed pieces in leading newspapers. A beleaguered

A Ceaseless Controversy

Safran's CIA-funded study, which argued that the United State's long-term objective in Saudi Arabia "should be to disengage its vital interests from the policy and fate of the Kingdom" (p. 461), was hailed by John Campbell as "surely the most comprehensive, informative and reliable account of Saudi foreign policy yet written." (*New York Times Book Review*, October 6, 1985.) In the jacket of the book, Hermann Eilts, a former American ambassador to Saudi Arabia, called it "an outstanding piece of scholarship," while Fouad Ajami declared:

"Its mastery of detail is awesome. Its command over its subject is rare and reassuring." The preface acknowledges financial support from the Rockefeller Foundation and the Rand Corporation, along with logistical support from CMES. Safran stated that he did not use any "privileged information of any sort," but instead relied entirely on open sources and declassified documents. He did not undertake any fieldwork and dismissed the "notion that 'having been' to Saudi Arabia is a warrant of validity for one's work." (Preface, p. 1.) ⊚

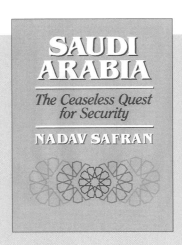

SAUDI ARABIA

The Ceaseless Quest for Security

NADAV SAFRAN

Safran was able to count on few supporters at Harvard. Several of his colleagues, including three of the six members of the CMES Executive Committee—Richard Frye, Wolfhart Heinrichs, and Abdelhamid Sabra—openly called for his immediate resignation once the sponsorship of the conference became public. At its annual convention in November 1985, the Middle East Studies Association of North America (MESA) added its voice to the outcry by "deploring" the violation of its resolution, passed only three years earlier, calling for disclosure of funding for research as well conferences and programs.[22] A group of junior faculty members and research fellows affiliated with CMES, some of whom would later attain senior positions in the field, insisted that the seminal issue was not so much one of procedure as it was of principle. "Regardless of whether any university rules or procedures have been violated, we believe that neither the Center for Middle Eastern Studies nor anyone who might be seen as acting in its name should either solicit or accept funds from the CIA or any other intelligence agency," they declared in an open letter to the dean. "If individual scholars chose to work for an intelligence agency that is their prerogative, but the Center as an institution should not be associated in any way with any such agency."[23]

Safran stepped down as CMES director at the end of June 1986. Long before then, the Center had become all but an empty shell.

The Center Restored

By almost any measure, the Safran saga was a harsh body blow to the Center for Middle Eastern Studies, damaging its reputation and eroding its support. It led to a questioning of the integrity of Middle Eastern studies centers across the United States. It raised fears among many scholars about their ability to do future research in the Middle East. And it cast a dark cloud over the Center as its continued existence was thrown into doubt. It was not until the end of the decade that the cloud lifted; the reverberations, however, would continue into the 1990s.

The mission of rescuing the Center was assumed by Roy P. Mottahedeh, a specialist in medieval Islamic history who became director in July 1987 following a one-year holding operation under Edward Keenan. A winner of the MacArthur Prize and author of such widely acclaimed works as *Loyalty and Leadership in an Early*

Islamic Society and *The Mantle of the Prophet: Religion and Politics in Iran*, Mottahedeh had studied with Gibb at Harvard, where he obtained a doctoral degree in history. In luring him from Princeton in 1986, Harvard prevailed in what for decades had been an elusive quest: the appointment of a senior historian in the Middle Eastern field. For CMES, the appointment offered the prospect that someone who had been removed from the infighting that erupted in 1985 would be able to repair the damage. *The Crimson*, which had devoted breathless coverage to the crisis, captured the general feeling of relief with the suggestion that CMES had chosen "a scholar of the 10th century in . . . an attempt to escape the ethical dilemmas of the 20th century."[24]

The survival of CMES was not a foregone outcome, however, and Mottahedeh did not assume it would be so. Mottahedeh recalls what he encountered when he came to Harvard. On the one hand, there was the admonition of Dean Spence—"He told me that if the Center seemed to be serving no purpose, he would disband it."[25] On the other hand, there was the advice of friends like Albert Hourani: "He told me that the Middle Eastern field at Harvard needed a scholar who would have his door open and be willing, as he put it, 'to think' with students. He persuaded me that I could best play this role in the context of the Center." That Middle Eastern studies at Harvard appeared to be shrinking reinforced the conviction that that a body like CMES was vital to energizing the field. But, having concluded that CMES, in his words, "very much needed to live," Mottahedeh discovered a disquieting setting. The controversy had left the faculty polarized and students embittered. The community of scholars with an interest in the Middle East had become so dispirited that few of them were willing to set foot in the Center—"it was as if the place had some kind of communicable disease." The recent upheavals, along with lingering uncertainties about the future of the Center, disrupted relations with outside supporters. Some of them delayed committed contributions; others withdrew them altogether. Fund-raising would continue to be undermined through the decade. Meantime, the Center faced severe financial stringency, with barely enough money to cover one and a half administrative staff positions and its outreach program. To add insult to injury, some of the benefactors who had abandoned CMES had begun to shift their attention to an upstart at the Kennedy School, the Institute for Social and Economic Policy in the Middle East, which focused on Arab-Israeli conflict resolution and had a director without either a

Roy P. Mottahedeh, Professor of History, and CMES Director from 1987 to 1990.

Harvard professorial appointment or scholarly expertise in the Middle Eastern field. The institute adopted the shorthand of "Middle East Institute" and presented itself, especially abroad, as the University's prime unit for Middle Eastern studies, thereby adding to the confusion about the status of CMES.[26]

Re-engaging faculty who had an interest in the Middle East and a stake in the Center became one of the first goals of Mottahedeh. He introduced a "Committee of the Whole" that brought together senior faculty in the field from different parts of the University. A forum for the exchange of ideas about the future of CMES and Middle Eastern studies at Harvard, it also served as a means of communicating the message that one of the primary purposes of the Center was to serve their interests. Mottahedeh also organized an Islamic Middle Eastern History Seminar series that drew scholars from a dozen universities in the area. The seminars, which called for a close reading of primary texts, included topics such as medieval Islamic treatises on economic morality and the *aja'ib,* or "the amazing and marvelous," in medieval Islamic culture. With the help of grants from the Mellon Foundation, CMES collaborated with MIT in organizing several important conferences: "Tribe and State Formation in the Middle East" in 1987 and "The Political Economies of the Ottoman, Safavid, and Mughal Empires" in 1988. The latter conference was repeated for five consecutive years, each on a different theme and with presentations from scholars in multiple disciplines. In combination, the substance of these activities signaled the redirection in intellectual energies at the Center under Mottahedeh. A visitor to CMES earlier in the decade would have encountered plenty of debates about the uses and misuses of missiles in warfare in the Middle East. Now, a more likely topic would have been the role of the *madrasah* in the transmission of learning in Baghdad in the eleventh and twelfth centuries.

That there had been a change in style was also readily apparent. Instead of the extravagant conferences of the past, the emphasis was now on the small, focused study group involving typically five to ten professors and students who would meet at least once a month over the course of a semester to engage in intensive exchange on a topic not covered in the regular curriculum. Study groups became one of Mottahedeh's innovations at CMES, and the appeal they generated prompted several other regional centers at Harvard to emulate them. By the end of his first year as director, no less than sixteen study groups had been formed, each with very modest funding. They were not all in history, and those in history were not all pre-modern. One study group, the political economy of resource windfalls, looked at the phenomenon of the "Dutch Disease" in the context of rentier states in the Middle East. Another explored theoretical works on historicism, structuralism, Marxism, and feminism, and their relevance to the study of the Middle East. Nevertheless, the overall change in emphasis was unmistakable. More common were topics like the strands of medieval hermeneutics or the status of Islamic law in Middle Eastern societies.

Mottahedeh also gave a solid push to Iranian studies and obtained seed money from the Ford Foundation for furthering research in that field. The Center launched a weekly seminar organized each semester around specific themes in Iranian history and society, such as "Groups and Associations in Modern Iran" and "Iranian Social History of the 19th and 20th Centuries." The occasion of the tenth anniversary of the Iranian revolution, coinciding as it did with the 200th anniversary of the French revolution, provided the impetus for organizing Harvard's first forum on the Comparative Study of Revolution in 1989–90. For some of the speakers at the forum—who included Patrice Higgonet, Simon Schama, Stanley Hoffmann, Richard Pipes, Benjamin Schwartz, and Theda Skocpol—this was the first time they had attended an event sponsored by CMES. Yet other small steps underscored the importance of scholarly research at the Center. For example, before the end of his term, Mottahedeh resuscitated the Harvard Middle Eastern Monographs. The series, initiated by Gibb in 1959 and intended to disseminate some of the work of research fellows at the Center, had suspended production in 1978. It was now relaunched and its scope redefined so as to include doctoral dissertations, other studies based on original sources, translations of non-Western original texts in Middle Eastern and Islamic studies, and CMES conference papers and proceedings.

Individually, each of these activities was unremarkable—they were the staple one would ordinarily expect of any area studies center at Harvard. But there was little about CMES that was ordinary in the 1980s. Together, therefore, these programmatic initiatives went a long way in reaffirming the intellectual mission of the Center and in rehabilitating its reputability. By 1990, Mottahedeh had succeeded in securing the Center's acceptance once again by the scholarly community both within and outside Harvard. Any lingering schemes involving a dissolution of the Center were interred. Even the partisan wrangling over the Arab-Israeli conflict that had embroiled the Center earlier in the decade had dissipated.[27] The governance of CMES was stabilized. Following the turmoil of late 1985, the CMES Executive Committee had been summarily disbanded by the University administration, which pronounced it to be "a divided body . . . that . . . cannot serve a useful function."[28] Responsibility for oversight of the Center and its policies had been assigned instead to the Standing Committee of the Faculty on Middle Eastern Studies. Under Mottahedeh, the Standing Committee reverted to its conventional academic review function and a new Executive Committee of CMES faculty was appointed to serve as the Center's internal decision-making and advisory body.

The Center's finances, however, remained precarious. Some donors did reappear. Gifts from private donors allowed for the sponsorship of a visiting Iranian scholar and also a visiting Arab scholar. And in 1989, CMES succeeded in obtaining its first major award in years from an educational foundation when the Mellon Foundation approved its application for a five-year grant of $575,000. The grant, the largest Mellon had ever made in Middle Eastern studies, paved the way for significant improvements in language instruction, especially in Arabic and Turkish, and an expansion of graduate and undergraduate scholarships for intensive summer language courses. It also facilitated a continuation of the Center's flourishing seminar programs. Nevertheless, the task of shoring up the Center's financial base, weakened not only by the withdrawal of traditional supporters but also by the burden of bearing the cost of several tenured faculty members, would have to await another decade.

The Return of History

The recovery brought about by Roy Mottahedeh entailed more than simply a restoration of the vitality and the respectability of the Center for Middle Eastern Studies. In more ways than one, it also involved a return to the more classical and purist orientation to scholarship that had animated the Center in its heyday. The return proved to be more than fleeting. The trajectory along which Mottahedeh steered the Center from 1987 to 1990 would be followed in its most crucial aspects by all three of his successors over the next fifteen years: William A. Graham (1990–96), E. Roger Owen (1996–99), and Cemal Kafadar (1999–2004). It would also have a direct bearing on many facets of the Center's existence, from the kinds of students it attracted and the range of thesis topics they selected to the type of image it projected within and beyond Harvard, and the nature of support it was able to marshal from different stakeholders. Generalizations about the Center can be fraught with hazards, especially for an entity that, far from being a monolith, has always been a setting of internal diversity. Nevertheless, CMES over this period of almost twenty years has maintained a distinctive approach to the field of Middle Eastern studies. The approach is comprised of a set of complementary characteristics that, in combination, have become integral to the Center's institutional identity. At least four major ones may be noted.

First, the Center has placed teaching at the core of its academic enterprise. Intimate familiarity with many aspects of the history and culture of the Middle East, a demanding standard of linguistic competence, sophisticated knowledge of classical texts and classical modes of inquiry, proficiency in the use of research methods and archival sources—for the Center's teaching mission, these objectives, in addition to the expectation of a thorough grounding in an established academic discipline, have assumed a status that is all but sacrosanct. Rigorous training, along with guiding and mentoring, has been a persistent preoccupation for senior faculty based at the Center. It has been especially so in the case of doctoral students, who the Center looks to as the next generation of leaders in the field. For the more transitory AM students, the task of advising has tended to be a more casual affair, although the two most recent associate directors in charge of the AM program, Laila Parsons and Susan Kahn, have attempted, with a measure of success, to place it on a sounder footing and to give the overall program greater coherence. To both sets of students, the Center has attempted to impart a message that is part of its ethos: the Middle East needs to be studied on its own terms and, therefore, it cannot be properly understood through the application of putatively universal conventions and categories of analysis. At stake here is more than a suspicion of the utility of disciplinary paradigms as determinants of what is to be studied and how it is to be studied. Rather, the message is premised on a conviction that Middle Eastern cultures and societies must be viewed from the inside rather than the outside and that such a perspective is possible only through knowledge of the history and modes of thought of its people.

Second, the Center has placed one field—history—at the apex of its intellectual interests. Although it was not always the case, Gibb's credo that "any program of regional studies without taproots is worthless, both academically and in its products"[29] has found a clear resonance at CMES since the late 1980s. For the Center's four latest directors, as for Gibb, the essence of these "taproots" has meant an overriding emphasis on the need for a profound and nuanced historical and cultural understanding of the Middle East. The premise has been that without a long-term perspective, a proper grasp of the region's problems of the twentieth century, or even of the nineteenth century, is likely to be elusive. The dominance of the history field has been evident in several tangible ways. Seven out of the twelve directors CMES has had in its first fifty years have come from the History Department. For at least three of the other five directors, history has been among their primary areas of research interest. And judging by the weight of senior faculty, traditionally the Center's greatest strength within Middle Eastern history has been in the pre-modern era. The concentration of history in the CMES doctoral program has not only been pronounced; it has become overwhelming in recent years. In the Center's first ten years, less than half of all joint PhDs were in history; over the last ten years, history has accounted for 90 percent of the total. As even a cursory look at the titles would suggest,[30] of the dissertations produced between 1995 and 2004, at least one out of every two are in pre-modern history. Unsurprisingly, CMES has not welcomed the prospect that history might be demoted by the march of the research agenda identified with the term "globalization." In one of the more forceful expressions of skepticism about that agenda, Owen has argued: "We must . . . continue to assert the importance of the study of history and the way that this can be used as a guide to the utility of previous theories of global/regional interactions which the present generation of globalists have conveniently managed to forget. . . . [H]istory itself becomes a weapon against the short term perspective displayed by most global social science."[31]

Third, CMES has accorded a peripheral position to contemporary themes and issues. The widely held notion that the Center has altogether neglected or slighted the modern and the contemporary, however, is misplaced. The generalization does not apply to many of the research projects to be found at the Center. Some of the most important research initiatives launched since 1990—for example, the Iraq Research and Documentation Project and the Contemporary Arab Studies Program—have focused on the present. Nor does it apply to the kind of researchers, such as visiting scholars and fellows, who have had appointments at the Center. Their range of interests has been more eclectic, perhaps much more so than that of the faculty, but it has been weighed heavily toward the contemporary. The current and unfolding realities in the Middle East have also been the thrust of the majority of fora sponsored by the Center in recent years. These have included not only perennials such as the Middle East Forum (formerly the "Brown Bag" Forum), and the Joint Seminar on Modern Middle Eastern Politics, organized jointly with the Weatherhead Center for International Affairs, but also newer seminar series, such as Gender and Health in Contemporary Muslim Communities, and Islam in Europe and America after September 11, both co-sponsored with the Center for European Studies. Nevertheless, the focus of research of the majority of the faculty associated with the Center has not been on the contemporary. As the discussion of history suggests, for a long time the pre-modern has been forte of the Middle East at Harvard. The generalization applies even more strongly to teaching. That the study of the contemporary Middle East has received short shrift in course offerings at Harvard is beyond dispute. It has been a complaint of many graduate students and it has been a concern of every recent director of CMES. The issue is addressed in several of the essays in Part III. However, the deficit has been not so much the product of deliberate choice on the part of the Center, although at times it has been interpreted as such, as it has been of the hiring decisions of individual departments. An emphatically contemporary approach to discourse on the Middle East would have come, most likely, from the social sciences. But, in the landscape of the Middle East at Harvard from 1990 to 2004, social scientists remained on the margins, even more than they had been in earlier decades. And, despite its constant pleading, the continued absence in disciplines such as government or economics of tenured professors with a specialty in the Middle East remained beyond the control of the Center.

Fourth, the Center has shied away from public policy debates and from policy-relevant research. Even when it comes to the Middle East, CMES has not been the first port of call within Harvard for reporters in search of a "sound bite" for the evening news or the next morning's newspaper. Faculty and other scholars associated with the Center have not made a habit of offering instant analysis of the crisis of the day or reciting menus of options for policy-makers. While there have been exceptions, the Center—to the chagrin of some, and to the relief of others—has distanced itself from the realm of policy and at times has even prided itself for doing so. The leaders of the Center have taken it as axiomatic that any meaningful effort to interpret the latest twist in chaotic events or to prescribe alternatives to decision makers must be rooted in a more than casual understanding of the region's historical complexities. All the same, only rarely have they ventured into policy analysis. Policy prescription has been even rarer. There have been calls—a few from inside Harvard, but most from outside—for policy work. The Center has resisted them, if only because this type of work does not fit easily within its culture. That CMES, in contrast to some other Middle Eastern centers in the United States, has become politically disengaged is an outcome that for the most part it has regarded with favor, given both its sense of what is and what is not critical to its mission and the lingering memories of its bruising experience of the mid-1980s.[32] Although seldom explicitly articulated, this stance has been of a piece with an approach to studying the Middle East that the Center has taken to be profoundly historical and humanistic. In the words of Kafadar, its most recent director: "Just as we cannot reduce history to a remote past, we cannot reduce the present to the immediate political encounters. Too often, the Middle East is viewed through the prism of the latest quagmire. We see plenty of this even here at Harvard. But the Middle East is much more than that and that's why we need to generate an understanding [of the Middle East] that has depth, nuance, complexity. And we always need to be sensitive to the larger historical and cultural context. We're not going to get that from the typical think-tank in D.C. Their mission is altogether different from ours."[33]

The 1990s and Beyond

The fifteen-year period from 1990 to 2004 saw notable moves to broaden and deepen the horizons of the Center for Middle Eastern Studies. While each of the three directors in this period brought to bear different emphases and interests, they have been generally complementary with each other and with the overall direction

The Center's inner circle in the mid-1990s. From left to right: Associate Director Susan Miller, Director William A. Graham, History Professor E. Roger Owen, Associate Director Thomas D. Mullins, and History Professor Roy P. Mottahedeh.

charted by Mottahedeh. William Graham, who would later become Dean of the Harvard Divinity School, emphasized the Center's concern not only with the Middle East as the region is conventionally understood but also with the larger world of Islam. Like Mottahedeh, Graham focused on making CMES into a center for Middle Eastern *and* Islamic studies. The Center was already recognized as the de facto locus of Islamic studies at Harvard. A new mission statement explicitly expanded the objective of the Center as encompassing the wider Islamic world in addition to the narrowly conceived geographical area of the Middle East.[34] It was evident, however, that moving the Center beyond its traditional moorings would not be a quick or easy project. Therefore, the ramifications of the widely shared view about the need to recast the intellectual and spatial reach of CMES—and by extension the Middle Eastern field at Harvard at large—have yet to unfold. Nevertheless, it was in the early 1990s and at CMES that these stirrings emerged at the University. An Islamic Studies Committee set up by CMES to spur the effort concluded that any serious endeavor in Islamic studies would need to be not only interdisciplinary in approach but also transregional and transnational in scope. The committee, led by Mottahedeh and Graham, recognized that such an emphasis would have far-reaching implications for the area studies orientation that has been the bedrock of the Center since its creation. The committee also concluded that while Harvard probably had the strongest concentration of scholarly expertise in classical Islamic studies among any university in the West, its weight in the modern area was weaker by comparison.

Among the activities instituted at the Center in the early
1990s was the Harvard Islamic Investment Project. The project,
undertaken jointly with the Harvard Law School's Islamic Legal
Studies Program and the Harvard Business School, resulted in a
major work on one of the more exotic areas of the international
financial services industry: Islamic banking and investment.[35] In
another collaborative initiative, the Islamic Studies Committee
joined forces with the Centre for Islamic Studies at Oxford
University to work on a multi-volume atlas of the social and intellectual history of the Muslim world. The research, a comparative
inquiry into the development and diffusion of ideas, beliefs, sects,
and groups in Islamic civilization, exemplified the increased attention to the world of Islam beyond the Middle East, as it also
included Muslim South Asia, Southeast Asia, Central Asia, and
Africa. Two other activities illustrated the growing interest in giving a more contemporary focus to research at the Center. The Iraq
Research and Documentation Project was founded at CMES in
1993 to create an archive for millions of government military and
security documents seized by rebels in the uprisings that swept Iraq
following the Gulf War of 1991. The project, led by Iraqi-born
Kanan Makiya, has provided an unusual picture of the inner
workings of the Saddam Hussein regime. The Moroccan Studies
Program, initiated in 1985 and funded by the Moroccan government, underwent significant development in the 1990s. The
program, directed by Susan Miller, who also was associate director of the Center from 1990 to 1999, has been the anchor for

research and teaching at Harvard on the Maghrib, thanks to such activities as organizing seminars and conferences, supporting courses and fellowships, and arranging visits by prominent Moroccan artists and intellectuals.

Harvard, and CMES, took a major step toward alleviating the seemingly perpetual problem of the imbalance between the premodern and the modern in the study of Middle Eastern history with the appointment of Roger Owen in 1993 as the first occupant of the newly endowed A.J. Meyer Chair. Owen, the dean of economic historians of the Middle East and author of landmark publications such as *The Middle East in the World Economy, 1800–1914* and (with Şevket Pamuk) *A History of Middle East Economies in the Twentieth Century*, came to Harvard from Oxford, where he had directed St. Antony's College Middle East Centre. In addition to courses in the Core Curriculum, notably "Making and Remaking of the Modern Middle East," Owen began to offer graduate seminars, covering such subjects as theoretical and empirical debates in the economic and social history of the Middle East. These seminars became a draw for many students at CMES. Perhaps Owen's most important influence at the Center —one that has been felt even before and after his relatively brief stint as director between 1996 and 1999—has been to re-engage the Center with the Arab world. Owen was more than a little conscious of the fact that many of the links CMES once had with the Arab Middle East had withered away after the passing of A.J. Therefore, he made one of his priorities the re-establishment of academic relationships with institutions and individuals in Arab countries. Motivating this effort is a conviction that the study of the Middle East must be a partnership with Middle Easterners. As Owen put it: "If I'm studying the economic history of Egypt, I should do it with Egyptian economists. But that's not easy to do. It's easier to collaborate with Turkish or Iranian economists because they have a larger presence in the United States. Besides, far more Turkish and Iranian scholars travel here than [do] Egyptians. The same, of course, goes for Israelis."[36]

Owen seized on the opportunity to give a programmatic expression at the Center to this interest in the Arab Middle East. In 1995, CMES launched a Contemporary Arab Studies Program (CASP) with the express purposes of sponsoring intellectual exchange with Arab universities, undertaking research projects on issues vital to the Arab world, holding seminars and workshops on current concerns of Arab society and culture, and strengthening

E. Roger Owen, A.J. Meyer Professor of History, and Director of CMES, 1996–1999.

the academic resources at Harvard for training a new generation of students in the field of Arab studies. CASP helped to support a new, and one of the Center's enduring, seminar series, the Arab Studies Forum. The Forum is chaired by Owen, who introduced it in 1996 in order to provide a platform for presenting some of the best work being done in the field. Under the aegis of the program, Owen also organized several international conferences, including two in 1995 and 1996 on issues of land and property in the Middle East,[37] and another in 1997 entitled "Challenges Facing the Arab World at the End of the 20th Century," which was designed to provide a Middle Eastern voice on the dominant perspective on globalization as well as on the areas of contestation in the notion of what constitutes the Middle East. CASP provided the impetus for the creation in 1998 of yet another project at the Center, the Arab Education Forum, which has dedicated itself to stimulating a dialogue on alternatives in education in Arab countries.

With programs in place for Iranian and Arab studies, it seemed only fitting that the Center would turn its attention to Turkish and Ottoman studies. Harvard was not a newcomer to this field. It was shortly after the turn of the twentieth century that the diplomatic historian Archibald Coolidge came to Harvard, where he taught Ottoman history for many years and left future scholars a collection of materials on the Ottomans that is one of the treasures of Widener Library. And it was in 1913 that one of Coolidge's students, Albert Howe Lybyer, published his classic on the Ottoman state that advanced the much-debated institutional argument known as the "Lybyer thesis."[38] Courses in Ottoman and Turkish history were taught over the years by several of the core faculty of CMES, including William Langer, Robert L. Wolff, Stanford J. Shaw, Richard D. Robinson, and Dennis Skiotis, who also served as associate director for many years. In addition, CMES had hosted as visiting scholars two of the century's leading Turkish historians, Fuat Köprülü and Halil İnalcik. Considering its strengths in fields beyond history—including language, philology, literature, art, architecture, anthropology, and economics—Harvard in 1990 could claim to have more resources in Turkish studies than any other university in North America. The Center did not have a formal program of Turkish studies. However, as an indication of the growing interest in the area, by 1995 fully one-third of CMES graduate students were concentrating on the

Ottoman and Turkish fields, all under the supervision of Cemal Kafadar, who came to Harvard in 1990 from Princeton.

The appointment of Kafadar in 1997 as the first Vehbi Koç Professor of Turkish Studies represented an important development in the invigoration of the discipline for the Center and for Harvard. The chair, named after one of Turkey's leading industrialists and philanthropists, was the product of a fifteen-year effort by CMES to secure a permanent endowment for Turkish studies. Kafadar established himself as a leading figure in the field through such works as *Between Two Worlds: The Construction of the Ottoman State*,[39] a significant contribution not only to the debates about the origins of the empire but also to the use of literary narratives in Middle Eastern historiography. His courses on the Ottoman state and society, along with more general offerings in the Core Curriculum, such as "The Middle East and Europe since the Crusades," marked the first sustained treatment of Ottoman and Turkish history for Harvard students in three decades.

Cemal Kafadar, Vehbi Koç Professor of Turkish Studies, and CMES Director, 1999–2004.

As director from 1999 to 2004, Kafadar presided over an explosion of interest in this field. Perhaps no single measure is as telling as the number of Ottoman and Turkish historians the Center has produced in recent years. For the latest crop, four out of the seven PhDs awarded in 2004 in the CMES joint program dealt with the Ottoman era.[40] Kafadar has undertaken several research projects that have given a further boost to Ottoman studies. Among these is one of the most ambitious projects in which the Center has ever participated: an effort to organize the mountain of information in the court records of Ottoman Istanbul across four centuries. Spearheading the work are Kafadar and Gülru Necipoğlu, the Aga Khan Professor of Islamic Art and Architecture and one of the core faculty of CMES, who has held this chair since 1993.[41] For the last fifteen years, they have led a team of researchers in sifting through millions of *qadi* court cases involving Muslims and non-Muslims, women and men, rich and poor. The project, described in Part II of this volume, plans to publish the court registers in scores of volumes and also to present them in electronic format using a context-sensitive concordance, an innovation in the field of Middle Eastern and Islamic studies. A more recently founded project, Historians of the Ottoman Empire, is aiming to provide the definitive biographical and bibliographic reference work for Ottoman history. The project, which Kafadar is organizing with the University of Chicago's

Cornell Fleischer and Hakan Karateke of NELC and CMES, will cover works not only in Turkish but also in other relevant languages. Two aspects of these projects are particularly noteworthy: they involve extensive collaboration with scholars in Turkey, Arab countries, and the Balkans; and they have directly engaged students at CMES. Several fora have offered a further stimulus to the field. The Center's Study Group on Modern Turkey, chaired by Kafadar and research associate Lenore Martin, began meeting in 2001 to hear an array of speakers, from scholars to diplomats, on vital issues in Turkey today. In recent years, CMES also has sponsored international conferences on themes ranging from the future of Turkish foreign policy[42] to a reflection on the state of Ottoman studies against the backdrop of İnalcik's contributions to the field.[43]

In addition to working on strengthening CMES's teaching and research programs, as well as attending to the quotidian demands that are part of the daily menu of any director, Kafadar actively pursued his interest in stimulating the cultural life of the Center. Perhaps more than any other of his eleven predecessors, he proved to be an ardent patron of the arts at CMES, supporting a wave of diverse music groups that emerged spontaneously and engaging the Center in a variety of film screenings and symposia. Kafadar also attempted to tackle what has become a growing concern at the Center: the financial hardships and uncertainties faced by many of its students, both AMs and PhDs. In an effort to increase its level of support, in 2000 CMES began offering summer research and travel grants to all doctoral students. Such measures are acknowledged to be but a modest step toward alleviating the funding problems of these students, many of whom devote the better part of a decade to fulfilling the demands of the program: from training in at least one language and regular coursework in one or more disciplines to field research in the Middle East and the writing of a dissertation. AM students, on the other hand, have had even fewer avenues for financial support from anywhere inside the University, while the many foreign students, whose presence is considered essential to preserving the cosmopolitanism of the Center, are generally ineligible for government fellowships in area studies. Finally, toward the end of his term, Kafadar put in motion a strategic initiative that is likely to have an important influence on the Center for years to come. The objective involves nothing less than arriving at an internal consensus about future directions for the Center and developing a long-term development plan, including a major fund-raising drive, to strengthen every facet of the life of the Center.

During this period, the Center also was confronted with the geopolitical upheavals triggered by the events of September 11, 2001, and by the war in Iraq that began in March 2003. These events evoked a response that revealed much about its priorities and emphases since the late 1980s. As would be expected of any such center, CMES organized a series of events, including seminars and workshops, to consider some of the larger questions raised by these turbulent developments. The Center also planned a project that would attempt to understand the consequences of 9/11 and of the struggle against terrorism for the Arab and Islamic world. Nevertheless, CMES did not rush to make itself more visible in the policy debates about a world crisis, or a convergence of world crises, centered in the Middle East. The Center felt it was incumbent on itself not to be deflected from the pursuit of its vision of historical and humanistic scholarship. Consequently, notwithstanding the occasional contributions to op-ed pages or appearances before the media by some faculty members, the voice of CMES during these crises has been relatively subdued. What is instructive, however, is that when it did choose to project its voice, the message it delivered was more often than not about the importance of understanding the complexities of history. Two examples, both of which are commentaries written in 2003 after the outbreak of the war in Iraq, illustrate the point. Other schools and centers at Harvard, notably the Kennedy School of Government and the Weatherhead Center for International Affairs, issued a steady stream of analysis about such matters as the deliberations at the United Nations Security Council or the effects of the "shock and awe" tactics of the US military. It was CMES that offered insights about the array of forces that have shaped the tortured history of Iraq and the political behavior of its people.

In "Keeping the Shi'ites Straight,"[44] written shortly after the invasion, Mottahedeh documented the perils of the failure to comprehend the country's sectarian majority. Public discourse, he noted, "almost universally skipped everything between 680 [the year of the murder of Husayn] and the 21st century." Mottahedeh then offered what amounted to a brief primer on Iraqi Shi'ism, in the process touching on the disappearance of the Twelfth Imam, the Hawza of Najaf, the structure of the religious hierarchy, and other issues essential for a proper grasp of the behavior of the Shi'ites—including the conundrum of why "they failed to welcome their liberators with rapturous joy." He argued that the Shi'ite clerics' "pragmatic approach to their flocks suggests that they are accomplished at adjusting to political realities if they have a say in matters vital to them" and concluded that it would be "very hard, and possibly very unwise, to build a new Iraq without allowing some of them to participate."

Owen, in one of his regular columns for the Egyptian week-ly *Al-Ahram*,[45] looked back at Hanna Batatu's *The Old Social Classes*,[46] a monumental work based on his 1960 dissertation at Harvard, to find clues about the contemporary political and social dynamics of Iraq. Owen noted, somewhat ruefully, that it would be virtually impossible to replicate the analysis of social structure carried out by Batatu, given the disruptions in communal and property relationships wrought by the Ba'athists and by the American occupation, and therein he espied some of the many unknowns about Iraq today. His predictions about the road ahead were far removed from the staple of both policy wonks and the quality media: "As Iraq moves towards national elections we shall certainly see more of communal leaders mobilising their communities behind national as well as communal ends. We shall also become increasingly aware of the pressures forcing all politicians working at the national level to do so in accommodation with their rivals. Whether it will produce a satisfactory result is another matter. Mutual distrust and fear will certainly play an even more pernicious role than it did in 1958–63 . . . We may indeed be faced with something that looks much more like Lebanon in 1943 than Iraq a decade or so later. It is here where we reach the point at which history is no longer much of a guide."

The CMES administration and staff as photographed in May 2004. Left to right: Ahmed Jebari, Staff Assistant; Kris Evans, Assistant to the Director and Staff Assistant; Susan Kahn, Associate Director and Director of the AM Program; Professor Cemal Kafadar, Director; Jonathan Ramljak, Coordinator of Publications, Communications, and Graduate Studies; and Barbara Henson, Financial Administrator.

Retrospective

The Center broke down barriers between departments. People from Government and Economics could come here and interact day by day with people from History or Fine Arts. CMES was a wonderful example of how area studies can be fertile and stimulating across disciplinary boundaries . . . We were able to bring some of the best minds in our fields to Cambridge. The result was a glorious environment for provincial beginners like me. It was a special moment, rich and lively.

    —Edward L. Keenan[47]

On its fiftieth anniversary, Harvard's Center for Middle Eastern Studies could look back with a measure of pride at what it had achieved since its founding in 1954. It had pioneered many facets of teaching and research in one of the more esoteric areas of inquiry in the academy. It had given coherence to an array of academic programs in a field widely acknowledged to be more disparate and more demanding than any other in the constellation of area studies. For these programs, it had offered a base of intellectual and institutional support that proved critical in nurturing and expanding scholarship on the Middle East. It had drawn human and material resources from across the University in planning, organizing, coordinating, and guiding the numerous activities required to fulfill its complex mission. As a result, the Center was instrumental not only in solidifying the position of Middle Eastern studies at Harvard but also in instilling a greater level of professionalization and systematization to the field.

Harvard had originally envisaged, in the words of a press release announcing the creation of CMES, "specialized training in a basic two-year course," leading to an AM degree in Middle Eastern Studies, that would prepare students "to enter at once upon government service or business careers in the Middle East."[48] The reality, of course, turned out to be markedly different, as the Center's priority in teaching quickly became the preparation of a new generation of scholars in Middle Eastern fields. The leading positions in universities across the United States and elsewhere attained by graduates of its joint doctoral program are testimony to the Center's success in this endeavor. From the University of California at Berkeley and the University of Washington in Seattle to Columbia and Princeton, the directors of Middle East centers have included products of CMES. Graduates of CMES have also played central roles in professional organizations dedicated to furthering the study of the field. Seven of the thirty presidents of the Middle East Studies Association between 1974 and 2003 were alumni of the Center.[49] The Center's alumni also have distinguished themselves in a variety of professions beyond the academy, including business, finance, government, diplomacy, law, and journalism.

Thanks in no small part to CMES, Harvard's course offerings on the Middle East, including both language instruction and departmental disciplines, have grown over a period of five decades from less than a handful to more than two hundred. As a result, thousands of Harvard students, especially undergraduates, have learned about a part of the world that would have remained a blank to them. During the same period, the number of faculty members associated with the Center has risen from four to more than sixty, fully one-half of whom are tenured. Today, they constitute perhaps the largest concentration of Middle Eastern scholars anywhere in the world. It is this assemblage, more than any other ingredient in Harvard's armamentarium of resources in this field, that has kept CMES at the top of its cohort of Middle Eastern and Islamic studies centers in the United States and abroad. For some of these faculty, along with many graduate students and even a few undergraduates, the Center has offered not only a vibrant setting through its panoply of activities related to the Middle East but also a primary intellectual "home" and a sense of community that is not easily found in the more diffuse academic departments.

The Center in 2004 showed few, if any, traces of the tensions and schisms that had convulsed it in the 1970s and 1980s. It had become one of the more pluralistic, even amicable, communities in Middle Eastern studies. A former associate director could credibly claim: "What stands out is the inclusiveness of the Center. That, and the pervasive tone of civility in the place. Yes, there are differences in pedagogy and in politics. Yes, we do have people of different persuasions—red shirts and green shirts. But this is anything but a divided Center. There's a total absence of rancor. There are loads of opportunities here and that's what seems to occupy the energy of everyone here."[50]

It is a community that has been enriched over the years by visiting professors and researchers whose ranks comprise a Who's Who of Middle Eastern studies. The Center continues to draw requests from around the world from senior and junior academics seeking a research affiliation through its program for visiting scholars and post-doctoral fellows. In addition, the Center attracts some of the best and brightest students who seek to specialize in the field. Indeed, notwithstanding the decline in levels of financial support and the vagaries of an already fiercely competitive job market, applications to its academic programs have never been higher than in recent years. In addition, CMES has remained at the top of the government funding league. As a federally funded Title VI National Resource Center, CMES is charged with fulfilling a function as a source of learning about the Middle East not only within its immediate surroundings but also in the wider New England area. The award by the Department of Education of a grant of almost $2 million for 2003–2006 to enable the Outreach Center to further its activities in support of this function, and also to provide Foreign Language and Area Studies Fellowships, represents an affirmation of the importance of the educational mission of CMES.

However, at fifty, the Center was also acutely aware of its limitations and failures. The principal rationale for the creation of the Center was a need to stimulate scholarship in a sorely neglected field. An annual report published at the beginning of its second decade insisted that while the Center had avoided a separation between classical and modern Middle Eastern studies, "it does recognize that departments and disciplines long established at Harvard provide a core for classical studies, whereas the Center is the one body in the Harvard community specifically charged with the task of adding the needed balance of modern studies."[51] Along several critical indicators, the Center has made limited headway in achieving this balance. Its predominant strength has remained premodern and has been concentrated in the humanities, a striking contrast not only with its mission but also with the expectations of many graduate students who seek an emphasis on contemporary and practical issues. The dearth of senior faculty who deal with these issues in teaching and research reflects, above all, Harvard's inability decade in and decade out to add in the social science disciplines sufficient capabilities to match the University's traditional excellence in pre–twentieth-century history; Ottoman, Iranian, and Islamic studies; and languages. The absence of such capabilities is reflected, in turn, in the Center's subdued engagement in discourse on the world after 9/11 and, more generally, in its relative detachment from many mainstream concerns affecting the Middle East today.

Well before the end of its fifth decade, CMES had achieved an objective that for years had seemed beyond its reach: a senior position in the History Department. By 2001, the department had no less than four positions in the Middle Eastern field.[52] Efforts over a span of more than ten years to replicate this success in Economics and Government became an exercise in futility. The weight of the Middle East field in both departments followed an identical script: it went from one junior appointment to the absence of any positions. The Center also was troubled by the continued absence of a Middle Eastern specialist in sociology. These imbalances resulted in a narrowing of the intellectual horizons of the Center in at least one critical respect: its teaching mission. Of the fifty-three students enrolled in the joint doctoral programs in 2003–04, forty-five were in History and Middle Eastern Studies. The once-thriving joint programs with Economics and Government had vanished. Aside from History, the two formal joint degree programs that remained were with Anthropology and Fine Arts. The Center also had established a concurrent degree program with the Law School, a notable exception to a generally failing record of attempts to collaborate with other schools. The daunting logistics of arranging a joint degree program with the Kennedy School of Government, along with the absence of a definitive commitment on the part of the School, led to the recent suspension of that effort.

What is perhaps most revealing about Keenan's statement above is its use of the past tense. That the Center "broke down barriers between departments" reflects an era when area studies, and the centers around which they converged, were regarded as an innovative and dynamic enterprise. "Area studies" was not the term of opprobrium that it has become in many quarters of the academy today. In its first two decades, the Center enjoyed the intellectual and institutional underpinnings for interdisciplinary collaboration that was both robust and extensive. The saga of the encounter between Middle Eastern studies and the social sciences at Harvard suggests that many of those underpinnings have eroded in the last two decades. Gibb's aspiration was to see area centers such as CMES "play the part of Trojan horse": instead of permanently cloistering themselves in a distant complex, all of its associated faculty members were to make sure that they were part of the core of their disciplinary departments. Only then, he insisted, would they be able to exercise any meaningful influence over these disciplines and, in the process, "radiate a knowledge and understanding of specific aspects of [Middle Eastern] cultures to their colleagues."[53] If this struggle was difficult for the Center during the heyday of area studies, it has become considerably more so in recent years. The Trojan horse role always presumed a firm base within departments. In many departments, particularly in the social sciences, the base did not exist or, when it did, it was tenuous and many of its holders remained on the periphery. The hope that CMES would be the habitat and the breeding ground of Gibb's "new kind of academic amphibian"—social scientists simultaneously at the cutting edge of their discipline and also at home in the history, culture, and languages of the Middle East—did not quite materialize. Some departments, especially the heavily quantitative social sciences, did not want amphibians of this sort; others considered the ones they encountered to be insufficiently amphibian.

Insofar as many faculty in Middle Eastern studies are marginalized, and also feel marginalized, CMES and Harvard are hardly unique. The problem has been longstanding and is pervasive in universities across the United States.[54] From the start, the Center waged a battle with other departments to secure acceptance and recognition. As its tenth anniversary report acknowledged, "By all odds the most difficult of the major commitments was to fashion a teaching program that would provide within the context of a large geographical area a training in a variety of traditional disciplines that would have integrity and unity of itself without diluting the academic quality of the students in relation to their chosen departments." But the difficulty did not stop there. "It was necessary," the report added, "to demonstrate to existing departments that a graduate program giving more emphasis to 'area studies' could be conducted without sacrificing any essentials of long-established disciplinary requirements."[55] Forty years later, the battle to convince the departments had yet to be won.[56]

The integration of the Center with the disciplinary departments, and of Middle Eastern studies into the University in general, stands as the unfulfilled promise of the last fifty years. Yet, to the extent that these are failures, it would be more than a little misleading to ascribe them to failures of the Center. The Center's institutionalized dependence on the departments has meant that it lacks control over the principal determinant of the direction of Middle Eastern studies at Harvard and its long-term future:

faculty appointments. Hence, "adding the needed balance of modern studies" or redressing the chronic imbalance between the humanities and the social sciences is beyond the capabilities of CMES. The Center can plead and cajole. Occasionally, it can put some of its money on the table in order to secure a temporary appointment. But it has no decision-making power in what matters most here: senior positions in the field. Some of the social science departments, especially Economics and Government, consider such centers as irrelevant to their interests. The ranks of faculty in these departments who might still attach some weight to the study of the Middle East per se have thinned to the point that today few, if any, are inclined to take up the cause of permanent appointments. What exists in the way of communication between CMES and these departments in recent years has been limited and episodic. Intimately related to all these concerns is what some take to be a factor that will have a decisive bearing on the future of Middle Eastern studies at Harvard: the nature and extent of the University administration's commitment.[57]

Quo Vadis?

On July 1, 2004, Steven C. Caton took over the directorship of the Center for Middle Eastern Studies. After a period of almost twenty years during which the leadership of the Center was dominated by historians, mostly with an emphasis on the pre-modern period, the ascension of a social scientist, an anthropologist with an interest in contemporary problems, marks a major change for the Center. It may even turn out to be milestone in a process that results in the Center reinventing itself. CMES took the first steps in this process during the period of transition from one director to another in the spring of 2004 when it engaged in an intensive stock-taking exercise that included a re-examination of its mission, deliberations on future initiatives, and the preparation of an ambitious development plan.

Caton's vision for the Center, as articulated in his fittingly titled essay, "Transitions," in Part III, is decidedly interdisciplinary. It also gives pride of place to transnationalism both as an intellectual paradigm and as an amalgam of phenomena with profound consequences for every major facet of life in the Middle East and beyond the Middle East. In at least two respects, neither of these

Gülru Necipoğlu, the Aga Khan Professor of Islamic Art and Architecture, and Wolfhart P. Heinrichs, James Richard Jewett Professor of Arabic, at a faculty retreat held on March 20, 2004, to discuss the mission of the Center.

emphases is a novelty for the Center. CMES has underscored the need for interdisciplinary approaches since its inception. Interdisciplinarity, in fact, was one of the justifications for the creation of a body outside existing departmental structures. And, even if they did not use the term, for both students of Islam and scholars of the Ottoman empire their subject matter was quintessentially transnational, given the porousness of borders and the fluidity of identities in the Islamic and Ottoman realms.[58] What perhaps can be regarded as novel, however, are the epistemological assumptions and implications, some of which are adumbrated in the essay. Also novel is the range of issues Caton highlights: to name a few, transgendered sexuality, mass media, informational flows, diasporic communities, and water resources. With the possible exception of the latter, these have not been the salient themes of research at the Center even during periods when contemporary questions received greater attention.

While the implications for research and teaching remain to be determined, Caton's call for moving beyond the erstwhile area-specific framework of inquiry poses yet another challenge to what CMES has done as area studies center. The call, which is echoed and expanded in several other essays in Part III, including William Graham's and Frank Vogel's, reflects a growing, although less than universal, consensus among Middle Eastern scholars at Harvard and elsewhere about the need to transcend the conventional boundaries of the Middle East as the region had been defined during the Cold War. Hence, studying the historic and emerging

Steven C. Caton, Professor of Contemporary Arab Studies, Anthropology Department, and Afsaneh Najmabadi, Professor of History and of Women's Studies, at the Workshop on Challenges in Sexuality Studies in and of the Middle East. The workshop was held at CMES on May 7, 2004, and was co-sponsored with the Harvard Committee on Degrees in Studies of Women, Gender, and Sexuality, which is chaired by Najmabadi.

linkages with Central Asia and South Asia would become much more than a passing concern. The inclusion in the mid-1980s of North Africa as part of the pedagogical and research mandate of the Center was an earlier step toward a reconceptualization of the Middle East beyond the traditional definition, as was the recognition, codified in a revised mission statement in the 1990s, that the intellectual reach of the Center included the wider world of Islam. However, the more expansive definition of the rubric of the Middle East envisaged in "Transitions" would require more than simply a spatial adjustment. The Center, according to this vision, would also strive to make inter-regional inquiry both comparative and collaborative.

In combination, these suggestions are in line with recent trends in the wider world of scholarship and funding. Cross-disciplinary, cross-regional approaches focused on specific issues and grounded in systematic comparison have been the essence of the reordered priorities in international programs of the influential private foundations, which have been the main impetus over the last decade behind efforts to "internationalize" or "globalize" area studies.[59] The Center's recent steps in rethinking the field also come at a time when Harvard has begun the most sweeping review of its undergraduate curriculum in thirty years.[60] Although the proposed changes are yet to be finalized, the emphasis on internationalizing the curriculum, including the likelihood that henceforth Harvard students will be encouraged or expected to spend some time studying abroad, suggests promising opportunities for CMES. The timing of this initiative is particularly significant. In the words of FAS Dean William C. Kirby, it is being undertaken "at a moment when the United States misunderstands the world, and the world misunderstands the United States more than anytime recently."[61]

The Center for Middle Eastern Studies in 2004 found itself at a juncture that few could have predicted fifty or even ten years earlier. On the one hand, both inside and outside the academy, knowledge and understanding of the part of the world it dealt with was pronounced to be more vital than ever. On the other hand, the field of Middle Eastern studies had never faced a crisis as severe as the ones it experienced after 2001. MESA President and former Harvard Professor Lisa Anderson bemoaned the "dreadful state" into which the region had descended.[62] The characterization appeared to apply with equal force to the field itself. Even among its leading figures, expressions of doubt about whether Middle Eastern studies had much of a future already had become commonplace. In addition, the field now faced a phalanx of polemicists who made a cottage industry out of attacks against Middle Eastern study centers, Title VI National Resource Centers, the Middle Eastern Studies Association—in short, against the profession and its institutions. Among the farrago of aspersions against the profession was a collective indictment for a failure to foresee the tragedy of 9/11.

However, for Middle Eastern studies, and for area studies in general, the more serious, and in the long run perhaps the more damaging, criticisms originated within the academy. To the older critiques of Middle Eastern scholarship as a tool for legitimating domination over the "Other" came the enfilades from the "hard" disciplinary-oriented social sciences, especially political science and economics. Many of the criticisms leveled against area studies, among which some of the most powerful originated at Harvard,[63] were familiar as they had been thoroughly rehearsed for decades: area studies are descriptive and atheoretical; they lack explanatory or predictive power; they are methodologically suspect and devoid of analytical rigor; they shy away from hypothesis testing and theory building; they are out of touch with disciplinary developments; they fail to offer insights that transcend time and place; they are provincial and irrelevant; they lead to work that is "mushy,"[64] etc. As it concerns the interaction between Middle

Eastern studies and the social sciences in particular, equally, if not more, serious are more recent arguments that substantive knowledge of areas is less than consequential in the first place. While there are many variants in these arguments, they converge in devaluing or dismissing the notion that an understanding of the particularities of regions is essential. Such are the claims of theories that ascribe uniformities in motivations and calculations to the rational choices of utility-maximizing individuals. Such are the claims of the neoclassical orthodoxy summed up in the term "monoeconomics," which rejects the notion that developing countries face economic circumstances sufficiently distinct from those of the developed countries as to warrant a recasting of conventional economic analysis, and which, in its insistence that universally valid laws apply to all countries regardless of how they are constituted, discards individual histories. And such are the claims of theories of globalization that see the homogenizing and leveling effects of economic integration as so potent and so pervasive that, once again, not only are the distinctive attributes of societies and cultures being reduced, perhaps on their way to being effaced altogether, but so is the need to devote much attention to studying them.[65]

For the architects of the Center for Middle Eastern Studies, these modes of parsing reality, each of which had plenty of adherents within the academy, must surely rank as one of the more remarkable conceits of the last fifty years. The suggestion that one can dispense with knowledge about the complexities and intricacies of regional, national, or local contexts would have been unthinkable, if not unfathomable. Equally so would have been the notion that the need to comprehend the specificities of history, culture, language, and thought is being rendered irrelevant both by the forces of international interdependence and by the insights afforded by more parsimonious and rigorous explanations grounded in theoretical and analytical approaches that have eluded area studies. Perhaps it is no small irony that, in 2004, it was turbulence in the Middle East, more than anything else, that appeared to confound claims about the irrelevance of history and culture for understanding behavior and outcomes.

Fifty years after its creation, the intellectual justification behind the establishment of a Center for Middle Eastern Studies at Harvard seemed to be as compelling as ever. The geopolitical landscape of 1954 had changed, but the declared imperative of confronting the problem of a paucity of knowledge and understanding of the Middle East was very much intact. The Center in 2004 began a process of rethinking its strategic enterprise in Middle Eastern studies and deliberating future initiatives that would build on its traditional strengths in the field and make way for new areas of inquiry and new frameworks of analysis. As it did so, both the opportunities and the constraints were as immense as any it had faced in its history. ☉

Notes

1. "Proposal for a Program in Middle Eastern Studies," October 28, 1952, Dean's Office, Faculty of Arts and Sciences (FAS), UA 111.5. 55.26 (Middle Eastern Studies, Center for), Box 13, Harvard University Archives, p. 1. The proposal is an early version of the one cited in note 2.

2. Committee on International and Regional Studies, "Proposal for a Program in Middle Eastern Studies," March 26, 1953, Records of President Pusey, UAI 5.169 (Middle Eastern Studies, 1953–1954), Box 20, Harvard University Archives, p. 1.

3. Dudley Hall, on 16 Dunster Street, was torn down soon afterward and replaced by Holyoke Center. CMES then moved to Coolidge Hall, 1737 Cambridge Street. Coolidge Hall, in turn, was demolished in 2002, to be replaced by the Knafel Center for Government and International Studies, upon which CMES moved into temporary headquarters at 1430 Massachusetts Avenue.

4. *In and Out of the Ivory Tower: The Autobiography of William L. Langer* (New York: N. Watson Academic Publications, 1977), p. 133.

5. The Committee on International and Regional Studies was renamed the Committee on Regional Studies in 1954.

6. "Literatures" was later replaced by "Civilizations" in the title, resulting in the current Department of Near Eastern Languages and Civilizations (NELC).

7. "Harvard University: Center for Middle Eastern Studies," meeting of the Executive Committee, International Training and Research," March 21, 1957, Ford Foundation (PA 57-141), p. 2. The generous assistance of Bruce Byers, Director of Information Technology at the Social Science Research Council, in sharing this and other material on the foundations is gratefully acknowledged.

8. Hamilton Gibb, *Area Studies Reconsidered* (London: School of Oriental and African Studies, University of London, 1965), p. 14.

9. *Ibid.*, p. 3.

10. *Ibid.*, p. 12.

11. Letter to President Pusey, Nov. 12, 1958, Dean's Office, FAS, UA 111.5. 55.26 (Middle Eastern Studies, Center for), Box 13, Harvard University Archives, p. 1.

12. Hamilton Gibb, "Program for Middle Eastern Studies," memorandum prepared for Rockefeller Foundation, Aug. 1956, UAV 569.12 ("Rockefeller Foundation," CMES Director's and Asst. Director's Files, 1958-68), Box 3, Harvard University Archives, pp. 10–11.

13. "Meeting of the President and Fellows of Harvard College," Dec. 16, 1963, and "Hamilton Alexander Rosskeen Gibb: Recommendation of the Dean of the Faculty of Arts and Sciences," Dec. 3, 1963, Records of President Pusey, UAI 5.169 (Middle Eastern Studies, 1963–1964), Box 300, Harvard University Archives.

14. Hourani's trenchant observation here is instructive, especially when one considers the enormous respect and affection he held for Gibb, whom he called "the great figure . . . even when physically absent . . . spiritually with us, the *murshid* guiding our steps in different ways." (Albert Hourani, *Islam in European Thought* [Cambridge and New York: Cambridge University Press, 1991], p. 61.) Gibb's administrative arrangements at Harvard, Hourani notes, "did not always have the results he intended, and those who observed him at work were never quite sure whether he had failed to understand the Harvard system or understood it rather too well. Faced with difficulties in a department he would go to a higher authority or just go his own way, and his construction had the essential fragility of a network of patron-client relations." (Hourani, "H.A.R. Gibb: The Vocation of an Orientalist," in *Europe and the Middle East* [Berkeley: University of California Press, 1980], p. 129.)

15. CMES, Annual Report, 1966–67, UA U569.158.18, Harvard University Archives, p. 2.

16. Harvard University, Graduate School of Arts and Sciences, "The Center for Middle Eastern Studies: Supplement to the General Announcement, 1956–57."

17. At FAS, a professorial appointment is normally in a department. Administratively, no department or discipline bearing the name of "Middle Eastern Studies" existed at Harvard.

18. Interview, Feb. 2004.

19. Safran was gravely ill by the time the preparation of this study was underway and, hence, a statement about his perspective on the events of 1985 and 1986 could not be obtained. He died of cancer on July 5, 2003.

In one of the few public statements on the occasion, Safran declared, "I had said at the outset that I had made an error in not informing the participants invited to the conference *as soon as* the CIA funding came into the picture. It was not there originally when they were invited, but only came later. I thought of the CIA contribution as being like another contribution coming to the Center. The Center receives contributions from a whole variety of sources which we do not necessarily disclose. We do not keep it secret, but we do not necessarily disclose it. I thought this was one of these things." ("Harvard's Nadav Safran Tells Story Behind Inquiry Ordeal," *The Jewish Advocate*, Jan. 16, 1986. Emphasis in original.)

Safran did selectively disclose the funding source. Consequently, some of the conference participants were aware of the CIA role before the public outcry, although most were not. Internal records also show that Safran was not wholly at ease about accepting CIA funding for the event. As late as the spring of 1985, he turned to several other sources to request alternative funding, a step that had been recommended by the Executive Committee, but was turned down. A letter to the Ford Foundation dated April 30, 1985, stated: "We at CMES don't mind being funded by [the CIA] as long as the proper standards of academic integrity and accessibility of results are maintained. We however, prefer for the sake of public peace of mind, funding from a more conventional source." ("Safran Correspondence," CMES Files.)

20. "Report on the Center for Middle Eastern Studies," *Harvard Gazette*, January 10, 1986. Hereafter, Spence Report.

Limitations on access to FAS records precludes a full account of the actions of the parties in the episode. However, a week before the leak and two weeks before the conference, Safran wrote Dean Spence and not only notified him about the conference but also addressed the contentious problem of its funding. "Funding for the conference," Safran noted in a one-page letter, "will be provided by the CIA—in the form of a $45,700 personal contract with me, as an 'independent contractor.' I, in turn, will write a check to CMES under the heading of 'recovered expenses' to cover the conference costs." Safran went on to explain why he had not communicated earlier about the matter: "I did not write to you sooner, as perhaps I should have, because four years ago, when I inquired about a similar case, I was told that there was no need to inform the University about personal contracts, as long as the pertinent rules regarding such contracts were observed. They are in this case: the conference is open to the public and the papers are all already available, and have in fact been put on reserve in the Coolidge Hall Library for the benefit of those who wish to consult them. I am writing to you belatedly because Dick Leahy [Associate Dean], who learned about the conference by chance, asked me to do so." (Letter from Safran to Spence, October 2, 1985, "Safran Correspondence," CMES Files.)

21. "These are clearly administrative errors in the Faculty of Arts and Sciences, not those of Professor Safran

or the CMES," the report observed, concluding that Safran "followed the policies and guidelines with respect to disclosure of individual contract. . . . He cannot and should not be held responsible for the Faculty's failure to conduct a complete review and to respond to the disclosure." (Spence Report.) The failure to examine the book contract meant that FAS was unable to determine whether it was an "institutional" contract, which would necessitate the application of University rules, or an "individual" contract, as Safran, who insisted all along that he was acting as an independent contractor, argued. Safran's study, *Saudi Arabia: The Ceaseless Quest for Security*, was published in 1985 by Harvard University Press under its Belknap label.

22. "Resolution Reaffirming Open Disclosure of Funds," *MESA Newsletter*, v. 8, no. 1 (Winter 1986), p. 8. MESA's censure of Safran was confined to the failure to disclose the conference funding. The 1982 resolution, adopted at MESA's meeting in Philadelphia, November 4, 1982, states: "[MESA], recognizing that the continued credibility and trust of the public in academic research on the Middle East rests upon an open and free disclosure of funding sources for such research, calls upon its membership to disclose fully in any written results [sic] and also to all persons involved in its conduct (i.e., participants, contributors, and subjects) all sources of support—other than personal—for that research." Less vigorously and less precisely, the resolution continued: "In addition, it calls on organizations and institutions in Middle East Studies to make regular disclosure of the sources of funding for their programs, conferences, and activities as they are announced and take place, and calls on its members to urge such disclosure." ("Attachment 2. Resolution: Disclosure of Funding," *MESA Bulletin*, v. 17, no. 1, July 1983, p. 119.) The 1985 resolution reaffirming open disclosure passed by 193 votes, but also drew eight negative votes and nine abstentions. (*MESA Newsletter*, Winter 1986, p. 8.)

While Safran may have violated professional norms, it is less than evident that he also broke with professional practice. Interviews with two directors of other Middle Eastern studies centers made it clear that, if a delineation of dollar figures from each contributor is the yardstick, they did not disclose all their funding sources. Nor did they believe that any major center did so. In that respect, Safran may have been a victim of selective enforcement of an otherwise unenforced, and perhaps even unenforceable, resolution. Disclosure of research consultancies has been yet rarer. Revealingly, the resolution passed in 1982 originally contained a third clause, which failed to win approval, declaring, "As a matter of principle, the Association also calls upon its membership to make public their research consultantships, official connections with governmental organizations of all countries, and sources of extramural research support." (*MESA Bulletin*, July 1983, p. 114.)

23. Letter to FAS Dean Michael Spence, reprinted in *The Harvard Crimson*, Oct. 25, 1985 and signed by Lisa Anderson, Associate Professor of Government; A. Tosun Aricanli, Assistant Professor of Economics; Selma Botman, CMES Research Associate; Mary Jo Del Vecchio Good,

Lecturer on Sociology; Zachary Lockman, Assistant Professor of History; Afsaneh Najmabadi, Visiting Lecturer on Government; and Paula Sanders, Assistant Professor of History.

24. "Evaluating Ethics in Academia," *The Harvard Crimson*, June 11, 1987.

25. Interview with Roy Mottahedeh, Dec. 2003. All subsequent quotations in this paragraph are from the same source.

26. The institute was disbanded toward the end of the 1990s.

27. Such partisanship had never been absent in the past. As former CMES Director Nur Yalman notes, "After the 1967 war, you could sense the increasing polarization among both faculty and students on the Arab-Israeli divide. Then came the 1973 war and that put everyone on edge. It was a very tense time at the Center, with passions raging everywhere. The wars were seen as struggles for survival for both the Israelis and the Palestinians." (Interview with Yalman, May, 2004.) The partisanship became overt once again in the mid-1980s. Even Dean Spence obliquely hinted at what had taken hold at the Center: "The task of the director of such a Center is inevitably made more difficult by deep divisions in the region from which it cannot be isolated." (Spence Report.)

28. Spence Report.

29. Letter to President Pusey, Nov. 12, 1958, Dean's Office, FAS, UA 111.5. 55.26 (Middle Eastern Studies, Center for), Box 13, Harvard University Archives, p. 5.

30. See appendix to section on alumni in Part II.

31. Roger Owen, "Gobalisation of Area Studies in America," *The Middle East at Harvard: Newsletter of the Center for Middle Eastern Studies*, 11 (Summer 1997), p. 6. Reprinted from *Al-Hayat,* Nov. 17, 1996.

32. As decisive factors behind the eschewal of more active involvement in the domain of policy and politics, these points were cited by all four of the most recent directors of CMES in interviews with the author in 2003 and 2004.

33. Interview with Cemal Kafadar, Feb. 2004.

34. A summary statement appears in "One View of the Center: A Word from the Director," *CMES Newsletter*, v. 1, no. 1 (Spring 1992), p. 2.

35. Frank E. Vogel and Samuel L. Hayes, *Islamic Law and Finance: Religion, Risk, and Return* (Boston: Kluwer, 1998).

An offshoot of the project, the Harvard Islamic Finance Information Program, began in 1995 and ran under the aegis of CMES until 2003 before it moved to the Islamic Legal Studies Program, Harvard Law School, where it operates under the rubric of the Islamic Finance Project.

36. Interview with Roger Owen, Feb. 2004.

37. The conferences resulted in a book published under the CMES Harvard Middle Eastern Monographs series: Roger Owen, ed., *New Perspectives on Property and Land in the Middle East* (Cambridge, distr. for the Center for Middle Eastern Studies by Harvard University Press, 2000).

38. *The Government of the Ottoman Empire in the Time of Suleiman the Magnificent* (Cambridge: Harvard University Press, 1913).

39. Berkeley: University of California Press, 1995.

40. See list of PhD graduates and dissertation titles in Part II. Like the Ottoman empire itself, the territory covered by these dissertations is quite broad, ranging from Egypt to the Balkans.

41. The first holder of the chair, which is a pillar of the Aga Khan Program for Islamic Architecture, was Oleg Grabar. The program, based jointly at Harvard and MIT, was established in 1979 to study Islamic art, architecture, and urbanism. Grabar directed the program at Harvard until his retirement in 1990.

42. The conference led to a published volume: Lenore G. Martin and Dimitris Keridis, eds., *The Future of Turkish Foreign Policy* (Cambridge, Mass.: MIT Press, 2004).

43. Formally the "International Congress in Honor of Professor Halil İnalcik: Methods and Sources in Ottoman Studies," the conference was organized jointly with the University of Chicago's Center for Middle Eastern Studies and held at Harvard, April 30–May 2, 2004.

44. In *Religion in the News*, v. 6, no. 2 (Summer 2003), pp. 1–5.

45. "Lebanon 1943, Iraq 2003," *Al-Ahram*, December 18–24, 2003.

46. The full title is *The Old Social Classes and the Revolutionary Movements of Iraq: A Study of Iraq's Old Landed and Commercial Classes and of its Communists, Ba'athists, and Free Officers* (Princeton, N.J.: Princeton University Press, 1978).

47. Statement by former CMES Director Keenan in written communication with author, April 2004.

48. "Center for Middle Eastern Studies Established at Harvard," *Newsletter*, Harvard Foundation for Advanced Study and Research, May 21, 1954.

49. Leonard Binder (PhD, 1956; MESA president, 1974); L. Carl Brown (PhD 1962; 1976); Richard T. Antoun (PhD 1963; 1983); Ira M. Lapidus (PhD 1964; 1984); John O. Voll (PhD 1969; 1993); Philip S. Khoury (PhD 1980; 1998); Joel Beinin (AM 1974; 2002).

50. Interview with Susan Miller, March 2004.

51. Center for Middle Eastern Studies, *Annual Report, 1964–1965* (Cambridge, Mass.: Harvard Graduate Society for Advanced Study and Research, December 1965), p. 12.

52. The appointment of Afsaneh Najmabadi in 2001 to the joint position of Professor of History and of Women's Studies added the fourth member to the existing contingent (Roy Mottahedeh, Roger Owen, and Cemal Kafadar).

53. *Area Studies Reconsidered*, pp. 6–7.

54. For two of many statements on this theme, see Leonard Binder, "Area Studies: A Critical Reassessment," in Binder, ed., *The Study of the Middle East: Research and Scholarship in Humanities and the Social Sciences* (New York: Wiley, 1976), pp. 1–28; and Rashid Khalidi, "Is There a Future for Middle Eastern Studies?" (1994 MESA Presidential Address), *MESA Bulletin*, v. 29, no. 1 (July 1995), pp. 1–6.

55. Center for Middle Eastern Studies, *Annual Report, 1963–1964* (Cambridge, Mass.: Harvard Graduate Society for Advanced Study and Research, December 1964), pp. 11–12.

56. The Center's past and present efforts to achieve legitimacy in the eyes of many departments was a recurrent theme in more than forty interviews conducted by the author in 2003 and 2004. The interviewees included Center directors, current and former faculty, alumni, members of visiting committees, and senior officials in the Harvard administration.

57. As a veteran of CMES put it: "We can plan this and we can plan that. But our destiny isn't entirely in our hands. It also depends on the [University] administration and the administration hasn't always been certain about what it would like to see. It doesn't quite know what to make of us. It doesn't seem to know what to make of Middle Eastern studies in general. At some point, it will need to make some hard choices. Is there a commitment to Middle Eastern studies? Exactly what kind of commitment? And what is it prepared to do to back it?" (Interview with CMES Executive Committee member, April 2004.)

58. As Cemal Kafadar notes, one of his priorities was "to recognize and act upon the transnational premise of working on an era that was not shaped on the basis of national identities and boundaries, which are often rigidly applied and diminish our understanding of the region's extraordinary cosmopolitan past. That's why I made it a point of inviting colleagues working on the Balkans or the Arab world during the Ottoman era to teach at Harvard. And that's why I've encouraged some of my students who are writing dissertations on the Ottoman period to take field exams in Greek or Armenian." (Communication with author, August 2004.)

59. As early as ten years ago, the Social Science Research Council, which had provided many of the intellectual foundations of area studies, began to disengage from traditional area-based research in favor of "thematic" or "functional" concerns, with emphasis on those that cut across regions and disciplines. (Descriptions and rationales are offered by SSRC President Kenneth Prewitt in "Presidential Items," *Items*, v. 50, no. 1 [March 1996], pp. 15–18 and in "Presidential Items," *Items*, v. 50, nos. 2–3 [June–Sept. 1996], pp. 31–40.) Other foundations, notably MacArthur and Mellon, have followed a similar path. Among the more important recent developments in area studies is the Ford Foundation's "Crossing Borders" initiative. The $25 million initiative reaffirms the importance of the traditional intellectual core of area studies—the study of history, culture, and languages—while supporting innovative projects that emphasize interdisciplinary and interregional approaches and collaborative partnerships involving both scholars and practitioners. (*Crossing Borders: Revitalizing Area Studies* [New York: Ford Foundation, 1999].)

60. A brief summary is to be found in "Undergrad Education Review Released," *Harvard Gazette*, April 29, 2004.

61. As quoted in "Committee Urges Harvard to Expand the Reach of Its Undergraduate Curriculum," *The New York Times*, April 27, 2004.

62. "Scholarship, Policy, Debate and Conflict: Why We Study the Middle East and Why It Matters" (2003 Presidental Address), *MESA Bulletin*, v. 38, no. 1 (June 2004), p. 4.

63. Among these critics, Robert H. Bates of the Government Department is at the forefront. See his "Letter from the President, Area Studies and the Discipline," *APSA-CP: Newsletter of the APSA Organized Section on Comparative Politics*, v. 7, no. 1 (Winter, 1996), pp. 1–2; "The Death of Comparative Politics?" *APSA-CP: Newsletter of the APSA Organized Section on Comparative Politics*, v. 7, no. 2 (Summer 1996), pp. 1–2; and "Area Studies and the Discipline: A Useful Controversy?" *PS: Political Science & Politics*, v. 30, no. 2 (June 1997), pp. 166–69.

64. The claim of "mushiness" is aired by Christopher Shea in "Political Scientists Clash over Value of Area Studies, *The Chronicle of Higher Education*, Jan. 10, 1997, pp. 13–14.

65. The latter, obviously, is no more than a crude summation of major strands of theories of, respectively, rational choice, development orthodoxy, and globalization.

A view of Harvard
from the Center's
conference room

PART II
A Look at the Center Today

51

Academic Programs, Students, and Alumni

In the academic year of 1642, six years after the founding of Harvard, its students began to devote every Thursday to the study of eastern languages. Befitting the College's religious origins—and a mission, in the words of an early tract, "[t]o advance Learning and perpetuate it to Posterity; dreading to leave an illiterate Ministry to the Churches"—the emphasis was on biblical languages. There was Chaldaic and there was Syriac. But most of the attention went to Hebrew, and for that the students had a manual of language and grammar that had been written recently by one of the greatest German polymaths of his day, Wilhelm Schickard, a Lutheran minister and student of oriental languages. Schickard had been appointed professor at the University of Tübingen, where he taught Hebrew and Aramaic, among many other languages, and it was there that he wrote *Horologium Hebraeum*. He is better known today for developing the world's first mechanical calculator, often called the "Schickard machine," a feat that has given him a hallowed place in the annals of computing. It was one of many devices, along with a machine for calculating astronomical dates and another for automating Hebrew verb inflections, that he invented after switching fields in mid-career and becoming professor of astronomy at the same university. Few Harvard students or their instructors were aware of Schickard's numerous advances in astronomy, mathematics, cartography, and engineering. Thursdays were consumed by the hard slog of puzzling through works like *Horologium Hebraeum*.

Although from the perspective of today it might have been narrowly defined, Harvard's interest in what today we call the Middle East was already established three centuries before the creation of the Center for Middle Eastern Studies. And at the center of that interest one element has been a constant: the study of language. For several centuries, the only languages that seemed to matter were Semitic and the study of these languages remained

Himmet Taskomur, PhD student in History and Middle Eastern Studies and a teaching fellow, at an Arabic class.

tied to biblical studies. Arabic was added to the curriculum as early as 1754, but it was taught as an adjunct to Hebrew. It was not until the formation of a Division of Semitic Languages and History in 1891 that Harvard developed a commitment to the larger field of Oriental studies. The historical and linguistic approach to the study of the Middle East would spread over the first half of the twentieth century and continues today within the Department of Near Eastern Languages and Civilizations (NELC). However, a commitment to Arabic as a medium to be valued in its own right was slow to emerge. As recently as 1950, Arabic was taught as an auxiliary to Hebrew.

An Expanding Curriculum

The establishment of CMES in 1954 marks the beginning of a transformation in academic programs on the Middle East at Harvard. The Center differed, and continues to differ, from the University's other centers in one crucial respect: teaching is a core part of its mission. Hence, the Center is responsible not only for conducting and encouraging research in the many unexplored areas of the history, culture, politics, and economics of the Middle East, but also for organizing programs of instruction at the graduate level in a variety of fields, from modern languages to the social sciences. As the Center is a coordinating body and not a department, it does not offer any courses itself. Instead, all courses are presented through the regular departments of the Faculty of Arts and Sciences (FAS) or professional schools such as the Harvard Law School, the Graduate School of Design, the Kennedy School of Government, or the Business School. The Center plays a critical role in teaching programs, nonetheless. It does so in at least two respects.

First, CMES remains the main body at Harvard that devotes sustained attention to promoting an integrated study of the states and societies of the Middle East. It is the faculty associated with the Center who have been the primary force behind the ongoing efforts to achieve a balance between classical and modern emphases in course offerings on the Middle East. Toward this end, the Center has provided not only the intellectual momentum within individual departments and across the University but at times even the financial support for temporary or permanent faculty appointments. Second, and perhaps more directly, the Center is involved in coordinating and supervising teaching programs in Middle Eastern studies. Degree programs in the field are overseen and administered by a standing committee of FAS, the Committee on Middle Eastern Studies, which is composed of CMES faculty and chaired by the Director of the Center. This body is reinforced by other committees based at the Center, such as one on Language Proficiency and another on Islamic Studies.

Collectively and individually, the faculty associated with the Center identify complementarities and cross-linkages that strengthen the interdisciplinary nature of the work of CMES-based AM and PhD students. In their role as academic advisors, they also attempt to ensure that all students pursue a coherent program that prepares them for their academic and career objectives and also fulfills departmental and University requirements. AM students are supervised by the director of the AM program. Each of the latest three advisors who have had this responsibility—Susan Miller, Laila Parsons, and, since 2003, Susan Kahn—has also been an associate director of the Center. The task of advising doctoral students, on the other hand, has been in the hands of senior faculty: today, in History, Cemal Kafadar, Roy Mottahedeh, Afsaneh Najmabadi, and Roger Owen; in Anthropology, Steven Caton; in Fine Arts, Gülru Necipoğlu and David Roxburgh.

Since its founding, the Center has aspired to forge a comprehensive and integrative teaching program, one that covers in depth and across a variety of disciplines the study of the languages, literatures, history, economics, politics, religion, and culture of a region whose boundaries have always been recognized as being more inclusive and more fluid than the conventional definitions dictated by geopolitical machinations or by academic bureaucracies. Given the enormity and the complexity of the geographical and temporal terrain, Harvard has never been able to satisfy all demands or needs in Middle East studies. In this, of course, Harvard is not alone. However, the increase in course offerings related to the Middle East provides a measure of the growth of the field since the creation of the Center. Even by the most elastic definition of what constitutes a course on the Middle East, the University could claim no more than five in the year before the Center opened. There were two courses in classical Arabic, one in modern Persian, and two in history—one Ottoman, the other Byzantine. Since 1954, the number of undergraduate and graduate courses on the Middle East, including languages, has grown to more than 200. Instruction has ranged from the pre-Islamic era to the contemporary period. The Center's particular emphasis, as reflected in the work of the majority of its faculty and doctoral students, has been on the classical Islamic and modern periods. The strengths and weaknesses of the curriculum are discussed in many of the essays in Part III.

Language instruction has always held a high place in the Center's pedagogical priorities. That the study of the Middle East and the Islamic world requires knowledge of a variety of languages is an assumption that has never been questioned at the Center, although it has been elsewhere. The Center, accordingly, has treated the acquisition of linguistic skills as a prerequisite for serious scholarship in any field of inquiry dealing with the Middle East. So heavy was the stress on these skills that CMES initially structured its teaching programs so that first-year AM students would spend fully one-half of their time studying languages. Today, language courses occupy about one-fourth of first-year course work for these students. Language is also an area where CMES has exercised the greatest influence in its attempts to develop both the quantity and quality of course offerings in the Middle East at Harvard. But it is also an area that has posed some of the greatest challenges. The co-existence of a multiplicity of languages within the heartland of the region; the sheer difficulties in mastering any one of them; the differences in idiomatic forms, both written and spoken, between modern and classical; and the uneven, often halting, progress in the development of teaching methods have always confronted students and faculty alike with

CMES Director Cemal Kafadar and graduating AM students at a reception in May 2004.

an extraordinary amalgam of hurdles. Nevertheless, from its early days, the Center has attracted exceptional talents in languages. A full tally of all the ones that Richard N. Frye, the Aga Khan Professor of Iranian and the Center's first associate director, taught over the course of his long career at Harvard may be impossible to establish. However, a perusal of course catalogues yields the following: for modern, Arabic, Persian, Turkish, Pashto, Kurdish (Sorani), and the dialects of Iranian (Baluchi, Ossetic, and Pamir); for ancient, Biblical Hebrew, Old Persian, Avestan, Middle Persian (Pahlavi), Sogdian, and Old Turkic, along with a survey of Middle Iranian, including Khotanese and Khwarezmian. Many others have followed in Frye's footsteps—from George Makdisi, Omeljan Pritsak, and Annemarie Schimmel to William Granara, Wolfram Heinrichs, and Wheeler Thackston.

Today's students specializing in Middle Eastern studies, like those of the seventeenth century, are expected to acquire a reading and speaking knowledge of at least one language. The backbone of the Center's degree programs are Arabic, Hebrew, Persian, and Turkish—the same four languages that the Center established at the outset as its priorities. Here, perhaps the Center's greatest contribution over the decades has been in pushing for modern forms and modern methods of instruction. This objective was not easily achieved. For years, the pleas for modern language training were met with the rejoinder, "If they want modern, let them go to Berlitz." Today, instruction in all four languages is offered in modern as well as classical forms, at all levels and degrees of intensity. As in other universities in the United States, enrollments in Arabic classes have surged in recent years, and, in the latest years for which numbers are available, they have approached 200. Although it has never been a formal requirement, or even an explicitly articulated preference, from its inception CMES faculty have encouraged degree candidates to study Arabic. Almost all doctoral students do attempt to attain a working knowledge of Arabic, regardless of any other Middle Eastern languages they select for specialization. The diversity of the Middle East necessitates instruction in yet other languages. Aside from the primary four, training in languages relevant to the Center's programs has included Armenian, Berber, Kurdish, Pashto, Urdu, and Uzbek. With the exception of Byzantine and Greek, almost all language instruction related to Middle Eastern studies is offered through NELC.

AM and PhD Students

While the requirements and the expectations have changed, in tandem with developments in Middle Eastern studies at large, there has been a continuity in the overall structure of the degree programs administered by the Center. As in the 1950s, the Center runs its own AM program and coordinates joint doctoral programs with other departments or schools. The master's program, leading to what is formally designated as an AM in Regional Studies—Middle East, requires two years of study and is designed to prepare students for careers in government, business, and other fields where they can use knowledge and skills related to the Middle East. AM students are expected to attain reading and speaking competence in one of the four core languages. They are also required to take two "bookend" courses: a survey of approaches to Middle Eastern studies that serves to expose them to the work of Harvard faculty in various disciplines as well as to the board of fare in the curriculum; and a research seminar that calls for the presentation of a substantial piece of work. The remaining coursework allows considerable latitude for choices across disciplines.

The joint programs for the PhD are of an entirely different order, as they call for the fulfillment of requirements of a disciplinary department or school and also those mandated by the Committee on Middle Eastern Studies. At the time of writing, the three formal joint degree programs were with Anthropology, Fine Arts, and History. In all three programs, students need to develop proficiency in at least one Middle Eastern language. In Anthropology, students must demonstrate a "through knowledge" of the modern version of one of the four main languages. "Thorough knowledge" is said to translate into a minimum of four years of language study and a final grade of at least B–. In History, there is a two-stage process designed to ensure the attainment of a threshold of linguistic skills that will allow high levels of scholarship and teaching. First, there is a test of evidence of proficiency in reading, accurately and fluidly, expository prose in one of the four modern languages; the requisite level is usually achievable with three full years of study. Second, there is the requirement of adequate mastery of the Middle Eastern language immediately relevant to dissertation research; in this case, mastery is normally attainable with four full years of language study and, in any case, it is to be confirmed in a separate field of the general exams. In both Anthropology and History, students are strongly expected to master at least two languages. Native languages cannot be counted toward any of the proficiency requirements. In addition, in all three departments, students must pass the regular proficiency examination in a European language: French, German, Italian, or Russian for Anthropology and History; or French, German, or Russian for Fine Arts.

In addition to the joint PhD programs, CMES students can pursue a concurrent degree with the Harvard Law School, thanks to the Islamic Legal Studies Program, leading to a JD or SJD and an AM in Middle Eastern Studies. The requirements for these concurrent degrees are complicated. Students have to apply for and be accepted independently by both the Graduate School of Arts and Sciences and the Law School. Simultaneous enrollment in the two schools is not allowed, nor is part-time residency. Instead, students must defer matriculation in one school, by taking a leave of absence, while attending the other. Students typically start by enrolling in the Law School, where they take a requisite number of courses in Islamic law and Middle East–related courses. Then they spend a year in the AM program at CMES, concentrating exclusively on courses on the Middle East. After obtaining an AM in Middle Eastern Studies, they return to the Law School to complete the law degree. The specific demands of the JD and SJD differ in both length and intensity, but in either case the concurrent program allows students to use courses taken for one degree as credit for the second degree, thereby reducing the total time and expense they would have to incur if they pursued the two separately.

As far as numbers are concerned, enrollments in both the AM and PhD programs reveal a picture of substantial continuity. A comparison of the figures for 1963–64, 1978–79, and 2002–03—corresponding to the 10th, 25th, and 49th years of the Center—shows roughly similar figures for the first and third of these years: the number of AM students was 27 in 1963–64 and 25 in 2002–03. The number for 1978–79—a total of 10, including both first- and second-year AM students—reflects the declining levels of government funding, the dwindling prospects in the job market, and the overall uncertainties the Center faced between the mid-1960s and mid-1980s. The number of PhD students registered in the three academic years stood at 16, 26, and 53, respectively. The rise in these numbers is explained more by the longer period of time students take to complete a dissertation—30 of the doctoral students in 2002–03 were in the sixth to "tenth year and beyond"—than by a growth in the volume of admissions. The figures for admissions, in fact, have been remarkably stable: 6 new students were admitted to the PhD program in 1963–64; 2 in 1978–79; and 6 in 2002–03. The ratio of AM to PhD students has also been stable. At the tenth year, marking the end of a period when the Center was building up the doctoral program, the ratio stood at more than 3 to 2. Over the last 25 years, it has been in the order of less than 1 to 2.

These numbers, of course, tell only part of the story. What is more revealing is the changing profile of students. The initial expectation was that the overwhelming majority of AM graduates—70 to 80 percent, according to original estimates—would go directly to careers in government or business. Only one-fifth of the graduates, it was assumed, would undertake further academic work, either at Harvard or elsewhere. Not for nothing was the AM program termed, and still is termed, a "terminal" program. The estimate proved to be roughly correct for the first 5 years. Beginning in 1960, however, a different pattern began to emerge: the Center discovered that more than 50 percent of AM graduates were pursuing more advanced degrees, usually PhDs. The pattern has continued to this day: well over half of AM graduates continue their studies. Exceptional ones have been accepted into one of the joint doctoral programs in Middle Eastern studies at Harvard. Another difference between initial assumptions and subsequent realities is to be found in the level of preparedness of incoming students. At first, CMES anticipated that few, if any students, would have a background in Middle Eastern studies and that none would have any language training. The latter assumption, in particular, has been misplaced. By the tenth year, the Center found that, even when native speakers from the region were omitted, one out of two incoming students had done formal coursework in one or more Middle Eastern languages. A surprising threshold of linguistic competence was to be found among AM and PhD students alike. This pattern, too, has persisted. Well over one-half of students who enter the program today have already studied a Middle Eastern language, in most cases Arabic, either during college or in more specialized institutions such as Middlebury College's summer schools or the Defense Language Institute of Monterey. Others have received language training through a stint with organizations like the Peace Corps. A few have even immersed themselves in language training in the Middle East, for example at the American University in Cairo or the American University of Beirut.

The PhD program has been highly competitive and selective and has become more so over time. The program has always been kept small and, with some notable exceptions, has tended to attract students who have already decided on a career in teaching and research in Middle Eastern studies. The 6 students who were admitted in 1963–64 to the PhD program came out of 9 applicants. By contrast, the pool of applicants from which the 6 were accepted in 2002–03 totaled 56. What has changed in the interim is not merely an increase in the number of students seeking the most advanced degree Harvard can offer in the field. Paradoxically, the increase has occurred in spite of the reduction of the disciplines with which Middle Eastern Studies can be combined. Of the 13 PhDs that had been conferred by 1964, only 6 were in History. Others were joint degrees in Middle Eastern Studies and Government (3), Near Eastern Languages and Literatures (2), Anthropology (1), and Linguistics (1). To these fields, the joint doctoral program later added others, notably Economics and Fine Arts, allowing CMES PhD students to specialize in a yet wider range of disciplines. For a variety of reasons, many of which are discussed elsewhere in this volume, this broad menu of choices no longer exists. By the end of the 1990s, only three departmental disciplines remained in the joint degree program: History, Anthropology, and Fine Arts. Of the joint PhDs in the last ten years, 9 out of 10 have been in History. And in 2002–03, out of the Center's 53 PhD students, 45 were in

History. One would have to go back to the early 1970s to find a dissertation on a topic like the measurement of rates of return and capital efficiency. However, these imbalances, although pronounced, are not necessarily indicative of the range of interests of students at the Center.

After Harvard

The Center for Middle Eastern Studies has attracted students from all over the United States, from large universities as well as small liberal arts colleges. It has drawn students from many European countries and even a few from African countries. It has had a contingent from Asia, including Japan, Korea, Malaysia, and Thailand. And it has been a magnet for students from almost every country of the Middle East. In the early years, almost all of the latter students came from the American University of Beirut or the Hebrew University of Jerusalem. Iranians and Egyptians began appearing in greater numbers in later decades. In more recent years, there has been a heavy influx from Turkey, which now tops the list of Middle Eastern countries of origin. CMES students have come from all walks of life—from the academy to the government, from the church to the military—and most of them have gone on to careers that have been related in one way or another to the Middle East.

By the middle of 2004, the Center's degree holders reached a grand total of 406. Of these, 119 are PhDs and the remaining 287, or 70 percent, are AMs. A concerted effort over a period of almost twelve months to track down all alumni yielded information on 259. The remaining 147, about one-third of the total, eluded both the reach of the Alumni Office, one of the most resourceful entities in the Harvard administration, as well as a variety of search methods employed by CMES. The overwhelming majority of these "unknowns" are AM graduates. The likelihood is that they comprise a substantial proportion of alumni who have opted for careers outside the orbit of the Middle Eastern field.

The majority of PhD alumni have gone into higher education. There have been some notable exceptions, however. A few PhDs have chosen a career in diplomacy, as exemplified by John Limbert (1975), whose stint in the US Foreign Service has included ambassadorial positions—and 444 days in captivity during the 1979–81 hostage crisis in Iran. Yet other PhDs have gone into banking and finance, for example Said Saffari (see page 65). Of the 259 identifiable alumni, more than 40 percent have had careers in teaching and university-based research. Within this concentration of alumni who have remained in higher education are many AMs who went on to obtain doctorates, confirming what we already know about the penchant of many of these graduates to seek more advanced degrees after leaving the CMES program. As more than 5 percent of the 259 alumni who are accounted for are still students, the proportion of graduates who end up in the domain of teaching and research approaches 50 percent. Public service and consulting constitute the next two largest categories of career choice, each accounting for about 10 percent of the total. Five percent of alumni have taken up non–university-based research. Business and industry combined make up slightly less than 5 percent, as do financial services, accounting included. Two other categories—law and a sector that subsumes journalism, media, and publishing—each accounts for around 3 percent. NGOs and nonprofit organizations together also comprise around 3 percent. The breakdowns of four other career categories—health services, military, technology, and library services—hover around 1 to 1.5 percent each.

Alumni of the Center are to be found at the commanding heights of the universe of Middle Eastern studies. Perhaps no other center has produced as many heads of Middle Eastern centers and institutes at leading universities in the United States as has Harvard's CMES. A partial listing of the directors of these centers includes Leonard Binder (PhD 1956) at UCLA and, earlier, at Chicago; Carl Brown (PhD 1962) at Princeton; Richard Bulliet (PhD 1967) at Columbia; Ira Lapidus (PhD 1964) at the University of California, Berkeley; and Zachary Lockman (PhD 1983) at New York University. They have had more than a few counterparts overseas, among them Eugene Rogan (PhD 1991), director of the Middle East Centre at St. Antony's College, Oxford, and Nadia El-Cheikh (PhD 1992), head of the Center for Arab and Middle Eastern Studies at the American University of Beirut. CMES alumni also have had leading positions in professional associations in the field. From no other center have come as many presidents of the Middle East Studies Association (MESA). Besides Binder, Brown, and Lapidus, former MESA presidents have included Richard Antoun (PhD 1963), John Voll (PhD 1969), Philip Khoury (PhD 1980), and Joel Beinin (AM 1974). Dozens of other CMES graduates have distinguished themselves in research and teaching both in the United States and abroad.

The Center's alumni have left their mark on the world of diplomacy, too. The Center has produced at least two foreign ministers, both PhDs: Mohamed al-Sabbah (1985) of Kuwait, and Surin Pitsuwan (1982) of Thailand (see page 65). Among several graduates who have put the knowledge of the Middle East they acquired at Harvard to work in postings in some of the region's trouble spots are Stephen Buck (AM 1965), who was Chargé d'Affaires at the US Embassy in Iraq and Consul General in Saudi Arabia; and David Mack (AM 1964), whose assignments included American Vice Consul in Baghdad in the mid-1960s, political officer in Benghazi in the 1970s, Ambassador to the United Arab Emirates in the 1980s, Deputy Assistant Secretary for Near Eastern Affairs in the 1990s, and currently Vice President of the Middle East Institute in Washington, DC. CMES graduates have also held senior positions in international organizations. They include Mona Khalil (AM 1988), Senior Legal Officer at the United Nations' Office of Legal Affairs; and Joseph Saba (AM 1971), World Bank Country Director for Iran, Iraq, Jordan, Lebanon, and Syria.

David Mack (AM 1964) in 1963 and in 2004.

Graduates of the Center have been equally prominent in the world of business and finance. They include Marilyn Edling (AM 1974), Vice President and General Manager of Enterprise Systems at Hewlett-Packard; and Craig Kennedy (PhD 1994), Vice President, Morgan Stanley, who appears to have made a seamless transition from analyzing dynastic relationships in fifteenth- and sixteenth-century Muscovy in a dissertation to analyzing problems of corporate governance in oil and other industries in Russia today. Then there have been alumni who have straddled many fields of endeavor. There is Paula Stern (AM 1969), a former chairwoman of the International Trade Commission, who has followed a career in trade and competition policy with leadership of an international advisory group in business and strategy, and a sideline of sculpting that has won her many awards. And there is Catherine Bateson (PhD 1963), who wrote a dissertation under the supervision of Hamilton Gibb, served as an Arabic instructor at Harvard, taught anthropology on four continents, became Dean of Social Sciences and Humanities at the University of Northern Iran before the revolution, published on linguistics and semiotics, ventured into books on personal exploration with themes of continuity, discontinuity, and ambiguity and titles like *Composing a Life*, *Full Circles*, and, most recently, *Peripheral Visions*—and all along could not help but be known first and foremost for being the daughter of Margaret Mead.

Catherine Bateson (PhD 1963) in 1965 and in 2002.

CMES Alumni in Academia and Beyond

A few of the many distinguished alumni of the Center for Middle Eastern Studies, pictured (in all cases but one) during student days at Harvard and more recently.

Leonard Binder (PhD, 1956)
The first graduate of the CMES joint doctoral program, Binder is among the handful of scholars consistently  recognized as having done work that is both at the forefront of theory-building in political science and a significant empirical contribution to the study of Middle Eastern politics. Revealingly, he is the only person to have headed a political science department and a Middle East center at two major universities—Chicago and UCLA. His major works include *Crises and Sequences in Political Development* and *Islamic Liberalism*.

Richard W. Bulliet
(PhD 1967)
"When it was determined that [Sir Hamilton] Gibb would not be able to resume his directorship  after his stroke, I was given the job of cleaning out his desk and closet. I smoked his last cigar and stole his umbrella. It was a very good umbrella and I was quite upset when a friend borrowed it and lost it." What Bulliet might have lost at Harvard he more than made up for at Columbia, where he is Professor of History and former director of the Middle East Institute. His latest book, *The Case for Islamo-Christian Civilization*, challenges the "what went wrong?" line of inquiry about Islamic history. It follows many other works on the subject, along with four novels (including *The Sufi Fiddle* and *Kicked to Death by a Camel*) set in the contemporary Middle East.

Philip S. Khoury
(PhD 1980)
Khoury, pictured with Albert Hourani during graduation, is  Professor of History and Dean of the School of Humanities, Arts, and Social Sciences at MIT. In a setting where engineers and scientists have reigned supreme, the deanship necessitates full-time bridge-building, especially between humanists and technologists, a demanding task for which he feels his years at CMES and Harvard offered solid preparation. His works include *Urban Notables and Arab Nationalism* and *Syria and the French Mandate*, which won the American Historical Association's George Beer Prize.

Eve Troutt Powell (PhD 1995)
She takes trapeze classes and she has been known to end speeches by reciting lyrics of pop hits like "32 Flavors." But Troutt Powell is likely to always be known for the MacArthur Prize that has given her a cult status, along with $500,000, just eight years after graduating with a joint degree in History and Middle Eastern Studies. An Associate Professor of  History at the University of Georgia, she is author of *A Different Shade of Colonialism: Egypt, Great Britain, and the Mastery of the Sudan*, which casts a light on the dark corners of racial identity within Egypt, demonstrating how the colonized was also a colonizer. Her latest work (co-authored with John Hunwick) is T*he African Diaspora in the Mediterranean Lands of Islam.*

John Abizaid (AM 1980)

General Abizaid was appointed in 2003 Commander of CENTCOM, which oversees operations not only in Iraq and Afghanistan but in the entire theater from the Indian Ocean to the Red Sea. Professor Nadav Safran, in one of the last interviews he gave before he died last year, was quoted as saying the 100-page paper on Saudi defense policy Abizaid turned in for one of his courses was the best he had read in all his years at Harvard. The exploits of this soldier's soldier caught the attention of not only Defense Secretary Donald Rumsfeld, but also Clint Eastwood, who reenacted in *Heartbreak Ridge* Abizaid's famed order to a ranger to drive a bulldozer, shovel raised, toward Cuban troops in Grenada, with his men advancing behind.

Sarah Chayes (AM 1988)

After CMES, Chayes spent five years with National Public Radio, earning awards for insightful, often searing, reporting in such trouble spots as Algeria, Lebanon, Palestine, Serbia, and Bosnia. Sensing that "the tectonic plates of history were shifting" after 9/11, a stint in Afghanistan left her with a yearning to go beyond reporting and to help the devastated country in its struggle to rebuild. A meeting with the Karzais led her to take up their offer to become field director for Afghans for Civil Society in Kandahar, the former stronghold of the Taliban. Dressed as a male, for two years she went about organizing community projects. In 2004, long after even the most intrepid NGOs had left the country, she was still in Kandahar, directing a dairy coop.

Surin Pitsuwan (PhD 1982)

Cosmopolitanism and international prestige have not made Pitsuwan forget his roots in the *pondok*, the traditional Islamic school, that his family ran in southern Thailand. The Malay-Muslim community of southern Thailand became the subject of his doctoral dissertation, which earned him a joint PhD in Government and Middle Eastern Studies. The integration of that community with the rest of Thailand remained a central concern after he returned home to a political career that saw him rise to the position of Foreign Minister from 1997 to 2001. A Member of Parliament, he is one of most articulate champions of reconciliation between Islam and the West. He is on many a short list for the next Secretary-General of the United Nations.

Said Saffari (PhD 1997)

Saffari still credits success in the world of banking to what he calls the "fluid architecture" of CMES, the opportunities to explore novel ideas, the venues for cultivating new relationships, all combined with a historical perspective on development inspired by Roger Owen and work for a project on Islamic banking and finance. A focus on economic

history and financial markets, and a dissertation on banking in Iran before and after the revolution, became the groundwork for a swift ascent in the rarefied realm of financial and strategic analysis that has taken him to the position of head of pan-European credit research for CSFB, London.

PhD Graduates and Dissertations, 1956–2004

2004

Diana Abouali, "Family and Society in a Seventeenth Century Ottoman City: The 'Alamīs of Jerusalem."

Giancarlo Casale, "The Ottoman Age of Exploration: Spices, Maps and Conquest in the Sixteenth-Century Indian Ocean."

Michael Connell, "The Nimatullahi Sayyids of Taft: A Study of the Evolution of a Late Medieval Iranian Sufi Tariqah."

Aykan Erdemir, "Incorporating Alevis: The Transformation of Governance and Faith-Based Collective Action in Turkey."

Ilham Khuri-Makdisi, "Levantine Trajectories: The Formulation and Dissemination of Radical Ideas in and between Beirut, Cairo, and Alexandria, 1860–1914."

Kristen Stilt, "The *Muḥtasib*, Law, and Society in Early Mamluk Cairo and Fustat (1250-1400)."

Cengiz Şişman, "When the Messiah Converts: Research on the Ottoman Origins of the 17th Century Jewish Messianic Movement."

2003

Tamara Chalabi, "Community and Nation-State: The Shī'ī of Jabal 'Amil and the New Lebanon, 1918–1943."

Karen Leal, "The Ottoman State and the Greek Orthodox of Istanbul: Sovereignty and Identity at the Turn of the Eighteenth Century."

Aslı Niyazioğlu, "Sheikhs in the Life of a Seventeenth Century Ottoman 'Alim: A Study on Nev'i-zāde Atayi's Ḥada'ikü'l-Ḥaqa'iq."

2002

Cemil Aydin, "The Politics of Civilizational Identities: Asia, West and Islam in the Pan-Asianist Thought of Okawa Shumei."

Sahar Bazzaz, "Challenging Power and Authority in Pre-Protectorate Morocco: Shaykh Muhammad al-Kettani and the Tarīqa Kettāniyah."

Leor Halevi, "Muḥammad's Grave: Death, Ritual and Society in the Early Islamic World."

Barak Aharon Salmoni (Kalfuss), "Pedagogies of Patriotism: Teaching Socio-Political Community in Twentieth-Century Turkish and Egyptian Education."

Deborah Tor, "From Holy Warriors to Chivalric Order: The 'Ayyars in the Eastern Islamic World, A.D. 800–1055."

2001

Nahīd Nosrat-Mozaffari, "Crafting Constitutionalism: 'Ali Akbar Dehkhodā and the Iranian Constitutional Revolution."

Ghada Osman, "The Christians of Late Sixth and Early Seventh Century Mecca and Medina: An Investigation into the Arabic Sources (Saudi Arabia)."

Iman Roushdy-Hammadi, "Recombination and Forensics: Cancer Risk among Two Cappadocian Communities in Turkey, Sweden and Germany."

Lucia Volk, "Missing the Nation: Lebanon's Post-War Generation in the Midst of Reconstruction."

2000

Dara Chafik, "History of the Heart and Cardiotherapy as Presented in Near Eastern, North African, and the Spanish Medical and Pharmaceutical Texts from the Ninth to the Thirteenth Century A.D."

Sharon Denise Lang, "Sharaf Politics: Constructing Male Prestige in Israeli-Palestinian Society."

1999

Saffet Hülya Canbakal, "Ayntab at the End of the Seventeenth Century: A Study of Notables and Urban Politics."

Julia Elyachar Dvorkin, "Egyptian Workshop, Global Enterprise: Visions of Economy and Urban Life in Cairo, 1900–1996."

Emily Ruth Gottreich, "Jewish Space in the Moroccan City: A History of the Mellaḥ of Marrakech, 1550–1930."

Relli Israel Shechter, "The Egyptian Cigarette: A Study of the Interaction Between Consumption, Production, and Marketing in Egypt, 1850–1956."

Levent Soysal, "Projects of Culture: An Ethnographic Episode in the Life of Migrant Youth in Berlin."

Nakeema Damali Stefflbauer, "An Analysis of Syrian-Lebanese Informal Trade: 1943–1993."

Derin Terzioğlu, "Sufi and Dissident in the Ottoman Empire: Niyazi-i Miṣri (1618–1694)."

1998

Misako Ikeda, "Sociopolitical Debates in Late Parliamentary Egypt, 1944–1952."

Amy Jo Johnson, "One Man's Impact: An Administrative Biography of Dr. Aḥmed Ḥussein: Social Reformer, Diplomat, and Idealist."

Salmaan Keshavjee, "Medicines and Transitions: The Political Economy of Health and Social Change in Post-Soviet Badakhshan, Tajikistan."

1997

Christin Marschall, "The Islamic Republic of Iran and the Persian Gulf States: Iranian Regional Foreign Policy, 1979–1994."

Said Saffari, "On the Rollercoaster of Development: Banking and Economic Growth in Iran under the Pahlavis and the Islamic Republic."

Tarik Mohamed Yousef, "Essays in Twentieth-Century Middle Eastern Economic Development."

1996

Najwa Al-Qattan, "Dhimmis in the Muslim Court: Documenting Justice in Ottoman Damascus, 1775–1860."

Richard Craig Foltz, "Uzbek Central Asia and Mughal India: Asian Muslim Society in the 16th and 17th Centuries."

1995

Moshe Gershovich, "French Military Policy in Morocco and the Origins of an Arab Army."

Harith Ghassany, "Kitman and Renaissance: Domination and the Limits of Development."

Eve Marie Troutt Powell, "Colonized Colonizers: Egyptian Nationalists and the Issue of the Sudan, 1875–1919."

1994

Craig Gayen Kennedy, "The Juchids of Muscovy: A Study of Personal Ties Between Emigre Tatar Dynasts and the Muscovite Grand Princes in the Fifteenth and Sixteenth Centuries."

Alisa Rubin Peled, "Debating Islam in the Jewish State: Formative Moments in the Development of Policy towards Islamic Institutions in Israel."

Janina M. Safran, "The Sun Rises in the West: The Ideology of the Umayyad Caliphate of Al-Andalus."

1993

Daphna Ephrat, "The Sunni 'Ulamā' of 11th-Century Baghdad and the Transmission of Knowledge: A Social History."

Sheila Hannah Katz, "Women and Gender in Jewish and Palestinian Nationalism before 1950: Founding and Confounding the Boundaries."

Frank Edward Vogel, "Islamic Law and Legal System Studies of Saudi Arabia."

1992

Nadia Maria El Cheikh-Saliba, "Byzantium Viewed by the Arabs."

James L. Gelvin, "Popular Mobilization and the Foundations of Mass Politics in Syria, 1918–1920."

Anne Thompson Sweetser, "The Power to Heal: Medicine and Society in the Pakistani Himalayas."

James Albert Toronto, "The Dynamics of Educational Reform in Contemporary Egypt."

1991

George Arthur Ashur, "The Kennedy-Nāṣir Correspondence: A Policy of Accommodation."

David Warren Lesch, "The United States and Syria, 1953–1957: The Cold War in the Middle East."

Meir Litvak, "The Shi'i 'Ulamā of Najaf and Karbala, 1791–1904: A Sociopolitical Analysis."

Roya Marefat, "Beyond the Architecture of Death: The Shrine of the Shah-i Zinda in Samarqand."

Eugene Lawrence Rogan, "Incorporating the Periphery: The Ottoman Extension of Direct Rule over Southeastern Syria (Transjordan), 1867–1914."

1990

Ghada Hijjawi Qaddumi, "A Medieval Islamic Book of Gifts and Treasures: Translation, Annotation, and Commentary on the Kitāb al-Hadāyā wa al-Tuḥaf."

1989

Zahra Faridany-Akhavan, "The Problems of the Mughal Manuscript of the Ḥamza-Nāma: 1562–1577: A Reconstruction."

1988

Maria Luisa Fernandez y Espinosa, "The Visual Competition of the Circassian Period Qibla Wall in Cairo."

Hasan Kayali, "Arabs and Young Turks: Turkish-Arab Relations in the Second Constitutional Period of the Ottoman Empire (1908–1918)."

1987

George Emile Bisharat, "Practicing Law under Occupation: Palestinian Lawyers of the West Bank."

Marisa Luisa Escribano, "The Endurance of the Olive Tree: Tradition and Identity in Two West Bank Palestinian Villages."

1986

Robert Lee Franklin, "The Indian Community in Bahrain: Labor Migration in a Plural Society."

Feredoun Safizadeh, "Agrarian Change, Migration and Impact of the Islamic Revolution in a Village Community in Azerbaijan."

1985

Mohamed Sabah Alsalim Al-Sabah, "General Equilibrium Analysis of Government Expenditures in an Oil Exporting Country: The Case of Kuwait."

Karen Pliskin, "The Dynamics of Semiotics: The Study of Silver Engravers and their Art in Shiraz, Iran."

1984

Selma Botman, "Oppositional Politics in Egypt: The Communist Movement, 1936–1954."

Lubomyr Hajda, "The Chyhyryn Campaign of 1678 in Light of Two Ottoman Gāza-nāmes."

Perween Hasan, "Sultanate Mosque Types in Bangladesh: Origins and Development."

1983

Zachary Lockman, "Class and Nation: The Emergence of the Egyptian Workers' Movement."

1982

Surin Pitsuwan, "Islam and Malay Nationalism: A Case Study of the Malay-Muslims of Southern Thailand."

1981

Rafique Habib Keshavjee, "The Quest for Gnosis and the Call of History: Modernization among the Ismā'ilis of Iran."

Judith Ellen Tucker, "Women and the Family in Egypt, 1800–1860: A Study in Changing Roles and Status."

1980

Sheila S. Blair, "The Shrine Complex at Natanz, Iran."

Jonathan Max Bloom, "Meaning in Early Fatimid Architecture: Islamic Art in North Africa and Egypt in 4th Century AH (10th AD)."

Uri Mordecai Gordon, "The Development of the Modern Turkish Press, 1945–1965."

Philip Shukry Khoury, "The Politics of Nationalism: Syria and the French Mandate, 1920–1936."

1979

Frederick Robert Hunter, "Bureaucratic Politics and the Passing of Viceregal Absolutism: The Origins of Modern Government in Egypt, 1805–1879."

Robert Lewis Walker, "Inflation in Saudi Arabia."

1978

Jacob Goldberg, "The Foreign Policy of the Third Saudi State: 1902–1918."

Franklin Pierce Huddle, Jr., "Railroads and Roads in Inner Asia: 1860–1940."

Daniel Pipes, "From Mawla to Mamluk: The Origins of Islamic Military Slavery."

1977

Mary-Jo Delvecchio Good, "Social Hierarchy and Social Change in a Provincial Iranian Town."

Constance Hilliard, "The Formation of the Islamic Clerisy of Fauta Toro, Senegal: 1670–1770."

1976

David Gregory Sharry, "The Fathomless Well: Organization of a Sufi Movement in West Africa."

1975

John Gault, "Public Utility Regulation of an Exhaustible Resource: The Case of Natural Gas."

1974

John W. Limbert, "Shiraz in the Age of Hafez."

1973

James Michael Allman, "Education and Social Change in Independent North Africa: Education, Family Planning and Fertility in North Africa."

Michael S. Horn, "The ʿUrābi Revolution Convergent Crises in 19th Century Egypt."

Orest M. Subtelny, "The Unwilling Allies: The Relation of Hetman Pylp Orlyk with the Crimean Khanate and the Ottoman Porte 1710–1742."

1971

Paul J. Magnarella, "Tradition and Change in a Modernizing Turkish Town: A Study of Kinship and the Family."

Dionysios Nikolaou Skiotis, "The Lion and the Phoenix: Ali Pasha and the Greek Revolution."

Thomas Reynolds Stauffer, "The Measurement of Corporate Rates of Return and the Marginal Efficiency of Capital."

1970

Mark Pinson, "Demographic Welfare: An Aspect of Ottoman and Russian Policy, 1854–1866."

1969

Carter Vaughn Findley, "From 'Re'is Efendi' to Foreign Minister: Ottoman Bureaucratic Reform and the Creation of the Foreign Ministry."

John Obert Voll, "A History of the Khat-mīyyah Tarīqah in the Sudan."

1968

Leon Charkoudian, "The Damascus of Muhammad Muhibbī."

Arthur Eduard Goldschmidt, Jr., "The Egyptian Nationalist Party."

Safiuddin Joarder, "The Early Phase of the French Mandatory Administration in Syria: With Special Reference to the Uprising, 1925–1927."

Avigdor Levy, "The Military Policy of Sultan Mahmud II, 1808–1839."

1967

Richard Williams Bulliet, "The Social History of Nishapur in the Eleventh Century."

Phebe Ann Marr, "Yāsīn Al-Hāshimī: The Rise and Fall of a Nationalist (A Study of the Nationalist Leadership in Iraq, 1920–1936)."

1966

John Joseph Donohue, "The Development of Political and Social Institutions in Iraq under the Buwayhids, 334-403H.: The Fall and Rise of the Caliphate."

Andrew Christie Hess, "The Closure of the Ottoman Frontier in North Africa and the Origin of Modern Algeria: 1574–1595."

Edward Louis Keenan, Jr., "Muscovy and Kazan, 1445–1553: A Study in Steppe Politics."

1965

Robert Mitchell Haddad, "The Orthodox Patriarchate of Antioch and the Origins of the Melkite Schism."

David Chapman Kinsey, "Egyptian Education under Cromer: A Study of East-West Encounter in Educational Administration and Policy, 1883–1907."

Robert Gerald Wilson, "The Monetary System of Egypt, An Interpretation."

1964

Munah Abdallah Khuri, "The Role of Arabic Poetry in Reflecting and Directing Social and Intellectual Currents in Egypt, 1882–1922."

Ira Marvin Lapidus, "The Muslim City in the Mamluk Period."

Milson, Menahem. "Kitāb Ādab al-Muridin of Abu al-Najib al-Suhrawardi."

1963

Richard T. Antoun, "Kufr al Ma, a Village in Jordan: A Study of Social Structure and Social Control."

Charles Berlin, "Elijah's Seder Eliyyahu Zuṭa."

Mary Catherine Kassarjian (Bateson), "A Study of Linguistic Patterning in Pre-Islamic Arabic Poetry."

Carla Joy Levine, "The Seljuk Vezirate: A Study of Civil Administration, 1055–1194."

Reuben William Smith, "The Kitāb al-Amwāl of Abu Ubaid al-Qasim ibn Sallam."

1962

Leon Carl Brown, "The Modernization of Tunisia: A Study of Ideological Changes under the Impact of the French Protectorate."

1961

Yusuf Kamal Hussein Ibish, "An Essay on Al-Baqillānī's Doctrine of the Imamate."

1960

Muḥammad ʿAbd al-Ḥayy Muḥammad Shaʾbān, "The Social and Political Background of the ʿAbbāsid Revolution in Khurāsān."

1959

Nadav Safran, "Modern Egypt in Search of Ideology."

1956

Leonard Binder, "Islamic Constitutional Theory and Politics in Pakistan."

Outreach

The outreach program of the Center for Middle Eastern Studies is a major vehicle for reaching out into the wider community and fulfilling the Center's function as a learning resource available to those not only within but also beyond its immediate surroundings. The program, which marks its thirtieth anniversary this year, parlays the intellectual resources of the Center into broad-based activities that have brought into CMES an important constituency: pre-collegiate educational institutions, the media, and the general public.

Although CMES has been networking with different segments of the New England community since the 1950s, it was not until the mid-1970s that a formal outreach program was instituted. The program was launched in 1974 by Barbro Ek, assistant to the associate director of CMES and an AM alumnus, at a time when world crises triggered by another Arab-Israeli war and the first oil shock thrust the Middle East onto the front pages. The outreach activities began modestly, with a series of introductory workshops on the Middle East for primary and secondary school teachers in the Greater Boston area. Soon, the outreach staff were finding themselves working overtime to meet the growing demand from teachers and librarians for curricula and other resource materials on the Middle East. In 1979, these activities were institutionalized in a Teaching Resource Center (TRC), housed at CMES. The TRC, which was renamed the Outreach Center in 2002, became the vanguard of a movement to prepare K–12 educators in the United States to teach students about the Middle East and Islam.

The TRC—and CMES—had its first full-time outreach coordinator in Catherine C. Jones, who spearheaded an expansion of its activities and resources over a period of ten years. The TRC developed what would become a sizeable library, consisting of a collection of books and periodicals for all ages, on the history,

Educators creating their own multimedia maps of the Middle East at an institute in the summer of 2004 on the theme "Perspectives on the Contemporary Middle East: Politics, Society and Culture." The institute was organized by the Outreach Center and hosted by the Education Cooperative in Dedham, Mass. From left to right: Darcie Lenhart, Wellesley Middle School; Ben Etscovitz, Pollard Middle School; Talya Wyzansky, Outreach Center intern; and Christine Carr, Hopkinton High School.

politics, geography, religion, cultural life, and social customs of countries in the Middle East and North Africa. In addition, it amassed an extensive compilation of works on folklore and literature in translation. Supplementing this material is what is now a substantial audio-visual collection of hundreds of films, filmstrips, videos, slides, cassettes, photographs, illustrations, posters, maps, and artworks covering all parts of the Middle Eastern and Islamic worlds. From the outset, these materials were made available on a no-fee lending basis and attracted instructors at all levels, from elementary teachers to university professors, in search of resources to enliven their classrooms.

Besides regular all-day workshops for educators, Jones launched a quarterly newsletter, *Middle East Resources*, distributed free of charge to thousands of teachers and librarians across the country, to publicize the activities of the TRC and to offer a variety of ideas for communicating knowledge and learning about the Middle East. Jones also wrote a book and an accompanying curriculum for the study of the encounter between Spain and Islam. Entitled *Islamic Spain and Our Heritage: Al-Andalus 711–1492 A.D.*, it is still used in middle and high school classrooms. Jones's contributions toward understanding the

Middle East were acknowledged shortly after her death in 2003, when the Middle East Outreach Council (MEOC) voted unanimously to give her a Lifetime Achievement Award. The Council, an organization of outreach coordinators that is affiliated with the Middle East Studies Association, was formed in 1981 through the initiative of several centers, prominent among which was CMES.

Jones was succeeded in 1989 by Carol Johnson Shedd, a teacher and librarian with a lifelong commitment to multi-culturalism. During Shedd's fourteen-year tenure as outreach coordinator, the TRC expanded both the scope and scale of its activities. Shedd continued the tradition of hosting professional development workshops, now with a special emphasis on inclusive approaches to Middle Eastern studies. She also led monthly discussion groups on Middle Eastern literature and developed multicultural curricula centered on the Middle East. The TRC's *Middle East Resources* was revamped from a newsletter to a "curriculum resource" that offered a thematic approach and included background readings, teaching suggestions, lesson plans, and bibliographies. One issue was devoted to women in the Middle East. Another focused on music of the Arab and Islamic world. Yet a third, entitled "What's in a Name," offered definitions for a compendium of terms, from "Black September" to "Muslim Brotherhood." In 1994, the TRC was awarded a grant by the Middle East Institute for developing teaching units on US foreign policy and intervention in the Middle East.

Shedd's special interest was in literature. In the October 1995 issue of *Middle East Resources*, she published a survey under the heading of "The Four Literatures of the Middle East" that included essays on Arabic, Hebrew, Persian, and Turkish literature. And under her editorial guidance, along with the help of CMES graduate students, the TRC produced what continues to be the Outreach Center's perennial bestseller: *Are You Listening? Voices from the Middle East*. The anthology, subsequently revised and expanded, consists of short stories, memoirs, and excerpts from novels, divided into sections such as "Growing Pains" and "Varieties of Love," all designed to give students a glimpse of some of the ways in which people in the Middle East respond to universals of the human experience. An introduction to the anthology, addressed specifically to teachers, contains a statement, perhaps as good as any mission statement, explaining why the

Barbara Petzen, CMES Outreach coordinator, and Dilek Barlow, CMES AM student and staff assistant at the Outreach Center.

CMES Outreach Center has devoted so much emphasis to attempting to counter the stereotypes and misrepresentations it finds in a good deal of present-day discourse on the Middle East in the United States:

> What is lacking in the images of the Middle East received by millions of Americans is a human perspective [that] fully conveys both the intricate nature of many of the region's conflicts and the personal experiences of those who live through them. The news media, the only way of knowing the Middle East for so many, often reduces the region to a limited number of categories, most of which are negative. In so doing, both the diversity of the area and its wealth of human experience are denied. (*Are You Listening?* Unit One [CMES, TRC, 1995], p. vii.)

Barbara Petzen, a doctoral candidate in History and Middle Eastern Studies, took over the position of outreach coordinator in September 2001, just days before the attacks of 9/11. What all along had been a demanding undertaking became much more so as the educational community and the public at large sought to come to terms with a cataclysm that for many defied comprehension. Petzen found herself responding to a flood of requests for information about the Middle East and the Muslim world. The Outreach Center continues to receive daily requests— through email messages, phone calls, and walk-in visitors—from teachers struggling to gain a better understanding of the Middle East and seeking resources and skills that might enable them to pass on the knowledge they acquire to their students. Recent requests for assistance have came from yet more unusual sources, for example converts to Islam in prisons who have asked to borrow books.

The Outreach Center, staffed by Petzen and a staff of CMES AM and PhD students, along with occasional volunteers, has intensified the effort to develop curricula and organize workshops for educators. The titles of two workshops reflect the post-9/11 world: "Teaching Beyond Terror" and "Afghanistan: History, Culture, and Politics." Other workshops for educators have included themes such as the Ottoman empire. The outreach staff have devoted considerable energy in recent years to working with schools and teachers. In 2002 and 2003, they visited around fifty schools to offer ideas and material for discussing the Middle East in the classroom. The greatest demand has come from teachers of courses on world history, international relations, foreign cultures, current events, and world geography. Petzen and her team have consulted on an individual basis with hundreds of teachers. Petzen herself frequently gives talks on subjects such as "Islam 101" or "Using Middle Eastern Literature in the Classroom." Although most of the visits have been in the Boston area and other parts of Massachusetts, the outreach staff has also organized workshops in school systems in other states of New England. Further afield, they have sent literature anthologies to Hawaii and a culture kit on the Arab world to the state of Washington. The day-to-day interaction with teachers has helped to identify gaps and needs and it has stimulated the development of new curricular materials, including topics such as the meaning of Ramadan, understanding Islam through the arts, the world of Islam beyond the Arab realm, and the spice trade and its connections over the centuries.

A notable aspect of the Outreach Center's activities in recent years has been increased collaboration with other organizations that have complementary skills and interests. These include its counterparts in some of the other regional studies centers at Harvard, for example, the Russian, East European, and Central Asian Studies outreach division of the Davis Center for Russian and Eurasian Studies. The Outreach Center has also worked with a variety of organizations beyond Harvard, including the African Studies Center at Boston University; the Massachusetts Foundation for the Humanities; the Concerned Scholars Action Group; Afghans for Civil Society; Dreams of Freedom, Boston's immigration museum; and even the Children's Museum of Boston, where it has addressed managers and interpreters on issues surrounding 9/11.

The newfound focus on collaborative relationships has allowed the Outreach Center to expand its programming and has given it new venues for its activities that it would not have had otherwise. The Center has engaged several professional development organizations as co-sponsors for its initiatives. Among these organizations are Primary Source, a nationally known nonprofit center for the culturally inclusive, multi-disciplinary study of history and the humanities; the Education Cooperative, which coordinates professional development and other services for fourteen school systems west of Boston; Educators for Social Responsibility, who develop curricula and conduct training on issues of intergroup relations, conflict resolution, violence prevention, and social and emotional learning; Facing History and Ourselves, whose mission is to engage students of diverse backgrounds in civic education; and Workable Peace, which provides training and curricular materials on conflict resolution. The Outreach Center has worked with these five groups in organizing a series of workshops for one hundred teachers in the Newton school district on the nexus of Islam, Afghanistan, and the United States.

Collaboration with such groups also contributed to two week-long institutes for educators that Petzen organized in the summer of 2004. The first, with the Education Cooperative, covered "Perspectives on the Middle East: Contemporary Politics, Society and Culture." The second, with Primary Source, had as its theme "The Genesis and Genius of Islam: The Founding, Expansion and Achievements of Islamic Societies." In addition, Petzen has assisted a host of organizations, such as the Massachusetts Foundation for the Humanities and the Harvard Institute for Retirement, in planning reading and discussion groups on topics like "Understanding Islam"; she also has appeared at their events to deliver lectures or lead study groups.

Moreover, the Outreach Center has ventured into the media world. It has provided much of the content and advised on many of the features of "Global Connections: Putting World Events in Context," a website developed by WGBH, Boston's public broadcasting producer. This interactive website (at www.pbs.org/wgbh/globalconnections/mideast/index.html) is organized around a timeline of Middle Eastern history from 1900 to the present; six thematic areas, including politics, religion, economics, culture, geography, and science and technology; and cross-cutting questions such as "What is the appeal of religious militancy?" and "What have been the effects of US foreign policies in the Middle East?" It also includes multi-media lesson plans and case studies on issues such as the responses of different communities to the events of 9/11. As with many other projects that have involved the Outreach Center, the purpose is to give educators and students, along with the curious public, material on the Middle East that is both informative and balanced.

In the wake of 9/11, the Outreach Center has also responded to calls from dozens of national and local news organizations seeking background information on the events of the day or asking for suggestions on experts to interview. Since its inception, the outreach program has served as a hotline for callers requesting immediate answers to questions as diverse as the following: "Who is the Israeli ambassador to the United Nations?" "What does Hizbullah mean?" "Where can I find a collection of Mullah Nasreddin stories?" "How do I cook *shwarma*?" The widespread availability of information online has not diminished the frequency of calls. But it has meant that many of the requests are less routine and require more complex answers. The Outreach Center also communicates to the public through a website, www.fas.harvard.edu/~mideast/outreach/index.html, which has recently added a searchable database of all its library materials, including videos and music.

As one of sixteen National Resource Centers, CMES is supported by the US government under Title VI and it is this support that funds much of the outreach activities. Harvard supplies matching funds and the work is further supported by occasional funding from outside sources, such as the Arabian American Oil Company (ARAMCO). The mission of the Outreach Center beyond Harvard, which is recognized in this support, has involved it in initiatives on the national stage. The Center continues to play an important role in the activities of the Middle East Outreach Council. The Center has taken the lead in collecting, reviewing, and digitizing teaching materials produced by all Title VI outreach centers in Middle Eastern studies as well as by other institutions and individual instructors. These materials have been put online in a searchable database, www.outreachworld.org, which aims to become a one-stop resource for teaching international and area studies and foreign languages in the pre-collegiate classroom. In addition, Petzen serves as ex officio member of the MEOC board in her capacity as editor of the Council's newsletter, *Perspectives*.

Comments Petzen: "What I originally thought would be a half-time job to help fund my dissertation writing has become a full-time obsession, a life's work."

Research Projects and Programs

Moroccan Studies Program

The Moroccan Studies Program represents one of the major steps by the Center for Middle Eastern Studies in recognizing that its teaching and research mandate encompasses more than the traditional heartland of the Middle East. Initiated in 1985 through a grant from the Moroccan government, it is the only program of any significance in the United States to be dedicated exclusively to the study of North Africa. Its purpose, according to the protocol between Mohammed V University in Rabat and Harvard, was "to contribute to the promotion and strengthening of friendship and understanding between the academic circles in the two countries." The program has expanded in scope beyond the initial emphasis on scholarly exchange to become the pillar of teaching and research on the Maghrib at Harvard.

The program is directed by Susan Miller, a senior lecturer in the Department of Near Eastern Languages and Civilizations and contributor of several works on Morocco, including *In the Shadow of the Sultan: Culture, Power, and Politics in Morocco* (co-edited with Rahma Bourqia) and *Disorienting Encounters: Travels of a Moroccan Scholar in France in 1845–1846* (tr. and ed. version of *The Voyage of Muhammad as-Saffar*). The program has sponsored a variety of activities, all designed to promote the study of a region that has been at the crossroads of Mediterranean, African, and Middle Eastern cultures from the early Islamic era to the present.

The centerpiece consists of courses on the Maghrib that have become a regular part of the Harvard curriculum. Besides Miller, in recent years two other CMES-based faculty members have offered courses with a direct focus on the region: Jocelyn Cesari and William Granara. In 2002, Miller and Cesari joined forces to teach "Politics, Society and Religion in North Africa from 1500 to the Present," a broad survey of the evolution of state-society relations in the area since the late medieval period. Miller has offered a course entitled "The Arab Mediterranean City," which traces the interaction between urban form and social praxis, using the Maghrib as a primary focus and supplemented by examples from Egypt and the Levant. Granara, who specializes in the history and culture of Muslim Sicily, has taught a seminar on Maghribi literary and cultural texts that explores the emergence of a Maghribi identity through an examination of works of the Arabo-Islamic cultures of al-Andalus, Sicily, and North Africa. The program has also sponsored visits by prominent Moroccan intellectuals. Among Moroccan scholars who have taught at Harvard over the last decade are Abdelfettah Kilito, who gave a course on "The Cult of Saints in Medieval Moroccan Literature"; Mohammed Kably, who offered "Society and Power in Medieval Morocco"; and Abdesselam Cheddadi, who taught two courses in Arabic: "Studies in Ibn Khaldun" and "Issues in Contemporary Arab Intellectual and Social Thought."

Saloua Zerhouni, Faculty of Law, Mohammed V University, Rabat, Morocco, and Susan Miller, director of the Moroccan Studies Program. Zerhouni spoke on "The Political Dynamics of the Islamists in the Moroccan Parliament" at a session of the Morocco Forum, May 5, 2004.

The Morocco Forum is another feature of the program. A monthly seminar series, the Forum has emphasized contemporary political and economic developments in the Maghrib, including such issues as political Islam and labor migration. In a less contemporary vein, the Forum has heard presentations on research in such topics as law and Sufism in the Maghrib and the historiography of medieval North Africa. Speakers have included many scholars from universities in North Africa and other parts of the Middle East, as well as European countries. Among those who have appeared before the Forum are Taieb Belghazi, Abdellah Hammoudi, Abdallah Laroui, Abderrahman El Moudden, Ahmed Toufiq, Lucette Valensi, Dirk Vandewalle, and William Zartman. The program has also sponsored several conferences, including "Representations of Power in Morocco and the Maghrib" in 1994; "Morocco in the Global Economy" in 1997; and, together with the Contemporary Arab Studies Program, "Algeria: State and Society in the Global Era" in 2001. In addition, it has helped to support several workshops, including one on "The State and Informal Economies in the Middle East and North Africa" in 1996 and another on "Contemporary Islamic Liberal Thought" in 1997.

Support to students for study and research is yet another component of the program. The program has awarded fellowships for undergraduate as well as graduate students to attend summer language courses in Fez. It also has given grants for dissertation research on topics related to Morocco. These have ranged from the social impact of structural adjustment policies of the 1980s and

1990s to the social history of the Jews of Marrakesh in the late nineteenth and early twentieth centuries. The program has helped to stimulate a two-way intellectual traffic between Harvard and the Maghrib by giving Harvard students direct exposure to the region and by bringing visiting scholars from Morocco to the University.

The program has not neglected the cultural side of the Maghrib. In 2000, it co-sponsored with the Department of Anthropology a North African Film Festival, which included feature films and documentaries from Algeria, Morocco, and Tunisia. In the fall of 2004, a major exhibition of Berber artifacts was due to open at Harvard's Peabody Museum of Archaeology and Ethnography. The exhibit, entitled "IMAZIGHEN! Beauty and Artisanship in Berber Everyday Life," is a joint initiative of the Peabody Museum and the Moroccan Studies Program. It is curated by Susan Miller and Lisa Bernasek, a doctoral candidate in anthropology who is writing a dissertation on museum culture. In conjunction with the exhibit, the program was planning an international symposium on Berber cultural revival.

The Moroccan Studies Program, which is made possible by grants from Morocco's Ministry of Education, builds on Harvard's already substantial resources on the Maghrib. The collection of Moroccana in the Harvard College Library, which includes more than 40,000 titles in Arabic, French, English, Spanish, and other languages, is perhaps the finest of any academic institution outside Morocco. The university's photographic, architectural, and ethnographic resources related to the Maghrib are also without peer in the United States. Maghribi studies, traditionally the preserve of French academia, were once a rarity in the United States. Thanks to the CMES program, that is no longer the case.

Contemporary Arab Studies Program

The Contemporary Arab Studies Program (CASP) was founded at the Center for Middle Eastern Studies in 1995 with a declared mission of "increasing mutual understanding between the West and Arab states" and also "encouraging the continued progress of the Arab world and its peoples." It was conceived of as a vehicle for channeling intellectual energies toward a part of the Middle East that had not received sustained attention at the Center or elsewhere at Harvard in prior decades. The program's focus on the Arab world, therefore, complements the Center's programs in Turkish, Iranian, and Maghrebi studies, as well as in the pre-modern and Islamic fields.

CASP has been directed since its inception by Roger Owen, the A.J. Meyer Professor of History and CMES Director from 1996 to 1999. Until his retirement in 2003, the program had an executive director in Thomas D. Mullins, who also was associate director of the Center. Its principal benefactor has been Khalid Alturki, head of a Saudi industrial conglomerate and, until recently, chair of both the CMES Advisory Council and the program's advisory committee.

CASP has set several specific goals for itself. For students, in particular, it hopes to create an environment in which issues pertinent to Arab society and culture can be explored through interdisciplinary initiatives, publications, conferences, and visiting scholars. It also aims to strengthen current teaching resources at Harvard through academic appointments in areas that are important to both the Arab and Western worlds. Toward the same end, it is dedicated to developing resources for the education and training of graduate students and returning professionals for public and private careers in the Arab Middle East. It has sought to offer traveling fellowships to Harvard students for field research and language training in Arab countries as well as financial assistance to outstanding students from these same countries to study at Harvard.

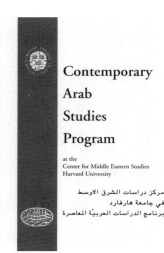

Contemporary
Arab
Studies
Program

at the
Center for Middle Eastern Studies
Harvard University

مركز دراسات الشرق الاوسط
في جامعة هارفارد
برنامج الدراسات العربيّة المعاصرة

As with all projects at the Center, research is a core ingredient. Here, the program has committed itself to undertaking research projects on problems of special interest and importance to the contemporary Arab world.

CASP has organized several major conferences at the Center. These have included a 1997 conference on "Challenges Facing the Arab World at the End of the 20th Century," which brought together leading scholars to grapple with a set of concerns that remain at the forefront of current debate about Arab countries today, including the resilience of authoritarian regimes, the changing position of the nation-state, the structural deficiencies in the economic realm, and the role of civil society and informal politics. They have also included two conferences on land and property issues, which have led to a CMES monograph (Roger Owen, ed., *New Perspectives on Property and Land in the Middle East*, 2000). CASP has co-sponsored several conferences within and beyond Harvard, including one in 2001 with the Moroccan Studies Program, on state and society in Algeria; and another, in 1997, with the Middle East Center of the University of Texas, Austin, on "The City in the Middle East: New Perspectives."

The program has given grants for assisting graduate assistance research. It has financed some of the costs of course offerings of visiting lecturers, including one by Ibrahim Oweiss of Georgetown University, who in the late 1990s taught on a topic that has become all but extinct in the Economics Department—economic development in the Middle East. CASP has provided support for yet other activities at the Center. It paved the way for the launching in 1998 of the Arab Education Forum, a project that has served as a platform for a discussion of alternatives in education among Arab countries, with a broader objective of nurturing authentic Arab visions to guide thinking and practice in education and learning throughout the Arab world. CASP has also provided support for the Arab Studies Forum, a seminar series instituted at CMES in 1996, and since then chaired by Owen, to discuss current research on subjects related to modern Arab history and society. In addition, the program has occasionally co-sponsored cultural activities, such as a concert of muwashshahat by the Tarab Chorus.

For Owen, the Contemporary Arab Studies Program has been a means of furthering one of his priorities at the Center: to forge ongoing relationships with Arab universities and research institutes. Hence, collaboration in research projects he has undertaken with institutions such as the American University in Cairo and the

American University of Beirut has been instrumental in fulfilling both a personal objective and one of the program's objectives. For CASP, the obstacles in maintaining regular contact with Arab scholars at Arab universities have been formidable; and they have become even more so in the twenty-first century. Owen sees another challenge facing the development of the program at Harvard: overcoming what he calls "the growing 'internationalist' assumption that the world can be understood by people who only know English, using categories like 'democracy' and 'liberalism' developed in the West." (Quoted in *The Middle East at Harvard: CMES Newsletter*, v. 8 [Summer 1995], p. 4.) For Owen, meeting this challenge necessitates not only advancing a winning argument for specialized knowledge of particular languages and particular histories, but also building a critical mass of scholars who are able to sustain a program of world-class teaching and research in Arab studies.

Arab Education Forum

For all his adult life, Dr. Munir Fasheh has been involved in education. But it was in the 1970s, when he was working as a mathematics teacher in schools and universities of the West Bank, that he began to question what he and probably no one else would deny: that schooling and literacy are essential for knowledge, understanding, and self-betterment in the world. As obvious as this truth is, it is not without its problems. Fasheh often recounts the story of how he first came to that realization. His mother was an "illiterate" seamstress who received orders from women to make clothing out of materials they provided her and, after taking a few measurements, she would cut the pieces of cloth and sew them together into a beautiful outfit. She had no formal schooling, but she had learned such basic mathematical operations as measurement and spatial patterning from practical experience. That she possessed this kind of mathematical knowledge was less surprising to Fasheh than that they had been invisible to him and to other literate and educated people, who assumed that "illiterates" necessarily lack skills acquired in school.

The Arab Education Forum's apprenticeship workshop that brought together illustrators from eight Arab countries for an intensive exchange with the renowned Egyptian artist and writer Mohieddin Ellabad in Cairo, January 2004. For AEF, the gathering, which gave the illustrators an opportunity to learn from each other as well as from Ellabad, is an example of the "learning communities" it seeks to stimulate.

Although Fasheh became critical of some of the negative assumptions about knowledge and learning that went into literacy and school programs, he was not prepared to dismiss such programs altogether. And while appreciative of the ways in which people learn through everyday practice and observation, he did not want to romanticize the school of hard knocks, either. The challenge for him was to unlearn the prejudices of modern education that blind one to diverse modes and alternative spaces of learning among people who can neither read nor write, and to provide the resources to enhance them. But how to bring literacy and other educational skills without stifling these "traditional" or "everyday" ways of knowing is just as challenging. And once in school, how can people be encouraged to learn how to learn, and, more profoundly, how to take charge of this learning process themselves rather than to accept blindly and uncritically what family, school, or the state sanction for them?

The Arab Education Forum is the latest of several initiatives in Arab education in which Fasheh has been involved over the last quarter century that attempt to address these questions. In the late 1970s, when Israel closed Birzeit University, where he had been dean of students, he embarked upon a project to teach mathematics to non-literate workers. As he describes the experiment, "I didn't start 'logically' by first teaching them the numbers and numerals, etc., but by choosing tasks that they were doing more or less daily"—such as learning to draw the road from their homes to the university or arranging chairs in big rooms and lecture halls according to the space in which they had to fit and the functions they were intended to serve. This was followed in 1992 by the launching of a reading campaign in Palestine. The campaign, assisted by the Tamer Institute for Community Development, which he had founded, set as its main goal to make reading into a habitual and enjoyable activity within the Palestinian community at large. The concern, however, was not just with literacy in the narrow sense of being able to read and write, but also with being able to learn and to produce. The objective, therefore, was to encourage people to use reading and writing skills to reflect on their thoughts and actions, often in dialogue with others in small interactive groups, and in particular to reflect on their own goals and aspirations for which they might believe that literacy is vital.

Meanwhile, Fasheh managed to take a break from these projects to get a doctorate in Education from Harvard University, at a time in the 1980s and 1990s when the academy was beginning to question the supposed differences between literacy and non-literacy

Arab Education Forum Director Munir Fasheh at AEF's first apprenticeship workshop, held in Cairo, January 2004. (See photograph on p. 86.)

and the benefits or merits of schooling. On one side were scholars like anthropologist Jack Goody or educationists like Angela Hildyard and David Olson, who argued that literacy is a practice that, once learned, will lead to specific cognitive and emotional developments that are not present in pre-literate societies, and that these developments are essential for success in school and in vocations, and even for the creation of modern subjectivity and the nation-state. On the other side of the debate were scholars like Paulo Freire, who argued that the conventional notions of literacy and education masked ideological functions in a class-dominated society. Fasheh's published writings reveal the important influence of Freire, but his views also resonate with other thinkers—anthropologists Brian Street and Shirley Heath, for instance—who developed a social or ideological model of literacy and schooling that was sensitive to differences in context and power relations. His overall approach, however, is not so much concerned with ethnographic description as it is with enabling people to think critically about their education and to determine how to make it serve their own needs and aspirations.

It was to this end that Fasheh founded the Arab Education Forum in 1998 under the aegis of the Contemporary Arab Studies Program (CASP) at CMES. The Forum is dedicated to stimulating a dialogue on education and learning, in the broadest sense of the terms, with a view to developing an authentic and shared vision across the Arab realm. It seeks to identify innovative projects in education and to provide a platform whereby such projects can be discussed and disseminated. It also aims to serve as a catalyst in building networks of practitioners and researchers who are engaged in inspiring

Participants at the second Conference on "Learning Societies/Diversity in Learning in the Arab World" held in Amman, Jordan, in April 2004 and organized by the Arab Education Forum in collaboration with UNESCO, Shikshantar (an education and development institute based in Rajasthan, India), and the Arab Theater Training Center.

activities in areas of formal or non-formal education. Fasheh's premise is that while there are many creative individuals and groups in the Arab world, they are but "streams," unknown, often marginalized, and typically isolated from each other. He regards the Forum as part of a sorely needed effort to connect those streams so they form a "river." By encouraging and supporting the process of innovation, the Forum aspires to promote what its mission statement calls "a culture of initiatives."

Among the Forum's own initiatives is a magazine it sponsors: *Qalb el-Umour*, which Fasheh describes as "an example of how to use the alphabet rather than be used by it." One begins with a community of people—of any age or background—and asks them to reflect on their values and hopes, to share and discuss these with each other, and to put together a magazine reflecting their diverse views. In "How To Eradicate Illiteracy Without Eradicating Illiterates?," a paper presented to the UNESCO roundtable "Literacy as Freedom" on the occasion of International Literacy Day, September 9–10, 2002, he described the magazine's distinctive approach: "No one approves, and no one edits . . . [L]anguage in the magazine is considered a tool for freedom (in expressing what exists inside the person and the interaction of what is inside with one's surrounding), and not a tool to evaluate through words such as 'right' and 'wrong.'. . . [W]e encourage people to share what they write with one another, and if, as a result of discussions, they feel they want to make changes, that's fine. But no one has the authority to correct another."

Over twenty magazines have been produced in several different countries, including Lebanon, Jordan, India, and the United States. Each publication is different in appearance and content and arises from the particular circumstances of the individuals and groups involved. For example, the first issue of *Qalb el-Umour*, released in September 2000, was put together by five students from different schools in Beirut. They entitled it *Laesh la*? ("Why Not?") and used their own funds to produce 100 copies for distribution across the Arab world. Another 1,500 copies were produced to meet growing demand.

As director of the Forum, Fasheh has also concentrated on organizing gatherings devoted to a dialogue on educational alternatives in the Arab world. The Forum has sponsored annual meetings in Lebanon, Jordan, and Egypt at which educators from many Arab countries discuss their educational ideas and goals for literacy. Topics have included the teaching of Classical Arabic to children under six years old, the histories of different Arab educational associations, reconsidering the "self as other," poetry for children, and the uses of video and other electronic media in school education. Proceedings of the annual meetings have been compiled and edited by Munir Fasheh and Serene Huleileh, the Forum's regional director, and published under CASP. The Forum has also co-sponsored conferences with UNESCO, the Arab Theater Training Center, and Shikshantar (India) to explore alternatives to traditional schooling in the form of "learning society networks." Other activities have included workshops on themes such as "regaining the uses of the senses in learning and teaching"; conventions of leading practitioners in various fields of educational and artistic endeavor, such as one that brought together accomplished illustrators from eight Arab countries; and *qalb el-umour* films by teenagers in Egypt, Jordan, Lebanon, and Palestine. A common thread in all these activities is to generate momentum behind the idea of diversity in learning and, toward this end, to establish "learning communities." The Forum has also developed a website in Arabic to serve as a resource center on education in Arab countries: www.almoultaqa.com.

Aside from seed money from CASP, the Arab Education Forum has been funded mainly by grants from the Ford Foundation. It has also received support from the Arab Fund for Economic and Social Development and the Khoudairi Foundation. Although it is perhaps too early to assess the impact of the initiative, Professor Roger Owen, director of CASP and a former director of CMES, has observed that the Forum has evoked an enthusiastic response in the Arab world. "They seem to have touched a deep chord among the many people who would like to find ways to energize the present systems of education and to make them more responsive to the social, moral, and imaginative needs of the young people of the contemporary Middle East."

Ottoman Court Records Project

The Ottoman Court Records Project, one of the more ambitious research endeavors to have involved the Center for Middle Eastern Studies in recent years, aims to organize the ocean of information in the *shari'a* court records of Istanbul between the middle of the sixteenth and early twentieth centuries. The records consist of approximately ten million *sijills*, or case entries, that were piled in large stacks in the headquarters of the Mufti of Istanbul, the Sheikhulislam, until Sultan Abdülhamid II (r. 1876–1909) decided to have them bound and organized chronologically for each of the district courts that functioned within the metropolis. The resulting archives of approximately ten thousand volumes (*defters*) have been kept intact, in the same building that houses the Müftülük today, decades after the secularization of the legal system in the republican era rendered the *shari'a* courts obsolete. Surprisingly, even though the records have been mined over the years by students of the Ottoman period, until recently a publication of any *defter* in full had yet to appear. The dearth of scholarly editions for the thousands of *defters* that exist in many other cities of the former Ottoman realm is equally striking.

Leading the effort to make the wealth of data in the court records available to the scholarly community around the world are two of the core faculty of CMES: Cemal Kafadar and Gülru Necipoğlu. Both scholars were born and grew up in Istanbul and in different ways both have dealt in their research with many of the concerns of the project. The Vehbi Koç Professor of Turkish Studies and a leading Ottoman historian, Kafadar has written extensively on the rise, transformation, and dissolution of the empire, a narrative that inevitably addresses questions of law, faith, and identity. He has also worked on numerous aspects of the social history of his beloved city, such as the rise of the coffeehouses in the 1550s and the revolts that raged in the seventeenth century. It was in the late 1980s, while he was teaching at Princeton, that he became intrigued with the idea of using computer technology to bring order to the court cases. For Necipoğlu, the Aga Khan Professor of Islamic Art and Architecture, the interplay between power and aesthetics has been a recurring theme and is the subject of several major works on Ottoman art that have earned her wide acclaim. The changes in the architectural and social landscape of Istanbul since the fifteenth century holds a special interest to her.

The project was launched in 1990 as Kafadar and Necipoğlu joined forces with Halil İnalcik, the doyen of Ottoman historians, who had pioneered the use of these court records as early as the 1940s. The initiative to organize the archives expanded into a larger team that has included scholars from several Turkish institutions, notably Istanbul and Sabanci universities. The principal achievement to date has been the preparation of forty volumes of *sijills* in different stages of readiness, including seven completed manuscripts. The first volume was due to be published in the fall of 2004, with others to follow within two-month intervals. The volume contains a complete court register and includes a scholarly transcription and facsimile. Considerable effort has gone into developing the conventions and protocols of standardized editing for this corpus before making it accessible to other researchers.

In addition to preparing the textual editions of these volumes for publication in conventional scholarly fashion, CMES faculty and students have been working on presenting the *defters* in electronic format. With the help of the Packard Humanities Institute, they have developed a software program for such procedures as lemmatization as well as a context-sensitive concordance. The concordance, which is to be appended to the published volume on a CD-ROM, promises to be a handy device for wading through the masses of data to be found in the *sijills*. The use of such an apparatus is perhaps a first in the field of Middle Eastern and Islamic studies. The long-range goal is to offer the material on the Web so it can be used by researchers anywhere in the world. The addition of yet other tools is being explored. As the *sijills* have entries in both Turkish and Arabic, the project has begun to consider developing software that can run bilingual and "bi-alphabetic" searches.

The court records are of inestimable importance for any effort to construct the fabric of social and economic life of a city that was the capital of an empire that covered almost two-thirds of the Middle East for the better part of four centuries. The records are also vital for understanding critical aspects of the political, administrative, legal, economic, and social structures of the empire and their transformation over time. Most of the records are the legacy of the proceedings of courts that were presided by *qadis*. The role of these *madrasah*-trained officials in the administration of justice is far from settled and it has often been distorted by such characterizations as Weber's famous concept of *kadijustiz* as a form of judicial legitimacy that does not rest on a consistent application of settled rules, or by Supreme Court Justice Felix Frankfurter's much-quoted declaration that "we do not sit like a kadi under a tree dispensing justice according to considerations of individual expediency." However, we do know that the *qadis* were more than merely judges in the strict sense of the term, as they also performed a variety of notarial and even some mayoral functions. Thus, the registers contain not only details of pleas entered and decisions rendered, but also registration of properties, certification of official and private documents, recording of business transactions, and information on economic matters such as prices and taxes. The cases heard by the *qadis* cover a broad range of issues, including marriage and divorce, disputes over inheritance and among neighbors, business partnerships and licensing agreements, petitions from individual proprietors and guild members, and crime. The parties included rich and poor, Muslims and non-Muslims alike.

Cemal Kafadar

The methodological problems in working through these documents can be daunting, both for members of the project team and for researchers who turn to the records as a primary source for scholarly inquiry. One of the purposes of the project is to offer a roadmap to assist the user in negotiating some of these problems. Putting some of the voluminous records in the public domain is also intended to facilitate comparative investigation, both over time and across space. Kafadar and Necipoğlu decided for practical reasons to limit the initial coverage to courts that functioned within the city limits of Istanbul. Eventually, they plan to include the records of other townships that were part of a metropolis that stretched across land and water. These include Eyüp, Galata, and Üsküdar, the latter containing the earliest existing *defter*, going back to 1512, in all of Istanbul. They also plan to include other kinds of records, notably *awqaf* (charitable foundations or trusts) that will reveal considerable information about the ownership and management of property as well as the social and political role of these institutions. Beyond Istanbul, they hope that the project will serve as a model for research projects on other cities under Ottoman rule—including Aleppo,

Gülru Necipoğlu

Halil İnalcik

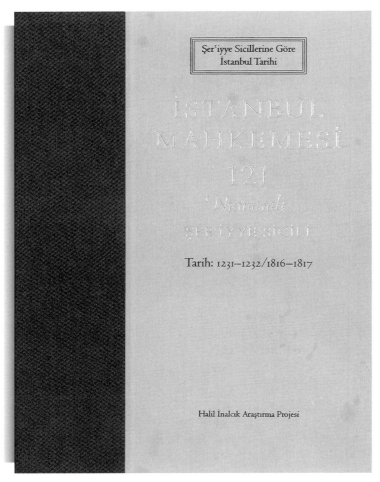
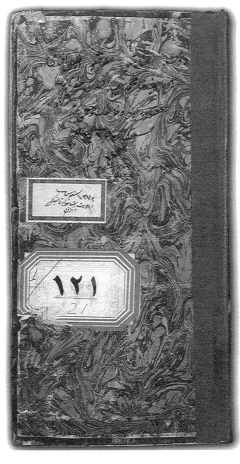

Şer'iyye Sicillerine Göre
İstanbul Tarihi

İSTANBUL
MAHKEMESİ
121
Numaralı
ŞER'İYYE SİCİLİ

Tarih: 1231–1232/1816–1817

Halil İnalcık Araştırma Projesi

Top left: *Istanbul Mahkemesi 121,* the project's first publication, scheduled to appear in the fall of 2004, and the world's first publication of a complete *defter* of Istanbul *shari'a* court records. **Right:** the 121st *defter* of the *shari'a* court records of Istanbul, on which the project's first publication is based.

Cairo, Jerusalem, and Sarajevo—where similar records exist in abundance and await organization. Meanwhile, the findings that are being unearthed are already working their way into research at Harvard. Students are using the *sijills* to glean insights into such question as the methods of dispute resolution used by Muslim communities or the role of the *qadis* in legitimizing the structures of wealth and power.

A second component of the project consists of an effort to map the information in the records to provide a graphical illustration of the social topography of Istanbul between the sixteenth and nineteenth centuries. As almost one-half of the documents involve real estate transactions and include descriptions of the locations of property, entire neighborhoods can be reconstructed and visually represented on sets of maps displayed on a monitor. The data,

Six of the *sijills* in the 121st *defter*. The cases pertain to a dispute over a coffeehouse in Topkapi; the setting of official prices for 25,000 bushels of wheat; the arrangement of a monetary agreement by the court; a dispute between the mounted porters' guild and the ferrymen's guild; the submission of a resignation from the stewardship of a foundation; and (shown in part) the transfer of a butcher business.

therefore, can be used to establish the physical coordinates of residential and commercial properties as well as public buildings, including both the monumental structures and more modest ones among mosques, churches, synagogues, and fountains. The result promises to yield a sense of the life of the city. Researchers would be able to use the computerized databases to arrive at a picture, for example, of what kinds of shops a particular neighborhood had, how rents for homes or shops fluctuated, who were the occupants of various buildings, what were the patterns of ownership in various quarters of the city, how many marketplaces existed at different times, and how street networks changed over the centuries.

For Necipoğlu, this aspect of the project is the most exciting and has the potential of the greatest pedagogical dividends, especially for courses in urban and architectural history. The hurdles to be negotiated are formidable, if only because of the sheer magnitude of Istanbul. Until it was overtaken by London and Paris in the middle of the eighteenth century, the city was larger than any other in Europe. During the course of its long history, it was burned and rebuilt many times, making any effort to determine changes over time an exceptional challenge. It is here that computer technology is allowing what would once have been inconceivable: the integration of maps, drawings, sketches, and other visual data with textual information. Students at Harvard have digitized the earliest street maps of Istanbul, which date back to the early nineteenth century, and are locating on these maps identifiable sites, relying on information extracted from the *sijills* and other sources of data. Work continues apace to identify with precision individual homes and shops in order to capture the social fabric of different neighborhoods. The project team is also mapping out dramatic events such as fires and revolts as they unfold in space and time.

The project has received support from a variety of sources. The Koç Foundation in Turkey and the Aga Khan Foundation in Geneva provided funding in the early phases. Since 1999, the Packard Humanities Institute has been a primary source not only of funding but also of technical assistance and scholarly collaboration, especially in the conception and development of software programs. The project has engaged four or five students a year, offering them both financial support and unique training in reading and analyzing some of the most important source materials on the social history of the early modern Middle East. The project has involved extensive collaboration among Harvard faculty and with universities in Turkey.

Historians of the Ottoman Empire

Historians of the Ottoman Empire is the latest research initiative undertaken by the Center for Middle Eastern Studies in support of the thriving field of Ottoman studies at Harvard. The project's objective is to produce a comprehensive biographical and bibliographic reference work on Ottoman history that will serve as a standard in the field. In contrast to earlier works in this area, the project plans to include all historians who lived and wrote within the far reaches of the empire, regardless of the language they used. Therefore, it will cover not only the many works of history that have been written in Turkish, but also ones in Arabic, Persian, Armenian, and Greek, among other languages.

Spearheading this effort are three passionate Ottomanists: Cemal Kafadar, Vehbi Koç Professor of Turkish Studies and Director of CMES, 1999–2004; Cornell Fleischer, Kanuni Suleyman Professor of Ottoman and Modern Turkish Studies at the University of Chicago; and Dr. Hakan Karateke, Preceptor in Modern Turkish at Harvard's Department of Near Eastern Languages and Civilizations (NELC). Karateke conceived of the idea of a major bio-bibliographical resource in Ottoman scholarship while he embarked on a teaching and research career in Germany in the late 1990s: first at Bamberg University, where he also obtained his doctorate on completing a dissertation, "Long Live the Sultan! Ottoman Ceremonies in the 19th Century," which was published in Turkish in early 2004; and later at the Free University of Berlin and the Institute for Advanced Study, Berlin. An appointment at NELC in 2002 and a position with CMES brought him to a university that had become one of the strongest bastions of Turkish and Ottoman studies in the West and where his ideas received an enthusiastic response.

The project was launched in the fall of 2003 with funding from the Packard Humanities Institute and an international advisory board consisting of fifteen experts from twelve countries. The two end products will be a published volume and an on-line encyclopedia, both carrying the title of "Historians of the Ottoman Empire." Both of these will works be edited by Kafadar, Fleischer, and Karateke, and each will contain more than one thousand entries on Ottoman historians. A CD-ROM version is also under consideration. The editors in 2004 began identifying and contacting prospective authors from around the world for these entries. The pool of contributors is not confined to the field's luminaries. Junior scholars, particularly from Turkish universities, who frequently write dissertations on lesser-known Ottoman historians, are also being approached. In an effort to maintain quality and ensure consistency, the editors have prepared elaborate and exacting guidelines to be followed in all submissions.

The project is due to be completed in 2007, but, long before then, once a significant threshold is reached, the mass of data it is accumulating will gradually be made available to researchers everywhere through the project's website: www.fas.harvard.edu/~mideast/historians. First drafts of articles, each containing extensive biographical and bibliographic information on a particular historian, are due to appear on this site in early 2005. In 2006, when the editorial committee expects to complete the writing and editing phase, the online database will have a panoply of search functions. In effect, a beta version of the final product will be released on the web. The website is also intended to serve the purposes of publicizing the project to the Ottomanist community around the world and eliciting feedback both on the overall concept and on specific entries.

The use of twenty-first-century technology aside, the project makes no claim to being the first of its kind. The compilation of *tezkires*, or bio-bibliographical dictionaries, on the grand and mighty in various fields has had a venerable pedigree, dating back to the sixteenth century, among Ottoman writers. Bursalis Mehmet Tahir's three-volume encyclopedia *Osmanli Müellifleri*, which was published between 1915 and 1924, is an exemplar of the genre. Even more influential is Franz Babinger's *Die Geschichtsschreiber der Osmanen und ihre Werke*. Notwithstanding its methodological shortcomings and substantive omissions, Babinger's work is still widely consulted, more than seventy-five years after it appeared. The project is picking up where Babinger stopped in 1927 and aspires to be nothing less than the most exhaustive and the most current work of its kind.

The typical entry is to comprise 1,500 to 2,000 words on a single Ottoman author and will contain a brief biography, details about each of the author's historical works, a summation of their contents, an evaluation of their historical significance, and a list of

The directors and some of the staff of the project at CMES.
Left to right: Erdem Çipa, Cemal Kafadar, Hakan Karateke, İklil Erefe, Richard Wittmann, and Nicholas Trepanier.

relevant manuscripts. The latter is far from incidental. For Karateke, in fact, perhaps the greatest single contribution the project stands to make is the provision of comprehensive and accurate lists of manuscripts of the works of these historians. There is to be a wealth of information, even on such matters as the location and availability of the manuscripts. Unpublished manuscripts will not be overlooked. If anything, they are to receive a priority. The level of detail in the database, therefore, is likely to be greater than what is found in most encyclopedia articles.

As with much of the Ottomanist's craft, few aspects of the project are straightforward. Even the definitional criteria of "historians" and "histories" is problematic, and has been made more so by the many developments in historiography, from the *Annales* school onward, over the last century. If only for the sake of manageability, the project has opted for narrower criteria, concentrating for the most part on writers who inhabited the Ottoman realm and whose works consciously included a pronounced "historical" content. The project will not throw into the mix geographers, as did Babinger. And Karateke has long since abandoned his initial idea of a bio-bibliographical reference work for all Ottoman literature.

A good deal of the spadework in the initial phase of the project has been done by graduate students at CMES, including Erdem Çipa, İklil Erefe, Susan Francia, Nicolas Trepanier, Richard Wittmann, and Cihan Yüksel. Together, they have combed through a huge body of secondary literature published since 1927. They also have pored over manuscript catalogues and a variety of published and unpublished works in search of references to manuscripts pertaining to Ottoman history. They have named the project computer "Ertogrul," after the earliest member of the Ottoman dynasty, in the hope that the project might turn out to be as successful, if not as enduring, as the empire itself. What they helped to unearth soon revealed both the vastness of the scholarly terrain and the magnitude of the task ahead. Whereas Babinger's 1927 opus listed 380 historians, some 900 historians surfaced during the first phase of the project alone. States Karateke: "The reference work might turn out to be a little bulkier than we thought."

Iranian Oral History Project

Habib Ladjevardi

The CMES-based Iranian Oral History Project (IOHP) has recorded the recollections of many of the people who played central roles in the political decisions of Iran from the 1920s to the 1970s. It has also garnered the personal accounts of influential individuals who were close witnesses of the political events of the country in those decades. The project has provided a unique source of primary material that will serve as an enduring archive for historians and others who study twentieth century Iran. It also has thrown open an unusual window on the country's turbulent past.

IOHP is the work of Dr. Habib Ladjevardi, a research associate and a former associate director of the Center. A Harvard MBA and Oxford PhD graduate, Ladjevardi left Iran after the revolution following two decades of leadership positions in business and education. The idea behind an oral history, he recalls, came from an encounter in 1980 with Edward L. Keenan, Dean of the Graduate School of Arts and Sciences and soon-to-be Director of CMES. "Ned told me if this were 1917, he'd want to able to record the memoirs of the people who were on the scene before and during the Russian Revolution. I had little idea of what an oral history is. But I realized that the political exodus from Iran offered a golden opportunity." The project was formally launched at the Center in 1981 and attracted support from a large number of donors, including the National Endowment for the Humanities and the Ford Foundation.

With a small group of scholars intimately familiar with Iranian history, and starting with subjects reckoned to have the lowest life expectancy, Ladjevardi proceeded to scout prominent members of the diaspora community. Some twenty-two years later, the project had yielded around 900 hours of audiotape and 18,000 pages of transcripts from 134 narrators. The interviewees, in Ladjevardi's words, covered "the whole gamut—vintage communists, religious zealots, diehard royalists, liberal nationalists, and more." Among the more important figures are Ali Amini, prime minister in the early 1960s; Shapour Bakhtiar, the last premier of the reign of Mohammed Reza Shah Pahlavi; Abolhassan Banisadr, first president of the Islamic Republic; General Hassan Alavi-Kia, deputy director of the State Information and Security Organization (SAVAK); Massoud Rajavi, leader of the resistance organization Mojahedin-e Khalgh; Abolhassan Ebtehaj, governor of the Central Bank and managing director of the Plan Organization; and Sir Denis Wright and Sir Peter Ramsbotham, British ambassadors in the 1960s and 1970s.

Ladjevardi has used a combination of unstructured and structured interviews to probe the experiences of these and other subjects during important junctures in Iran's recent political history. He harbors no illusions about the objectivity of the testimonies. Many of the interviews included self-serving statements; a few were patently disingenuous. Nevertheless, even the prevarications, evasions, contradictions, omissions, allusions, and silences can be revealing. To elicit a greater level of candor, and to allay the suspicions of reluctant participants, he made them aware of other personages whose accounts were being recorded for posterity. He also gave them an option, which one-third of the narrators chose to exercise, of stipulating a window during which their memoirs would be kept under wraps. Harvard's commitment to honor such restrictions through a formal letter of agreement proved instrumental in opening doors to a wider segment of the Iranian political elite.

The interviews, averaging six hours each, have yielded a wealth of insights about Iranian politics and society. As such, they have become an invaluable resource for scholars working on modern Iran. For many years, two libraries—Harvard's Houghton and Oxford's Bodleian—have offered access to all the unrestricted tapes and transcripts. In addition, CMES has published ten volumes of individual memoirs. Almost from the start, however, Ladjevardi eyed developments in technology as a potential for making the entire collection available to a worldwide audience and preserving it for generations to come. In 2004, the project took a major step toward achieving this goal by securing funds for digitizing both the audio and text versions and, with the support of the Harvard Library's database management and delivery services, making it accessible to anyone in the world with an Internet conection. Soon, millions of Iranians will be able for the first time to read and hear the words of the actors of a recent past that for many of them remains elusive.

Planning under the Shah

Ladjevardi is fond of saying that a random selection of any four tapes of interviews recorded by IOHP would provide a good clue behind the fall the Shah. "The Shah," he notes, "pulled all the strings and when he was no longer around there was no-one else to pick them up." The excerpt below, extracted from one interview, offers a glimpse at the effects of the Shah's methods on economic planning and budgeting in the 1970s. The statement, which appears in both the Farsi original and in translation, is by Abdolmajid Majidi, director of the Iranian Plan and Budget Organization during the last six years of the Shah's rule. ☉

[اعلیحضرت] خیلی خوب تصمیمی گرفتند و خیلی منطقی مطالبی را که به عرضشان رسانده می‌شد قبول می کردنیم در بعضی موارد نه، برعکس، خیلی سریع از رویش ردمی شدنیم می‌گفتند ، «نخیر. این است و جز این نیست. » « ماهمه اش یک مقدار در تاریکی و با حدس و پیش بینی کار می کردیم و برنامه ریزی می کردیم و تنظیم‌بودجه می کردیم لذا قبل از این که ما اصلاً مطلع بشویم که‌درآمد نفت دارد بالا می رود، مقدار زیادی تعهدات شده بود. خوب، از قبیل همین که می گویید مسئله خرید کنکورد، مسئله خریدهای‌نظامی که‌تعهدات خیلی‌عمده ای بود... اینها همه یک اطلاعاتی بود و برنامه هایی بود که تصمیماتش گرفته شده بود. [بعداً، به ما ابلاغ می‌شد که باید برای اینها اعتبار بگذارید. حالا این در زمینه نظامی بود. در زمینه غیر نظامی هم همین طور ًبود،‌یم تعهداتی که شده بود روی مثلاًذوب آهن تعهداتی که می شد از نظر پتروشیمی، تصمیماتی که روی توسعه‌صنعت‌گاز و پتروشیمی‌گرفته می‌شد... متأسفانه در جریان گسترش و تصمیم گیریش نبودیم. اینها معمولاً به ما ابلاغ می شدتم موقعی که یا تصمیم قطعی گرفته شده بود یا این که در شرف گرفته شدن بود.

His Majesty was generally a very logical decision-maker. But sometimes he tended to pass over critical issues quickly, exclaiming, "No. My decision is final.". . . We often labored in the dark and with guesswork to develop plans and prepare budgets. Before we knew that oil revenues were going up, major financial commitments had already been made, such as for the purchase of the Concorde airliners and military hardware. These were all decisions that had already been made. [Later on] we would be instructed to include these financial commitments in the budget. This was [the pattern] in the military sector. It worked the same way in the non-military area, like the commitments for the steel mill and for the expansion of petrochemicals. Unfortunately, we were not involved in the decision-making [process]. These [decisions] would normally be passed down to us as orders for implementation.

Iraq Research and Documentation Project

For Kanan Makiya, the rumors of truckloads of government documents seized by Kurds in the uprising that erupted toward the end of the Gulf War of 1991 were too intriguing to ignore. A visiting scholar, and later a research associate at CMES, Makiya had left his ancestral home in Baghdad in 1968 to study architecture in the United States and never returned. He had given up the practice of architecture and had started writing books about his troubled homeland under the pseudonym of Samir al-Khalil—first *Cruelty and Silence*, which became a best-seller after the invasion of Kuwait; and then *The Monument*, a study of the vulgarities of art and power under the regime of Saddam Hussein. A trip to northern Iraq later in 1991 confirmed the stories that huge quantities of classified military and security papers had been pilfered from government buildings and stashed away, many in ammunition boxes in caves. In 1992, his research into these papers resulted in the award-winning televised documentary *The Killing Fields,* which exposed the horrors of the *Anfal* campaign against the Kurds. The research became the inspiration for the launching in 1993 of the Iraq Research and Documentation Project (IRDP) at the Center.

Kanan Makiya

With funding from the Bradley Foundation, the Iraq Foundation, and the National Endowment for Democracy, the project set for itself the task of becoming a major resource for the study of Iraq by collecting and organizing the material that had begun to emerge about the Ba'athist regime. The specific means would be to integrate the material into a computerized, multimedia database system. The information came in a variety of forms and from a variety of sources. There were taped interviews with eyewitnesses and survivors of massacres. There were audio tapes and videotaped records. And there were the suitcases of documents that Makiya, the project director, had brought from his visits to the safe havens in northern Iraq, along with a cache of papers he had obtained from the Kuwaiti government. But all along his eye was on a larger prize: the mountains of documents the Kurds had turned over to the United States for safekeeping.

For several years, the papers remained in the hands of the Department of Defense, which scanned and digitized them. They were pored over by the Defense Intelligence Agency and by Human Rights Watch, but were not in the public domain. However, the Senate Foreign Relations Committee, which was formally in charge of the documents, had promised Makiya that he would receive a copy and, in 1999, 176 CDs were turned over to CMES. IRDP then entered a new and more intensive phase as it assembled a five-member team to design and operate the software to process the documents and to develop a website that would allow others to access its databases and other information. The core of the collection consists of two sets of material: the "North Iraq Dataset," containing 2.4 million documents, mostly ones seized by Kurdish rebels; and a "Kuwait Dataset," consisting of 725,00 documents captured by American forces in Kuwait during the Iraqi retreat in 1991. By the end of 2003, the labor-intensive process of sorting through these documents page by page—annotating, indexing, classifying, evaluating, and summarizing—in order to make them usable to other researchers had covered about one-tenth of the datasets. The project had also translated several hundred of the more important documents.

The papers, many of them handwritten, were all produced by official organs of the Saddam Hussein regime. They include texts of the Revolutionary Command Council and presidential decrees, official orders and correspondence, bureaucratic directives and instructions, investigative reports and guidelines, military and paramilitary rosters. The majority originated from the Ba'ath Party and security, intelligence, and military agencies. For the researchers at the IRDP, a perverse dividend seems to have come from one of the pervasive features of the Iraqi bureaucracy under the Ba'athist regime: its insistence on recording its activities in meticulous detail. The networks of the party, army, security, and intelligence were all required, therefore, to maintain comprehensive records of their operations. The records served multiple purposes, including the assignment of responsibilities for decision making and the provision of evidence of compliance with instructions. In addition, for many zealous officials—from party functionaries to prison torturers—the reports were a means of securing rewards for the fulfillment of duties.

In combination, the paper trail examined by IRDP helps to weave a picture of the inner workings of a regime that, even after its overthrow, is imperfectly understood. The documents provide details of the bureaucratic apparatus of the state and the instruments of monitoring and control. They cast a light on the channels of command and communication. They reveal the reach of the Ba'ath Party and its position at the pinnacle of the power structure. They highlight the web of surveillance by different intelligence agencies and offer clues about the rivalries among them. They show how the regime manipulated the tribal system so it could be used as a tool of social control. They detail the methods used to vet and grade loyalty to the regime. One document outlines "A Plan of Action for the Marshes," which called for poisoning water and burning homes in Iraq's southern marsh areas. Others records the program of relocations that marked the start of the *Anfal*.

CMES saw the potential that the IRDP collection would offer for the study of Iraq what the "Smolensk Papers," also housed at Harvard, had done for scholarship on the early decades of the Soviet Union. For Makiya, the insights that might be gleaned from the data could help to recast the study of the Middle East. "This material," he says, "takes us away from the 'us' versus 'them" kind of writing on history and society. It takes us right down to the inner machinery of a repressive state—to the belly of the beast. It moves us away from all the ideological categories—Zionism, imperialism, etc.—that have stifled a great deal of discourse on the Middle East." Beyond that, he sees the prospect that the research that will come out of such a project will have a major effect on the identity of Iraqis and other Arabs in the long run: "In the future, Iraqis, and Arabs as a whole, are likely to have a humbler sense of who we are. We will have a better sense of our human frailties and we will have a basis for acknowledging what we did to each other." The records, he hopes, will also affect how Iraqi history is written by future Iraqi historians. "All this will help Iraqis move away from the bombast and puffery that for too long been the hallmark of political discourse in the Arab world—and which are the hallmarks of the documents themselves."

The IRDP collection no doubt is but a fragment of the official records of the Ba'athist regime that have been unearthed, and that remain to be unearthed, in the wake of the invasion of Iraq in 2003. However, IRDP has provided the foundations for an archive of primary material that is likely to be useful to those studying Iraqi politics, culture, and society for decades to come.

A Word from "Chemical Ali"

*T*he subject matter in the documents that are the core of the Iraq Research and Documentation Project ranges from the banal to the horrific. There are reports on payment of government salaries and procurement of military clothing; and there are orders for the execution of adversaries and the elimination of villages. The communication below took place a few months after the appointment of Ali Hassan al-Majid, first cousin of Saddam Hussein, as head of all security, military, and civil affairs in northern Iraq. Al-Majid, dubbed "Chemical Ali," has been accused of being the mastermind behind the poison gas attacks that led to the deaths of thousands of Kurds in Halabja and other parts of northern Iraq in 1988. The "King of Spades" in CENTCOM's deck of playing cards, and No. 5 on its Iraqi "Top 55" list, he was captured by Coalition forces in August 2003. The following [IRDP-NIDS-2379420] is a reproduction of the digitized version of an advisory sent to a military command and a translation by IRDP researchers. ☺

One Arab Nation With an Eternal Message
The Ba'ath Arab Socialist Party
The Qutr of Iraq
Northern Organization Bureau Command

Number: 5083 (Secretariat Office)

Date: 22nd August, 1987

Confidential and Personal
To: First Corps Command
Subject: Execution of Criminals

Comradely Salute,

[Re:] your personal and confidential letter [No.] 352
dated 8th July, 1987.

The valiant comrade, Ali Hassan al-Majid, Commander of the Northern Organization Bureau, has commented as follows on your aforementioned letter:

"We do not object to the decapitation of traitors, but it would have been preferable had you first sent them to Security for interrogation. Prior to their execution, [security personnel] might have found significant information that could have been useful."

Kindly review . . . Respectfully,

[Signature]

Tahir Tawfiq
Secretary of Northern Affairs Committee

Copy to:
Command of al-Rashid Military Branch
General Military Intelligence Directorate

Please review the above Command's letter.

Respectfully.

Visiting Scholars and Research Associates

The designations have differed over the years, as has the range of backgrounds and interests, but from the outset the Center for Middle Eastern Studies has attached great importance to the presence of scholars who devote a period of time at the Center exclusively or primarily to research. In its first fifteen years, the Center spent more than $500,000 of its own resources on some 100 appointments of research fellows. The fellows, all of whom worked in residence at the Center and most of whom received grants for one or two years, included some of the most prominent figures in the field—John Batatu, Robert Fernea, Benjamin Halpern, Kepal Karpat, Walter Laqueur, Ragaie El Mallakh, and Şerif Mardin. While the wherewithal to maintain the earlier levels of support has waned, along with the capacity to physically accommodate them in offices at its premises, the enthusiasm on the part of the Center for visiting scholars, as well as the attraction the Center holds for these researchers, is very much intact.

The Center has always been a magnet for a select number of individuals outside Harvard who have a serious interest in Middle Eastern studies and who seek to spend some time away from home. In the main, they have been academics, but occasionally the visitors have come from the worlds of diplomacy, business, journalism, and NGOs. Aside from the ability to avail themselves of the library and many other resources at Harvard that are vital to their research, CMES offers them an opportunity to participate in conferences, seminars, lectures, and other Center activities, and thereby engage in a regular exchange of ideas with faculty, students, and other scholars affiliated with the Center. For the Center, in turn, these visitors, especially ones from the Middle East, enrich its intellectual community in tangible ways, enhancing the quality of its seminars and colloquia, adding new perspectives and dimensions, and imparting an immediacy to discourse on many issues that would otherwise be missing.

In any given year, the Center has a contingent of about twenty visiting scholars. Some are senior faculty spending a year's sabbatical at Harvard; others are at the beginning of their academic careers. Most engage in full-time research; a few combine research with teaching, substituting for regular faculty on leave or supplementing existing course offerings. Some, especially post-doctoral fellows, occasionally intersperse research toward a publication with auditing lecture or seminar courses. The research specialties have covered a broad terrain. Work on the court records of seventeenth century Ottoman Istanbul is to be found alongside an inquiry into current problems of Turkish foreign policy; Iranian currents in medieval hermeneutics alongside problems of strategic policy and planning in Iran today. The majority of the scholars rely on outside sources of funding. That CMES has been unable in recent years to offer either space or funding has not appreciably lessened interest in the program: the Center continues to receive applications from around the world for visiting scholar and post-doctoral fellow appointments.

A distinct class of visiting scholars at CMES consists of a limited number of researchers appointed either through the Center's dedicated endowment funds or through other special funds managed by the University but directed primarily toward the Center. These funds have included the Center's Goelet Fund for Islamic Studies, which has supported Gibb Fellows. The Iranian scholar Abdolkarim Soroush was the Center's latest Gibb Fellow, from 1999 to 2001. The Yarshater Visiting Fellowship in Iranian Studies, a gift from the Persian Heritage Foundation, is aimed at bringing promising younger scholars to the Center. Among recent appointees are Farhad Atai and Mohammad Bazargan. Yet another fund, the CMES Iranian Studies Fund, formerly the Hassan Nemazee Fund, has supported two other Iranian scholars at the Center in recent years: Hossein Modarressi and Ahmad Mahdavi-Damghani.

Research associates are yet another category of scholars at the Center. These associates have had a more permanent presence at CMES and also a more active involvement in Center activities. They include directors of research projects, such as Munir Fasheh of the Arab Education Forum and Habib Ladjevardi of the Iranian Oral History Project. They also include scholars who are engaged in research on some of the most contentious political and social issues today in the Middle East and beyond the Middle East. The interests of these scholars, as well as the roles they have played at the Center and in the general Harvard community, have varied widely, as the following profiles of three current research associates—Jocelyne Cesari, Salmaan Keshavjee, and Sara Roy—suggest.

Jocelyne Cesari

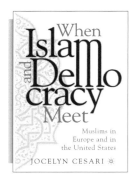

French-born Jocelyne Cesari came to Harvard in 1998 as a Fulbright Scholar after working in Europe for the better part of a decade on a topic that many of the scholars she initially encountered in the United States considered to be of marginal interest: the role of Muslims in the West. She soon became an associate of CMES, where she discovered that the topic was regarded as anything but marginal. Events have subsequently conspired to ensure that it remains center stage.

A political scientist by training, with a doctorate from University of Aix-en-Provence and a background in political sociology and ethnic studies, Cesari has been a steadfast believer in the need for interdisciplinary approaches in any serious effort to understand the interaction between Islam and the West. The relatively brief period she has spent at Harvard, which has been sandwiched between two years of teaching and research at Columbia University, seems to be a study in a determined attempt to cross disciplinary divides. She has chaired the Islam in the West Study Group, which is co-sponsored with CMES, the Center for European Studies (CES), and the Law School's Islamic Legal Studies Program. She has also co-chaired a CMES-CES seminar on Islam in Europe and America after September 11. She has offered courses on subjects such as "Global Islam" in the departments of Anthropology and Government as well as at the Divinity School. In the Fall of 2004 she began an appointment as Visiting Associate Professor of Islamic Studies at the Divinity School, where she teaches a course entitled "Islam in America." She also has been coordinator of the Provost Interfaculty Program on Islam in the West.

Cesari began her research career with an examination of the political emergence of the Muslim minority in France. There, she sought to trace the complex adaptations of religious practice and organization by French Muslims to the pull of a secular state and society. She then extended this inquiry to the wider setting of Europe, and in 1998 founded a network of scholars from six other European countries to design research projects of a comparative nature with hypotheses and data intended to be of use to policymakers who deal with problems of immigration, race, ethnicity, and multiculturalism. The latest phase of her research has expanded the empirical framework to the United States. Among her goals is a systematic assessment of the consequences of 9/11 for Muslim communities in Europe and the United States. Cesari has attempted to disentangle the array of forces that have contributed to definitions and redefinitions of Islamic identities in Western countries. Of particular interest to her are the roles of the transnational networks that have emerged through the spread of diasporic communities. She also has tried to come to grips with the effects of the perception of Islam as a closed system devoid of the possibility of change and of the more recent but still evolving construction of Islam as the dominant enemy of the West.

Cesari's major works include *When Islam and Democracy Meet: Muslims in Europe and in the United States* (New York: Palgrave, forthcoming), *Musulmans et Républicains: les jeunes, l'islam et la France* (Brussels, Editions Complexe, 1998), and (with Bernard Botiveau) *Géopolitique des islams* (Paris: Economica, 1997).

Salmaan Keshavjee

Salmaan Keshavjee's focus is the intersection of health care, social change, and human development in the Middle East and Central Asia. As he makes clear in his essay in Part III, the larger issues at stake in this nexus are simultaneously intellectual and practical. It would be difficult to appreciate what he means by the simultaneity, or what it means for him, without knowing something about his penchant for crossing not only boundaries and disciplines but also institutions and professions.

Keshavjee was born in Nairobi, Kenya, to a family that had descended from the nineteenth century Indian migration to South Africa. In the early 1970s, during the exodus of Asians from East Africa, the family moved to Canada. After a degree from Queen's University, Ontario, he came to Harvard, where he earned an AM in Middle Eastern Studies before heading to the joint doctoral program in Anthropology and Middle Eastern Studies. His dissertation, "Medicines and Transitions: The Political Economy of Health and Social Change in Post–Soviet Badakhshan, Tajikistan," examined a disintegrating health system buffeted by the economic and social dislocations that accompanied the sudden juncture of capitalism, communism, and Islam. Before he had completed the final chapter, he enrolled in the Stanford School of Medicine in 1998. He finished the dissertation during his first year as a medical student; in his second year, he taught a course in Stanford's Department of Cultural and Social Anthropology. He graduated with an MD in 2001, when he returned to Harvard to begin a residency in internal medicine at Brigham and Women's Hospital (BWH), where he is also a research fellow in its Division of Social Medicine and Health Inequalities. He is due to complete his training next year and has accepted an offer to join the Medical School as a faculty member.

At BWH, Keshavjee has spent a good deal of time working on a project to treat drug-resistant tuberculosis in Siberia. He has also received funding from the MacArthur Foundation to examine the role of NGOs in global health policy, again with a focus on TB in Siberia. While the setting is removed from his area of immediate interest, the Middle East and Central Asia, for Keshavjee there are important lessons for the task of devising and managing health care in many other countries with equally limited infrastructure and scarce resource. He has already gone to Syria for advisory work on setting up a similar project in Damascus and is planning to do the same in Turkey. And throughout, the anthropologist in him casts an eye on the second-order social and cultural ramifications of his work beyond Siberia.

Meanwhile, Keshavjee has continued to pursue the line of research that he began with his dissertation. At Harvard Medical, he also has a position as a research fellow in the Department of Social Medicine. The department holds special appeal for him because one of its missions is to address the global health problems of low-income countries. Its faculty include anthropologists, sociologists, historians, ethicists, and clinicians who do teaching and research on the social and cultural aspects of health care.

Keshavjee's goal at CMES is to develop a program for research and teaching on issues related to health and development in the Middle East and other parts of the Muslim world. He has begun a dialogue on such a program through two of his activities at the Center: the CMES Working Group on Health and Social Change in the Middle East and Central Asia, which he founded in 2001 together with Professor Mary-Jo Good and Diana Abouali; and a CMES Seminar on Gender and Health, co-chaired with Abouali and co-sponsored with the Department of Social

Medicine. His aspiration is to position the Center to become a major player, through research and policy work on the region, in the global health initiative that is being planned by Harvard.

Dr. Keshavjee's publications so far have appeared mainly in medical journals. The titles of two of his articles in the *Journal of the American Medical Association* offer a hint of his broader interests in the field: "A Doctor's View of Medicine and Misery" (March 7, 2001) and "Medical Anthropology: Providing an Insight into the Social, Political and Economic Determinants of Health" (October 2, 1996).

Sara Roy

It was fieldwork for a dissertation at Harvard that took Sara Roy in 1985 for the first time to the West Bank and Gaza. For the last twenty years she has continued to conduct research in a land where few other American scholars tread. She has lived in refugee camps, experiencing first-hand the patterns of daily life of people under occupation. She has also produced some of the most important, and also some of the more controversial, works on the effects of the occupation.

Roy's major work, *The Gaza Strip: The Political Economy of De-Development* (Washington, D.C.: Institute for Palestine Studies, 1995), presented an exhaustive examination of changes in Gaza's economy over a period of three decades. It argued that politically motivated Israeli policies, reinforced by the failures of Palestinian leadership, had not only distorted but altogether forestalled development in Gaza. The expropriation of Palestinian land and water, the integration of the territory's economy with Israel's, the diversion of Palestinian resources to meet Israeli needs, and the emasculation of economic and social institutions had left an economy bereft of the capacity for structural transformation, she concluded. A postscript to the second edition, published in 2001, presents the case for the persistence of "de-development." The economy of the West Bank and Gaza in the wake of Oslo agreements, she argues, has been a story of continued stagnation and deterioration.

Roy's current research, funded by a grant from the MacArthur Foundation, looks at recent changes in the Palestinian Islamic movement and attempts to assess the implications of an apparent shift in emphasis by its constituent organizations from political and military action to social work and community development. The findings will appear in *Between Extremism and Civism: Political Islam in Palestine* (forthcoming). Another soon-to-be-published volume, *Scholarship and Politics: The Israeli Occupation, the Palestinians, and The Failure of Peace—The Selected Works of Sara Roy*, will bring together some of her many articles on Palestinian issues and the Israeli-Palestinian conflict. Unsurprisingly, her work, along with her outspoken criticisms of the occupation, has drawn more than a few detractors, not all of whom are mollified by her poignant assertions that as a child of Holocaust survivors she feels morally obligated not to remain silent about the deprivations she has witnessed.

Dr. Roy, whose intellectual background is in political economy and international development, has been a consultant to the United States Agency for International Development on projects related to the West Bank and Gaza. She also has worked on projects for private organizations such as the Center for Economic and Social Rights. At CMES, she co-chairs with Professor Roger Owen the Middle East Forum (formerly the Brown Bag Forum). She also is co-chair of the Joint Seminar on Modern Middle Eastern Politics, which CMES runs with the Weatherhead Center for International Affairs.

Seminars and Conferences

Each year the Center for Middle Eastern Studies sponsors several speaker series covering a wide range of topics. Since 2000, the Center has offered on average sixty public lectures a year. The majority of the presentations are on the contemporary Middle East and most take place within the Center's seminar room in a setting that allows for close interaction between participants—students, faculty, and other Boston-area scholars—and speakers, who include prominent academics, analysts, diplomats, and journalists from around the world. The seminars are organized around themes developed by Center faculty and associates. In recent years, the series have included the following:

Middle East Forum

Co-chairs: CMES Research Associate Sara Roy and Professor of History Roger Owen

The Middle East Forum, formerly the Brown Bag Forum, brings scholars from a variety of fields to discuss their research and topics of current interest. Recent talks have included "Pluralism in the Arab World: A Critique of the *Arab Human*

Sara Roy, CMES Research Associate; Professor Rashid Khalidi, Edward Said Chair in Arab Studies, Columbia University; and Hilary Rantisi, Associate Director of the Middle East Initiative, Kennedy School of Government, at a talk co-sponsored by the Middle East Forum and the Middle East Initiative, on May 5, 2004. Khalidi spoke on "Resurrecting Empire: America and the Western Adventure in the Middle East." Roy is holding a copy of Khalidi's recently published book bearing the same title (with a subtitle of "Western Footprints and America's Perilous Path in the Middle East").

Development Report," by Niloofar Haeri, Professor of Anthropology, Johns Hopkins University; "Hizbollah and Israel: New Rules for the Game," by Daniel Sobelman, correspondent, *Jane's Intelligence Review*; and "The Economic Viability of a Future Palestinian State," by Ephraim Kleiman, visiting professor, Economics Department, MIT, and Patinkin Professor of Economics, Hebrew University of Jerusalem.

Joint Seminar on Modern Middle Eastern Politics

Co-chairs: CMES Research Associates Lenore Martin and Sara Roy and Cabot Professor of Social Ethics Herbert C. Kelman

Pasi Patokallio, former Finnish Ambassador to Israel and Cyprus; and Lenore Martin, CMES Research Associate, at a presentation on March 25, 2004, before the WCFIA/CMES Joint Seminar on Modern Middle Eastern Politics. Patokallio, who was also a WFCIA Fellow, spoke on "The EU and the Palestinian-Israeli Conflict."

The seminar, co-sponsored by CMES and the Weatherhead Center for International Affairs (WCFIA), marks its thirtieth anniversary in 2005. For all but the first two years, its guiding force has been Kelman, a pioneer in international conflict resolution. Consequently, the seminar has focused on the Arab-Israeli conflict and what has been intermittently called the "Middle East peace process." Other topics have included problems of state formation, the role of religion in politics, the dynamics of inter-Arab rivalry, and the Middle Eastern policies of the United States and the United Nations. A sampling of recent presentations: Shibley Telhami, Anwar Sadat Professor for Peace and Development, University of Maryland, "The Arab-Israeli Conflict: Do They Ever Learn?"; Hafez al-Mirazi, Washington bureau chief of Al Jazeera, "Madison Avenue v. the Arab Street: U.S. Public Diplomacy and the Arab Media"; and George Abed, director of the Middle East Department, International Monetary Fund, "Unfulfilled Promise: Why the Middle East and North Africa Region Lags Behind in Growth and Globalization."

Islam in the West

Co-chairs: CMES Research Associate Jocelyne Cesari and Center for European Studies Affiliate Jonathan Laurence

Since its creation in 2001, this seminar has looked at the political and social consequences of 9/11 on Muslim communities in Europe and the United States, the influence of proliferating transnational Muslim networks, the debates over multiculturalism as they affect Muslim newcomers, and problems of political and legal integration of Islam in the West. Speakers have included Talal Asad, Professor of Anthropology, City University of New York, who gave a presentation on "The Formation of Secular Muslims

A panel on "The Concept of Tolerance for Muslims in the West" at the Seminar on Islam in the West, May 4, 2004. The two speakers were Sherman Jackson (center) Professor of Islamic Studies, University of Michigan; and Qamar-ul Huda (right), Professor of Theology, Boston College. Ali Asani (left), Professor of Indo-Muslim Languages and Cultures, Harvard, moderated the panel.

among Muslims in the West," and Tariq Ramadan of Fribourg University, who delivered a talk entitled "To Be a European Muslim: Questions of Pluralism and Tolerance Revisited in a Democratic and Secular Context."

Study Group on Modern Turkey

Co-chairs: CMES Research Associate Lenore Martin and Professor of History Cemal Kafadar

This forum, launched in the fall of 2001, is one of many initiatives that reflect the growing interest of the Center over the last ten years in Turkish studies. Balancing the research projects devoted to the Ottoman period, the study group has focused primarily on modern and contemporary issues. Topics have ranged across a broad spectrum of political, economic, cultural and social concerns affecting Turkey. Talks and speakers have included "Turkish-U.S. Relations," by Morton Abramowitz, former U.S. Ambassador to Turkey; "The Gender Dimension of Poverty in Turkey," by Ayse Ayata, Professor of Political Science, Middle East Technical University, Ankara; and "The AK Party's First Year in Government," by Metin Heper, Professor of Political Science, Bilkent University, Ankara.

Morocco Forum

Chair: Susan Miller

The forum, organized under the auspices of the Moroccan Studies Program, concentrates on political and economic developments in the Maghrib today as well as issues of historical concern in the region. Among recent speakers and presentations, the Center has heard Driss Maghraoui, Center for International and Area Studies, Yale University, on "Fragments of History in

Colonial Morocco: Prostitution in the Quartier Reserve of Casablanca"; Rachid Tlemcani, Institute of Political Science and International Relations, University of Algiers, on "Elections and Political Development in Algeria"; and Gregory White, Department of Government, Smith College, on "Morocco's Parliamentary Elections: First-Hand Observations of a Regime Transition."

Conferences

The Center each year organizes several conferences that bring together large groups of scholars from around the world. Generally open to the Harvard community as well as to scholars at other universities in the wider Boston area, these conferences provide an opportunity for an intensive exchange of ideas and for the development of research projects. The themes have been as varied as those of the faculty, students, and researchers at the Center. Among the many conferences sponsored by the Center in recent years are the following: the "International Congress in Honor of Professor Halil İnalcik: Methods and Sources in Ottoman Studies," organized jointly with the University of Chicago's Center for Middle Eastern Studies; "Challenges Facing the Arab World at the End of the 20th Century"; "Muslim Societies and Islams in the Age of Globalization and Postmodernity"; "Perspectives on Ibn Khaldun and His Times"; "History as Mythical Discourse in Modern Arabic Literature"; and "Symposium on the New Turkish Cinema."

Scholarly Publications

From the outset, the Center for Middle Eastern Studies has made it a priority in the area of research to make known to the academic community at large the work of its faculty, fellows, and research associates. In addition to the numerous books and monographs published through a variety of outside channels by these scholars, the Center itself has been directly involved in producing publications. Like the research interests of Center, these publications have covered a wide geographic, disciplinary, and temporal range.

Before it was five years old, the Center already had two thriving publication series. The first, labeled Harvard Middle Eastern Studies, was introduced in 1958 and comprised books published by Harvard University Press. Some of these works received financial support from the Center. All were the products of scholars associated with the Center and all went through the regular editorial process the University Press uses for all its publications. The first two were David Finnie's *Desert Enterprise: The Middle East Oil Industry in its Local Environment* (1958) and A.J. Meyer's *Middle Eastern Capitalism: Nine Essays* (1958). Subsequent books in the series included major publications such as Ira Lapidus' *Muslim Cities in the Later Middle Ages* (1967), Ben Halpern's *The Idea of the Jewish State* (1969), Richard Bulliet's *The Patricians of Nishapur* (1972), and Nadav Safran's *Egypt in Search of Political Community* (1981).

In 1959, CMES launched a second publication series, Harvard Middle Eastern Monographs, consisting of more specialized works intended for a more limited readership, although some of them sold out within short order. The monographs are edited and published by the Center itself but distributed by Harvard University Press. CMES initially conceived of the series as part of a conscious effort to emphasize research on modern aspects of history, economy, and

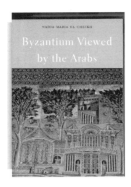

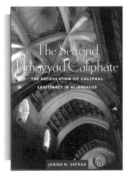

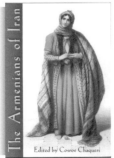

A sample of works published by the Center under its Harvard Middle Eastern Monograph series.

society in the Middle East. Revealingly, about one-third of the early monographs were on economic issues. Among these were *Syria: Development and Monetary Policy* (1959), by Edmund Asfour; *The Industrialization of Iraq* (1961), by Kathleen Langley; *The Economy of Morocco: 1912–1962* (1964), by Charles Stewart; *The Economy of the Israeli Kibbutz* (1966), by Eliyahu Kanovsky; and *High-Level Manpower in Economic Development: The Turkish Case* (1967), by Richard Robinson.

In 1978, after the appearance of the two-volume *City in the Desert*, by Oleg Grabar et. al., the monograph series suspended publication. In the mid-1980s, during its short-lived venture into the policy world, the Center produced five brief works under a new title, Harvard Middle East Papers: Modern Series. The papers included *When Oil and Politics Mix: Saudi Oil Policy, 1973–1985*, by David Golub, and *Khomeini, the Islamic Republic of Iran, and the Arab World*, by Marvin Zonis. In 1990, during his last semester as director of the Center, Roy Mottahedeh relaunched the monograph series and redefined its purpose to include works based on dissertations, translations, and CMES conference papers and proceedings, all conforming to the review and evaluation standards of Harvard University Press. Since the relaunch, twelve volumes have been published. Most of the works have dealt with different aspects of Middle Eastern and Islamic history. However, the series has also included two titles in women's studies—*Women's Autobiographies in Contemporary Iran*, edited by Afsaneh Najmabadi (1990), and *Hermeneutics and Honor: Negotiating Female "Public" Space in Islamic/ate Societies*, edited by Asma Afsaruddin (1999). In addition, there has been a volume on economic institutions, namely *New Perspectives on Property and Land in the Middle East*, edited by Roger Owen (2000). The monograph series is overseen by an editorial board currently chaired by Habib Ladjevardi, CMES Research Associate and Director of Publications.

The Center also publishes a journal, the *Harvard Middle Eastern and Islamic Review*. Introduced in 1994 on the occasion of the fortieth anniversary of CMES, the journal was initially intended as a platform for the presentation of Harvard's scholarly activity on the Middle East. In a statement in the inaugural issues, CMES Director William Graham wrote: "Its primary audience is Harvard's own scholarly community, although our hope is that other scholars will also find in it stimulating matter for debate and research." Although the journal has subsequently expanded its scope to include contributions from outside Harvard, it has retained its objective of presenting a diversity of perspectives on a diversity of topics related to the Middle East and Islam. Reza Alavi, the founding editor, seems to have established the orientation of the journal when he wrote, in an introduction to the second issue: "Taken as a whole, [its contents] are a part of our effort to revive an awareness that the Middle East is not synonymous with conflict, but has been, since time immemorial, as much a vibrant region of art, thought and culture as one of politics and war."

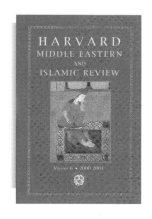

Accordingly, the journal has been decidedly eclectic. An article on the Shi'ite ulema of Najaf and Karbala during the Tanzimat is to be found alongside a survey of computer software in Arabic for the Apple Macintosh; an essay on the tottering Arab-Israeli "peace process" next to a discourse on whether Persian bureaucrats really ran the Mongol empire. Among the specially notable articles that have appeared in the journal are Roy P. Mottahedeh's "Clash of Civilizations: An Islamicist's Critique"; H.E. Chehabi's "The Imam as Dandy: The Case of Musa Sadr"; Cemal Kafadar's "The Question of Ottoman Decline"; and Beatrice Gruendler's "Ibn al-Rūmī's Ethics of Patronage."

The *Review*, a refereed publication, is now run by graduate students at the Center. Its seventh volume was planned to appear in the Fall 2004 and to feature studies on the *muhtasib* in a variety of settings, from Seljuk Anatolia to Mamluk Cairo.

Detail of the new Center for Government and International Studies (CGIS) complex under construction in 2004. CMES is expected to move into its own building in the CGIS complex in 2006.

PART III

The Future

Meeting the challenges of a changing field

Transitions

Steven C. Caton

Steven C. Caton is Professor of Contemporary Arab Studies in the Anthropology Department. He assumed the position of Director of the Center for Middle Eastern Studies on July 1, 2004. His earliest research was in anthropological linguistics and poetics, which resulted in *"Peaks of Yemen I Summon"* (University of California Press, 1990), an ethnography of language, oral poetry, and political culture conducted in a highland tribe of Yemen. A dispute that broke out in the village where he was living during the fieldwork for that book in 1980 drove him to his next interest, the anthropological study of events, which he analyzes in *Yemen Chronicle* (Hill and Wang, forthcoming). He also has written on film, Orientalism, and anthropology in *Lawrence of Arabia* (University of California Press, 1999), and with Harvard students he is working on a comparative study of film industries in the Middle East and beyond. In 2005–2006, he plans to do field research with Yemeni scholars and students on the politics of water scarcity and degradation in the Sana'a Basin, Republic of Yemen.

Since the tragic events of September 11, 2001—not to speak of their aftermath, which is still unfolding and may be with us for some time to come—centers of Middle Eastern studies have become embroiled in political controversy, the likes of which they perhaps have not experienced since their founding after World War II.

For example, some of the charges now leveled against some of its scholars, especially of Islam, are that they have been blind to the threat that certain groups in the area pose to "democracy" and "Western civilization" or that they have not been even-handed in their coverage and critique of regional politics. Whatever one might think of these charges, one has to take seriously the efforts of some people to try to curtail or even cut off research funding to centers of Middle Eastern studies that are not thought to be working on agendas congenial to more conservative outlooks. But the threat to centers such as the one at Harvard goes far beyond the campaign of certain self-appointed watchdog groups. Provisions of the US Patriot Act, along with measures taken by US Immigration, have had and will continue to have a potentially damaging or even intimidating effect on scholarship undertaken in the name of Middle Eastern studies. Their impact can be felt in long delays in, if not outright denials of, visas to the United States for foreign scholars who wish to come to this country to pursue higher education or attend workshops and conferences for the sake of information exchange. The potential surveillance of scholars and their research, pertaining to what are deemed sensitive areas of research on the Middle East, is also always a possibility. And with US policies inflaming public opinion in the region, scholars holding US citizenship have begun to have serious doubts about their safety when traveling to certain parts of the area for purposes of research or scholarly exchange, preferring to turn to venues closer to home or just biding their time until the situation in the region, it is hoped, improves.

Yet, even before September 11, more general and longer-term trends, largely epistemological in nature, had caused many scholars to question what was meant by "Middle Eastern studies" and to wonder whether the concept had not to be reinvented and, hopefully, reinvigorated, if it was not to be abandoned altogether. For one thing, there was the trenchant critique of Orientalism, articulated most influentially by the late Edward Said, the impact of which was to induce scholars to re-examine the terms in which the history and life of the region had been represented and to interrogate the complicity of this knowledge with the project of European colonialism.

But post-colonial theory, which has emerged as a thriving field in the wake of Said's historic intervention, is only one of several exciting critiques of knowledge that have been important in re-conceptualizing the "object of study" in the humanities and social sciences in the last forty years—among them gender, sexuality, and feminist theory, as well as media and cultural studies. Surely the continued intellectual vibrancy of area centers will depend on the extent to which they not only foster research on the Middle East in such long-established disciplines as economics, politics, history, art history, religious studies, linguistics, sociology, and anthropology, but are also able to make room for these more recent fields of inquiry and engage with them constructively. Finally, even the concept of "area studies" has come under critical pressure of late from a number of different quarters. Some question the continued salience of a research paradigm developed during the Cold War and quite deliberately harnessed to its political agendas, when the world has changed so dramatically since then. In particular, globalization and transnational phenomena have made it questionable whether areas can be treated as more or less self-contained entities and, if they cannot, what this might portend for the organization of research in terms of area-specific projects.

These are challenges any center for Middle Eastern studies such as ours must confront if it is not to appear hopelessly naive or out of touch with some of the most important critical currents of our time. They are to be faced, however, not as portents of the demise of our historic enterprise but as opportunities for strengthening and re-conceptualizing the field. Indeed, it is profoundly

"[T]here has never been a greater need for in-depth and informative research on the Middle East of the sort that area centers provide."

ironic that these challenges come at a time in the history of the United States when there has never been a greater need for in-depth and informative research on the Middle East of the sort that area centers provide. If it is doubtful that area research—and particularly on the Middle East—can ever be the same after September 11, 2001, this certainly does not mean that it is any less pertinent. How, indeed, to make it pertinent in many different ways is the overall goal of our planning for the Center's future.

The Priority

The most important way to enhance Middle Eastern studies at Harvard University is to increase the number of full-time faculty who teach and do research on the region, especially on contem-porary politics, economics and business, public media and society, legal studies, modern history and literature, and other vital topics. The priority of the Center in the next five to ten years will be to work with Harvard's central administration and development office to make it possible for the world's greatest and most distin-guished scholars in these areas to teach at Harvard, to collaborate with University departments in program development, and to mentor students at the undergraduate and graduate levels who wish to pursue academic and professional careers related to the Middle East. It is hoped that Harvard will be able to hire out-standing scholars not only from the United States and Europe but also from countries of the Middle East, reflecting not only com-pelling scholarship emerging from this region but differing intel-lectual viewpoints as well. Such scholars will attract more students from the region to Harvard, adding to an already diverse interna-tional student body, and will facilitate study abroad for under-graduates seeking such an experience in the Middle East.

If, for reasons already mentioned having to do with post-9/11 developments, it is difficult for scholars from the Middle East to come to the United States, every avenue should be pursued to make intellectual exchanges happen through teleconferencing, the Internet, and other forms of electronic technology. Of course, we should continue to do everything in our power to bring outstand-ing faculty to Harvard through full-time appointments, in visiting positions, and in face-to-face meetings such as conferences and workshops, but when such faculty are unable to come to the United States or to Harvard we must seek virtual means by which

"If it is doubtful that area research—and particularly on the Middle East—can ever be the same after September 11, 2001, this certainly does not mean that it is any less pertinent."

to learn from, and exchange ideas with, them. All major centers of Middle Eastern studies in the United States today face the crucial questions: what facilities are available, not merely at their own university but also in Cairo, Beirut, and Dubai, for such technologically mediated exchanges? If they are not already in place, what might be done to create them?

Dissemination of information on the Middle East to the general public in the United States has always been a top priority of the Center at Harvard, particularly in response to ongoing events; yet still more could be done in this regard. Of course, the US public is reached not only by powerful media but also in more grassroots ways, through lectures given by faculty and advanced graduate students in classrooms and school auditoria, church halls, and bookstores as well as the facilities at the Center. Given the longer time frame for presentations and more open-ended format for discussion, in contrast to what is usually possible on media programs, these occasions might be more opportune for general education and genuine dialogue, and though they might not reach as broad an audience, their impact may be deeper or more profound in the long run.

Clearly people learn not only in formally didactic settings such as interviews and lectures but also by watching documentary and even fiction films. The Center has, from time to time, collaborated with the Harvard Film Archive in acquiring films by Middle Eastern filmmakers to house in the University's permanent collection, but this endeavor has not been carried out in an extensive or systematic fashion. Feature-length films are as important in this regard as documentaries for purposes of teaching and research. Given that there have been thriving film industries in Egypt and Iran since at least the 1920s, to name only two famous examples, every effort should be made to add to Harvard's collections of such films, along with films from other countries both inside the Middle East and outside it. Such an effort is not without its difficulties. Sometimes the available prints of films are not in the best of condition and require expensive restoration; in other instances, the translations into English are not of the highest quality and would best be served by new subtitles. This work has already been begun by Dr. Iman Hammadi, Joint PhD in CMES '01, but it is expensive and painstaking and requires far more resources than are currently available.

Finally, another potent but perhaps underutilized resource at Harvard for the public viewing of the cultures and histories of the

> "[I]f . . . it is difficult for scholars from the Middle East to come to the United States . . . we must seek virtual means by which to learn from, and exchange ideas with, them."

Middle East is its extensive museum collections, the quality of which is unique among universities in the world. The Sackler, the Fogg, and the Peabody all have sumptuous collections that include not only paintings, sculptures, tile work, and textiles but also photographs and ethnographic objects on or from the Middle East. Impressive exhibitions have been mounted of these collections by faculty affiliated with the Center, and it is essential that curation of such exhibits be expanded in the future. The Peabody Museum of Ethnography and Archaeology has also of late become involved in the study and display of its collections related to the Middle East. As this volume goes to press, an extraordinary collection of Berber material culture, which will be open to the public in 2004–2005, is being put together by Dr. Susan Miller of the Moroccan Studies Program and Lisa Bernasek, PhD student in Anthropology and Middle Eastern Studies.

Another exhibit pertaining to the Middle East, which will run through 2005, is a set of historic ethnological photographs taken of the Marsh Arabs in southern Iraq during the Field Museum Expeditions to the Near East in 1934. The curator is Omar al-Dewachi, an Iraqi doctor and PhD student in the Anthropology Department. Given the extensive collections of material objects and photographs of Middle Eastern provenience in Harvard's Peabody collections, it could be argued that considerably more could be done to bring these images of the Middle East before the museum-going public.

Aside from these efforts, the Center for Middle Eastern Studies will also attempt to meet the challenges posed by a post–September 11 world by sponsoring workshops, conferences, and other forums to advance discussion on a host of scholarly topics that are at the forefront of humanistic and social scientific knowledge. Let us consider some of these in turn.

New Areas of Inquiry

The field of critical inquiry initiated by Said's interventions in the late 1970s, post-colonial theory, has grown in influence and affected a host of disciplines dealing with the Middle East. At the same time, it has grown beyond the terms in which Said had originally cast the debates—an altogether healthy outcome for a developing field. This has partly been the result of conversations with colleagues working on colonial regimes and their systems of

> ☉ "The dichotomies of the 'Orient' versus the 'West' that once dominated the paradigm have given way not only to a more heterogeneous view of each but also to an understanding of a more complex relation between them."

knowledge in other regions of the world, such as South Asia, but it is also because of influences from psychoanalytic theory and post-structuralist thought, which have together enriched our notions of knowledge, power, and fantasy. The dichotomies of the "Orient" versus the "West" that once dominated the paradigm have given way not only to a more heterogeneous view of each but also to an understanding of a more complex relation between them. The notion of the stereotype that underwrote these dichotomies has become more nuanced with the introduction of the idea of ambivalence and the role it plays in their construction. Finally, though it may still be controversial to claim it, colonial power is as often seen to be a result of the complicity of indigenous elites as it is of the extension of power of the European or American metropole. The importance of studying Orientalism goes beyond the critique of knowledge about the Middle East or the understanding of the political function of such knowledge in the relations we have with this region of the world; it is also to understand how Europe has needed "Others" for the creation of its own traditions and philosophies that did not simply emerge autonomously within Europe's imagined borders.

Since at least the 1970s, gender has been at the cutting edge of research in the humanities and social sciences and it continues to be so. Not only has the representation of the "lived experiences" of women in different places and times been an important agenda, the variable constructions of masculinity and their impact on women's lives have now also emerged in relation to it as important topics of investigation. This is not just an empirical matter: it is an interesting question of whether feminist theory can account for these differences where masculinities are concerned. How the bodies of women have been and continue to be sites of political contestation within and between nation-states—and often through violent means—is as compelling a question after the Taliban and the Second Gulf War as it was before. The rise and fall of feminist movements, the extent to which they may have been influenced by their counterparts in Europe and the United States (and yet have concerns that differ from them and cannot be readily addressed in Euro-American terms), and the sometimes problematical relationship that international feminisms have had as a result of these differences: these topics are all of vital concern. Moreover, sexuality—and here we are speaking not only of heterosexuality but also of bi-sexuality, homosexuality, and transgendered sexuality—has emerged as an important topic of

> "How the bodies of women have been and continue to be sites of political contestation within and between nation-states—and often through violent means—is as compelling a question after the Taliban and the Second Gulf War as it was before."

> "[I]t is now as legitimate to study 'the Middle East' in, say, Boston or Hamburg as it is in Cairo or with a bedouin tribe in Arabia."

empirical research and also of theory, though it remains a somewhat vexed question as to whether it is best explored under gender studies or under its own theoretical rubric. Related issues of prostitution and pornography are no less germane. Yet the exploration of these topics, particularly of sexuality and prostitution, is not without its challenges in many regions of the world where such topics are often surrounded by taboos and sometimes actively repressed. Indeed, perhaps this is where we have reached the political limits of inquiry, at least for the time being. Nevertheless, we remain ignorant of them at our peril, not only where the protection of the rights of women, homosexuals, and young persons more generally are concerned, but also for the understanding of the spread of infectious diseases through different sexual practices.

Cultural studies and mass media studies have also emerged in the last three decades as researchers have become increasingly more attuned to the spread and importance of mass media in modern life; and yet their impact has been felt more strongly in research on Europe and the United States than on the Middle East, even though obviously the latter, too, has had its share of powerful newspaper syndicates, television programming, and film industries. Initially interested in the way in which film, radio, and television mediated the culture of dominant groups in society, in addition to the mass or popular culture of subaltern groups seeking alternative forms of expression that match more closely their own experiences, cultural studies has now branched out to include the study of the commodification and consumption of images and sounds coming from the West and circulating elsewhere in the global marketplace or, conversely, the ways in which images and sounds emanating from regions such as the Middle East are commodified and consumed in the West. This is as true of the way in which cigarettes were marketed in nineteenth-century Egypt as it is of North African rai music sold in the United States today. Cultural studies has also become closely allied to film studies and film theory, and the methodology has shifted from a primarily textual (or filmic) approach to research on processes that lead to the production of such texts as well as their reception and the links these may have to larger political, social, and economic movements in the public sphere. Such an approach depends on more than historical archival research. It also requires extensive fieldwork; it is here that younger scholars are breaking new ground in the way film and television are being studied.

The Pull of Transnationalism

The intellectual landscape has changed dramatically since area studies were founded, but obviously the world has changed, too. There is, of course, the collapse of the Soviet Union and the end of the Cold War, which has now been replaced by the war on terrorism and the emergence of "new" areas such as the Balkans and Central Asia, which have had important historic connections with the area called the Middle East. More subtle perhaps is the phenomenon of transnationalism and how it has motivated a reconsideration of what is meant by area studies. By transnationalism we have in mind a host of trends that include the rise of "global cities" (that is, cities such as New York or Dubai in which high-tech firms dominate the service economy and tie its flows to financial and informational circuits around the world); "migrant circuits" (which involve travel by migrant workers to the United States and Europe, often for economic or political reasons, and their frequent return to their homelands in areas such as the Middle East or to far-flung migrant groups of Middle Eastern origin); and "diasporic" groups that have lived in this country or elsewhere for historically longer periods of time and whose members often have complex cultural identities and political allegiances to their home countries in the Middle East. Indeed, transnationalism is one of those research paradigms like post-colonial studies that has emerged with remarkable intellectual force in the last two decades to influence the ways in which we understand media and information flows, global capitalism (particularly as it pertains to migrant labor), and the forging of "hybrid" cultural identities. The possible implications of transnational phenomena for area studies might be posed by the example of New York City and its large and diverse Middle Eastern immigrant population: what does it mean to draw boundaries around an area when this population is larger and more cosmopolitan than many cities located in what is usually referred to as the area of the Middle East? Or, to put it differently, it is now as legitimate to study "the Middle East" in, say, Boston or Hamburg as it is in Cairo or with a bedouin tribe in Arabia. What is interesting is not the mere displacement of a population from one area to another but precisely the connections and tensions that exist between them, and that means bringing areas studies from different regions into conversation with each other, be they Middle East, on the one hand, and North America or Europe or South Asia or Southeast Asia, on the other.

> "It is also within the framework of transnational studies that one of the oldest and most important topics of research and teaching on the Middle East has been reconceptualized, namely religion."

"[I]t is surprising how little is said about the need to redress the conditions that make terrorism and other forms of political violence seem compelling."

It is also within the framework of transnational studies that one of the oldest and most important topics of research and teaching on the Middle East has been reconceptualized, namely religion. Take, for example, Islam. The figures for the numbers of Muslims in the United States vary from as low as four million to as high as eight, depending on the source. The Council on American-Islamic Relations averages the number to around six million people. According to the Pluralism Project of the Harvard Divinity School, this puts the number of Muslims slightly behind Jews in this country, and makes it the third largest religion in the country. Similar trends and statistics could be cited for countries in Europe. One wants to know how well or poorly such groups are faring in their adopted countries, how their religious practices have been received, and how their own religious commitments have developed or changed over time. For example, are they becoming more or less secular? Are they adhering to the religious traditions of their countries of origin or are they developing new ones, the product of their experiences in new circumstances? And do these "diasporic" groups have an influence on their religious counterparts in the Middle East? Given that the study of Islam intersects with that of the tradition of legal thought, the Islamic Legal Studies Program at Harvard has been crucial for probing such questions in the textualist tradition.

Islam is not, of course, the only religion of Middle Eastern origins. Indeed, one of the challenges of Middle Eastern studies is to deepen its understanding of Islam while avoiding the temptation of reducing the area's religions to Islam. How have Judaism, Christianity, Zoroastrianism fared in the face of different national politics, and how have they withstood various transnational pressures? What are their links to their diasporic co-religionists outside the Middle East?

Though the Middle East has not been untouched by globalization, it could be argued that, taken as a whole and relative to other regions of the world such as Latin America or Asia, it was left behind in the period of unprecedented growth and development that took place in the 1980s and 1990s, thereby deepening poverty in a region that already was one of the least affluent in the world but has one of its highest population growth rates. Of course, with poverty come problems in health care, not to mention feelings of hopelessness and despair that impel some to political violence, including terrorism. Indeed, in the talk about the war on terrorism, it is surprising how little is said about the need to redress the conditions that make terrorism and other forms of political violence seem compelling, for whatever reasons, to those suffering from extreme want or debility. In conjunction with the Medical School and with the School of Public Health, the Center has been studying systems of public health in the region, an initiative it hopes to expand in the future with an even greater sense of urgency and commitment.

Exacerbating the problems of poverty is a rapidly diminishing water supply in a region that overall is one of the most arid on earth. Barring the discovery of new water resources, the development of a technology that will make drinking water safe and widely available at an affordable price, or a means to transport water in bulk from regions that have a surplus to ones with a deficit, conflicts over water in the Middle East will only worsen over time. This a problem that the Center for Middle Eastern Studies has concerned itself with in the past and that various initiatives are trying to broaden, for clearly the problem has not lessened or gone away. It has to be tackled in interdisciplinary terms, involving as it does economics, engineering, politics, sociology, anthropology, and public health; and if technological solutions cannot be found or are not sufficient, the question remains of how suffering and political conflict over diminishing water resources can be mitigated. Though it could be argued that the problem of water and the politics of want that it occasions are most severe in the Middle East, it is obviously not the only region in the world that suffers from these problems in this age of global warming. In other words, this is one of those problems on which a number of centers, each focusing on a different region of the world, might fruitfully exchange information and compare responses as well as possible solutions.

> ⊙ "The challenges that the field of Middle Eastern studies faces in the next decades are thus manifold, complex, and even daunting in scale— but they are also reasons for reshaping the field, not for abandoning it."

The Road Ahead

The challenges that the field of Middle Eastern studies faces in the next decades are thus manifold, complex, and even daunting in scale—but they are also reasons for reshaping the field, not for abandoning it, least of all at this historical juncture when the destiny of our nation and the nations and peoples of the Middle East are more fatefully intertwined than ever before. Above all, we

"Mindful of the great work ahead of us, we are nonetheless inspired by the possibilities and opportunities that the future portends."

must do more to bring outstanding scholars who work on the contemporary Middle East to Harvard in full-time, tenure-track appointments. We must also do everything in our power to facilitate the travel of scholars between the Middle East as well as the United States and Europe and to promote the free exchange of ideas and information, in "cyber" space as much as in "real" space. We must strive to protect and promote the academic freedom of speech and inquiry of all scholars, but particularly those working on or in the Middle East, whether in the Middle East itself or in this country. The intellectual challenges a center for Middle Eastern studies such as ours must confront in the next decade also include the following. How can we build on the historic strengths of area studies, such as language learning and disciplinary specialization, while at the same time opening up the field to newly emergent, interdisciplinary formations such as gender and sexuality studies, post-colonial theory, cultural studies, and the study of public media? How can we retain a conceptual toe-hold on trends that are global in scope, such as transnational circuits of migrant labor and the flows of economic transfers and information exchange, while retaining a focus on a particular area such as the Middle East? And, given an increasingly globalizing world, how can we foster interchanges between centers of area research that are confronting similar phenomena of populations, commodities, money, and ideas criss-crossing the borders of different regions of the world?

Mindful of the great work ahead of us, we are nonetheless inspired by the possibilities and opportunities that the future portends.

Extending the scope of that infamously vague term, "Middle Eastern"

A Vision for the Center

William A. Graham

William A. Graham, Murray A. Albertson Professor of Middle Eastern Studies and John Lord O'Brian Professor of Divinity, is Dean of Harvard Divinity School. A member of the Faculty of Arts and Sciences since 1973, he holds a joint appointment in the Department of Near Eastern Languages and Civilizations (NELC) and the Study of Religion. He was Director of the Center for Middle Eastern Studies from 1990 to 1996. His scholarly work has focused on early Islamic religious history and textual traditions and problems in the history of world religion. His major publications include *Beyond the Written Word: Oral Aspects of Scripture in the History of Religion* (Cambridge University Press, 1987) and *Divine Word and Prophetic Word in Early Islam* (Mouton, 1977). He is co-author of *The Heritage of World Civilizations* (6th rev. ed., 2003) and *Three Faiths, One God: The Formative Faith and Practice of Judaism, Christianity, and Islam* (Brill, 2002), and co-editor of *Islamfiche: Readings from Islamic Primary Sources* (IDC, 1982-87).

My particular vision for the Center for Middle Eastern Studies involves both sustaining our current strengths and significantly expanding them.

The first part of this vision is geographically inclusive and expansive. Since the beginning of my six-year tenure in the early 1990s as CMES director, I have been convinced of the intellectual logic, as well as the institutional need, of extending the geographical scope of that infamously vague term, "Middle Eastern," to include more than just the Egypt to Oxus regions, largely because it is necessary to think of Mediterranean North Africa as well as Northwest India, parts of Central Asia, and even the Sudan and Horn of Africa as belonging historically in important ways to the southwest Asian–eastern Mediterranean world, even as they simultaneously have belonged in other important ways to West Africa, South Asia, East Asia, and East Africa, respectively. The reach of Arabic cultural and religious linkages into Africa, and of Turkish and Persian cultural and religious linkages into Central and South Asia, in diverse instances is easily documented, and to understand the "Middle Eastern" Nile to Oxus "heartlands," one cannot do without these linked neighboring regions. This vast "greater Middle East" has been in many ways both a culturally and an economically interconnected area of the world since at least the early Islamic era, and it deserves to receive attention in one place beyond the teaching departments at Harvard—namely in the Center for Middle Eastern Studies. If it does not, the "outlier" regions will be neglected in our curriculum and in our thinking. The recent expansion of the Asia Center at Harvard to include South Asia has not changed the logic of a CMES purview that includes in relevant ways and moments more than the Arabic/Persian/Turkish "heartlands." Thus I would hope that in the future CMES will be attentive to, and concerned with, support of scholarship involving this larger geographical realm; such attention and support will also serve to ally the Center with colleagues and initiatives in Asian and African studies in particular.

Second, I would like to see CMES continue to build on its venerable tradition of insisting that Harvard offer both strong historical, cultural, and religious studies covering the Middle Eastern/Near Eastern world from its beginnings to the present and also strong social scientific studies of the modern and contemporary Middle Eastern world. The Center has never been content to be just another "modern area studies" center in the limited sense of focusing only on contemporary affairs and policy-oriented studies; it has always represented a concept of area studies that sees them as interdisciplinary work on a given world region with both historical depth and contemporary coverage. Our ability to do both here has never been as good as we would like it to be, but we have never been and never should be content with less than excellent coverage on both fronts.

Third, the Center for Middle Eastern Studies that I envision would be one with a stronger faculty cohort within Harvard. We currently lack regular appointments in social science departments outside of Anthropology (e.g., Government, Economics, Sociology). Nor is there significant Middle East expertise in most of the faculties other than the Faculty of Arts and Sciences (FAS) at Harvard. And in FAS we cannot allow a shrinking of our current strengths in history, art history, religious and cultural studies, or in anthropology and the spectrum of subfields covered by the Department of Near Eastern Languages and Civilizations: there must be growth or at least a sustaining of existing strengths here as well. A vibrant Center needs an active cohort of scholars in diverse disciplines from the teaching departments of the University, not only in FAS but other faculties as well.

Fourth, a great desideratum for CMES is the development of the capacity to offer significantly greater financial support for more of the highly qualified graduate students in various fields who want to specialize in one or anther aspect or field of Middle Eastern studies. Greater support for the best students (and more of them) is essential to a really successful Middle Eastern studies center and a successful Middle Eastern studies presence at Harvard. We have a strong Middle East faculty presence here already, and hopes of making that still better in the future. We could probably get almost all the best students who apply to us if we could be more fully competitive with other institutions in the financial aid packages we offer in the different doctoral programs, not to mention the AM in Regional Studies, where we generally give little if any financial aid to applicants.

Fifth, and finally, I hope that a significant part of the future of the Center will be a continuing and even heightened emphasis upon the two-way flow of contact between Harvard and the Middle East region itself. In the first instance, this involves increasing our financial capacity to support our own students and faculty in travel to and residence in various countries of the Middle East. In the second, it involves increasing our financial capacity to bring more students and visiting (as well as permanent) scholars of Middle Eastern nationalities and/or Middle Eastern residence to study and do research at Harvard under CMES auspices. Just as we need to continue to insist that our students spend as much time as possible in the region, we need to continue to bring more students and established scholars to CMES from the Middle East itself. This requires substantial resources that are currently not sufficient. Finding such resources needs to be an important goal, for that is the means of ensuring the existence of the important and irreplaceable opportunities for learning that the two-way flow of scholarly and human contact provides. Furthermore, finding these resources will allow us to develop for our Harvard programs and scholarship a series of serious intellectual alliances and contacts across the area of our concern. Only in this way can we serve adequately the increasingly complex demands of quality scholarship for deep and extensive linguistic expertise, first-hand experience of the region, and thereby serve the larger purpose of increasing both knowledge and understanding of the Middle East inside and outside the academy.

All of these ideas are aimed at strengthening the core programs and mission of CMES and making them more relevant to the changing global realities of a world in which the Middle East very likely will continue to play a major part for a long time to come. To persist in doing this, and to do it better than we have in the past, we need to work constantly and simultaneously on intellectual issues such as those discussed in the first of my five points above, and on issues of infrastructure such as those raised in my last three points. Both kinds of concern are important to a stronger and adequate twenty-first-century Center for Middle Eastern Studies at Harvard University.

One final matter also deserves attention: the lack at Harvard of a Center for Islamic Studies that would stand alongside CMES as a focus for the historical, cultural, and religious study of the

> "Just as we need to continue to insist that our students spend as much time as possible in the region, we need to continue to bring more students and established scholars to CMES from the Middle East itself."

wider Islamic world around the globe. Since this latter world encompasses not only the Muslim Middle East but also the many other parts of the globe where the vast majority of Muslims live, it deserves the scholarly focus of a separate entity. A Center for Islamic Studies would in no way displace CMES, but could relieve it of the need to try to deal with the vast history and extent of Islamic religion and civilization alongside Middle East history, politics, economics, culture, and religion in a more geographically delimited set of contexts. To give CMES full scope for adequate treatment of the region from North Africa to Central Asia both historically and in the present day, another center is needed to attend to the history, civilization, and religion of Islam. Such a division would match also the general division that obtains in the modern academy between Middle Eastern area studies and Islamic studies. With two such centers at Harvard, we would only strengthen our capacity to train the very best students from this country and around the world in these two major fields of scholarship. Such a development would be the culminating success of the last half-century of scholarship at Harvard that CMES largely initiated and long has nurtured here under its auspices or with its material support.

Forging links with colleagues in other fields of History and in other disciplines

History

Cemal Kafadar

In a certain sense, interest in Middle East history goes back to the founding era at Harvard, long before the term "Middle East" had been coined and a History Department established. Increase Mather (1639–1723), who graduated from Harvard College and later served as its president, was one of many seventeenth-century intellectuals in western Christendom to write a chiliastic tract in which the setting of the millennial scenario was, naturally, the area that is now called the Middle East—as analyzed in one of seven dissertations completed under the History and Middle Eastern Studies program in 2004. In the meantime, the nature of academic interest in and approaches to the Middle East have undergone dramatic changes.

Whether it was driven by millennial enthusiasm or by more sober concerns, the proto-history of the study of the "Middle East" was closely associated with biblical studies and Semitic languages. It was the transformation of Harvard from a provincial institution into a modern research university during the nineteenth century that eventually ushered in signs of a serious interest in the study of Middle East history. For the first modern instruction in the field, we have to look to Archibald Coolidge, a diplomatic historian who introduced Harvard students to some of the mysteries of the Ottoman empire. One of his students, Albert Howe Lybyer, produced what may well be the first significant monograph in the United States on the Ottoman state—based on his 1909 dissertation and published in 1913 in the Harvard Historical Studies series—when the empire was still part of the political scene of Europe and Asia. After World War I, in the wake of seismic shifts in the political landscape of the region, both Coolidge and Lybyer were busy writing books and essays on "the question of the Near East."

When William Langer mobilized forces at Harvard to establish a Center for Middle Eastern Studies after World War II, he

Cemal Kafadar is Vehbi Koç Professor of Turkish Studies in the History Department. He was Director of CMES from 1999 to 2004. His study of early Ottoman history, *Between Two Worlds: The Construction of the Ottoman State,* has been translated into Arabic, Greek, and Turkish. Ever in search of hidden troves in archives and libraries, his serendipitous discoveries there have led to works on autobiographical writing and to the editing of a Sufi lady's mid-17th-century dream log. He is also pursuing his interest in the narratives of modernity and tradition through research projects related to Ottoman social and cultural life in the early modern era. He plans to publish a book on one of his central concerns, the politics of "crowds" and rebellions in Istanbul from the late 16th to early 19th centuries. Meanwhile, his essays and lectures on the topic will appear in *Rebels Without a Cause? Janissaries and Other Riffraff of Ottoman Istanbul* (forthcoming). He continues to work on related topics, including the history of coffeehouses, uses of the night, and communities of dissent.

> "[T]he main challenge for the future is not in securing new History appointments but in deepening and broadening our coverage."

already had a scholarly record going back to the 1920s that gave firm recognition to the importance of Middle East history. As Langer notes in his memoirs, Coolidge inspired in him a life-long interest in "the Near Eastern Question" and, hence, from the outset he included the subject in his teaching and publishing. The creation of the Center also owed much to the energies of Richard Frye, whose appointment to an assistant professorship in History and the Committee on Comparative Philology in 1949 signaled the arrival for the first time of a scholar who could do research in Middle Eastern history using Middle Eastern languages. After the establishment of CMES, Middle East history received a big boost, if not a regular home within a department, through the appointment of Sir Hamilton Gibb as University Professor.

In the following decades, the faculty providing instruction on the Middle East mushroomed and, although not all of them were historians, they came to include some of the most prominent scholars who have worked on historical aspects of Middle Eastern societies and cultures. Whichever department they saw as their home, and whatever their own disciplinary preferences, more than a few Harvard professors—among them, George Makdisi at NELC, Oleg Grabar in the History of Art and Architecture, Muhsin Mahdi at NELC, and Abdelhamid Sabra in the History of Science—made immense contributions to the study of Middle East history, not only through their own work but also by inspiring students to undertake original research projects in the field. Eminent figures in Middle East history at leading universities in the United States, and in the region itself, have came out of the ranks of Harvard alumni.

And then there were historians like Robert Lee Wolff, the Byzantinist and Balkanist, or David Landes, the economic historian, who did not necessarily think of themselves as historians of the Middle East, but played considerable roles in that vein, nonetheless. A number of scholars—Stanford Shaw, Ira Lapidus, Richard Bulliett, Dennis Skiotis, Zachary Lockman, and Will Rollman, to name a few—served as junior faculty before they moved to distinguished careers at other institutions.

Still, reports of visiting committees from the 1970s and the early 1980s perceptively and persistently pointed out that the Center, although it flourished in certain respects, needed a solid base in History, both intellectually and institutionally. Partly as a consequence of CMES's success in responding to that challenge since the mid-1980s, the situation is radically different today. Thanks to four senior appointments in less than two decades (Roy Mottahedeh, Roger Owen, Cemal Kafadar, and Afsaneh Najmabadi), the Middle East is now firmly embedded in the History Department, the disciplinary home of historical research and writing at Harvard. All of us have served and continue to serve CMES in different capacities, while the Center has provided and continues to provide a home for a good part of our intellectual and social activities. Most students of Middle East history at Harvard are accepted through the joint degree program, and most of the PhD students at the Center are students of History.

Enhancing, or even maintaining, the current level and scope of relevant work in the discipline at Harvard will be an important concern in the near future, due to pending retirements, when some of our current strengths will come under jeopardy. Still, the main challenge for the future is not in securing new History appointments but in deepening and broadening our coverage. Appointments in Economics, Political Science, or Sociology, for instance, would not only allow meaningful coverage of the contemporary Middle East—an area where Harvard certainly needs more faculty and more courses—but would also be quite a boon to historical studies themselves.

In fact, groundbreaking work in Middle East history has not been limited to members of the History Department. Revealingly, one of the most significant events in the study of Middle East history in the late 1980s and the early 1990s at Harvard—a series of workshops on the political economies of the Ottoman, Safavid, and Mughal empires—was organized by Tosun Aricanli, then an associate professor in the Economics Department. Aricanli was supported by two directors, Roy Mottahedeh and William Graham, both scholars of Islam, when he organized those workshops. CMES has played a pivotal role in making such history projects possible, by providing not only funding and institutional support but also a congenial home.

There is more fertile ground today than there has ever been before for engaging in conversations with historians in other fields and with colleagues in other disciplines. Not only do many of us have overlapping interests and research agendas, but we also share common concerns in some of the methods and approaches that enhance our analytical arsenal, as the examples of gender or post-colonial studies suggest. Such dialogues are facilitated by

> "Such dialogues are facilitated by developments in Middle Eastern studies that would have surprised, perhaps even disappointed, the founders of CMES."

> "Middle East historians have come to think of themselves first and foremost as historians. That simple step has worked wonders."

developments in Middle Eastern studies that would have surprised, perhaps even disappointed, the founders of CMES.

During the last three decades of the twentieth century, students of the Middle East started to reimagine their field with a new critical spirit. Both the conceptualization of "the Middle East" as a region that defines the boundaries of an object of study and the whole notion of "area studies" came under intense scrutiny. Scholars working on various countries and themes that fell under the institutional umbrella of Middle Eastern studies grew dissatisfied with relegation to the status of "area experts" and the intellectual marginalization often implied by their discipline. This was not simply a matter of identity and recognition, but an intellectual quest to refine methods and practices in order to achieve an understanding of the societies and cultures of the region that is deeper than what has been allowed by a heavily philological approach or a narrowly political focus. With this quest has also come an intellectually ambitious search for ways to enrich the broader discourse in the human and social sciences, both empirically and theoretically.

Historians of the region, too, were uncomfortable with a legacy shaped within the Orientalist tradition. Even when touched by the growing influences of the social sciences, they were typically situated on the periphery of their discipline, in the role of providers of "case studies" for different theories, particularly those of the modernization school that reigned supreme for at least two decades after World War II. Since the 1970s—even earlier in the case of pioneers like Roger Owen and Roy Mottahedeh—Middle East historians have come to think of themselves first and foremost as historians. That simple step has worked wonders, thanks also to historians of Europe who started to question the Eurocentric view of world history. Evidently, debates around Orientalism have not only fostered increasing sophistication and self-reflexiveness within the field but also rendered it much more relevant for historians of other areas and for scholars of other disciplines.

In the mid-twenty-first century, all this may look banal, but what used to be the histories of other peoples, or even of peoples without history, started to be woven into "history itself." During this process, Middle East historians, like historians of other areas, have recognized and adopted fresh interpretive strategies that were inspired by social and cultural anthropology, among other sources, as history-writing became more comfortable with interdisciplinarity. For better or for worse, the so-called linguistic turn in history and new forms of textual analysis have had as much influence in Middle East history as in some other fields. Some of the most interesting work in gender history has been conducted by historians of the Middle East. Transnational and transregional history has made such an impact in the field that some of the recent dissertations are hard to classify simply as "Middle East studies."

However, the ongoing search for interdisciplinarity, transnational perspectives, methodological sophistication, and theoretical finesse can be too much of a good thing, especially in a field where the traditional apparatus of scholarship—for example, critical editions of sources and reference materials—remains relatively underdeveloped. The temptation to be at the cutting edge needs constantly to be balanced by fidelity to the standards of what is considered by some to be old-fashioned historiography, based on well-honed philological skills and solid empirical research. It is with that sensibility that Middle East historians at Harvard have developed projects (such as Mottahedeh's "library of the Islamic world" or Kafadar's "registers of the Ottoman *shari'a* courts") to provide serialized editions and translations of sources that, we hope, will in turn facilitate a new generation of social and cultural historical studies here and elsewhere.

In fact, the menu of skills associated with historical scholarship is evolving, and becoming more complicated, under pressure from both intellectual currents and technological changes. Our capabilities for instruction and training need to keep up with all this. Some students question the conventional boundaries between fields and disciplines, such as the one between Byzantine and Arab or Ottoman studies, and take the next step to learn the requisite languages. Some students of European colonial history seek to utilize, in addition to European sources, documents that provide indigenous perspectives from the Middle East. There are those who wish to look at East Asian and Middle Eastern experiences in the age of modernity, using archival materials in both regions, in order to do justice to their transregional research agenda. Issues concerning the configuration of space or visual idioms are so central to the projects of some that they look for training in the history of art and architecture or in the anthropology of visual cultures. There is an increasing number of students who emphasize "minority" languages (Greek, say, or Armenian) in addition to one or more of the "basic foursome" (Arabic, Hebrew, Persian, and

> "Transnational and transregional history has made such an impact in the field that some of the recent dissertations are hard to classify simply as "Middle East studies."

Turkish) because of their interest in subaltern groups or because they wish to move beyond the essentializing tendencies of a field that has traditionally privileged the "Islamic" at the expense of the "Islamicate."

Exciting as these developments may be, they also offer challenges to our resources, both human and financial. The growing emphasis on new combinations of linguistic skills, and the search for familiarity with a variety of regions and their scholarly resources, render additional funding needs all the more acute for CMES, since students can hardly afford to spend a summer without language courses and/or travel and they cannot do this without external support. Language instruction on campus, too, needs to be enhanced and placed on a more secure ground through endowed funds.

The growing use of electronic media not only helps language instruction, of course, but also offers some new possibilities for research that might be facilitated by the Center. The transition from conventional modes of instruction and research, based on card or book catalogues and printed or manuscript materials, to research using the Internet is full of hazards as well as joys, however, especially for students who would like to imagine that "it's all already there on the Internet." Close cooperation with Middle East librarians and technology experts will be needed for faculty and students to navigate the incomplete, and often erratic, contours of the information highway.

Among practical difficulties, restrictions on travel to and from the region, as well as outright censorship, should also be mentioned. Such curtailments, be they based on circumstances or political decisions, not only impede the flow of ideas and scholars, and access to archives and libraries, but also undermine possibilities for much-needed cooperation with institutions and colleagues in the Middle East.

As students of Middle East history develop new research agendas and strategies, new links are forged between CMES and colleagues in other fields of history or in other disciplines, at Harvard and elsewhere. It is not unusual these days to find a CMES History student whose thesis advisors include an anthropologist, or a legal scholar, or a historian who works on another region. This is primarily a matter of intellectual choices, but students also realize that their chances are thereby strengthened in the job market since demand for instruction in world history (with a

> "The growing emphasis on new combinations of linguistic skills, and the search for familiarity with a variety of regions and their scholarly resources, render additional funding needs all the more acute."

focus on a particular region) is rapidly growing, and world history itself is becoming a more rigorous field than it used to be.

Links to other fields and departments are facilitated, of course, by the work of scholars of other areas, especially those who are constructing their own projects in ways that bring them and their students closer to us. Sugata Bose and Robert Travers, for instance, are great assets for Middle Eastern studies because of their own broad conception of the study of South Asian and British colonial history. Sven Beckert's research on cotton and the global economy in the nineteenth century implies that he casts his net much more widely than is usual for an American historian and conducts research on Egypt, among other places, thereby making it possible for an Americanist and an Ottomanist to imagine collaborating on the organization of a conference and an edited volume on the history of globalization. In the same light, the strength of international history at Harvard, as developed by Akira Iriye and Ernest May, and, it is hoped, to be continued after their retirement, hardly needs to be mentioned.

Middle East historians also stand to benefit from, as they already contribute to, the institutionalization of Islamic studies through new appointments at the Divinity School. The examples could easily be multiplied, and it should be admitted that there are precedents for such collaboration across fields and disciplines. Yet it is clear, and we need to come to terms with the fact, that historians of the Middle East now find themselves within new networks and crosscurrents created by an unprecedented surge of interest in transnational and transregional perspectives. This is all the more relevant for a field in which historiographies have been shaped to a large degree by nations (e.g., Arabs or Turks) as timeless units of analysis and national or religious identities as ahistorical fixtures.

Shared concerns, both substantive and methodological, imply that there are abundant opportunities for Middle East historians, faculty and students alike, to imagine or partake in collaborative ventures across the University. Initiatives should be taken toward joint courses, conferences, and projects, with an eye to enriching the intellectual life of the campus and to advancing the field of Middle East history itself. And collaboration should be imagined, obviously, not only across different areas of historical research but also across disciplines and programs. Critical developments in film studies, for instance, seem to offer fresh tools for historians to reconsider questions of historical narrative or issues related to the

"... all the more relevant for a field in which historiographies have been shaped to a large degree by nations (e.g., Arabs or Turks) as timeless units of analysis and national or religious identities as ahistorical fixtures."

> "'[D]oing Middle East history' means 'doing' much more than the Middle East, strictly defined, and 'doing' much more than history, strictly defined."

representation of the Middle East in particular, possibilities already explored by a number of colleagues in anthropological and literary studies. Middle East studies is already fortunate in sharing one of its historians, namely Afsaneh Najmabadi, with the program in Studies of Women, Gender, and Sexuality and CMES can, through workshops and film series, for instance, play an important in role in enhancing the study of Middle East gender history. Environmental history, to give another example, has not yet made significant inroads in Middle East studies, but there are many colleagues on campus who are among the foremost students of the environment, in the Middle East and elsewhere. In that respect, the collaborative venture envisioned by Steve Caton to study "water in the Middle East" could be a dream project since it would bring historians together with students of anthropology, economics, business, public health, and landscape design, toward a deeper understanding of the past and the present of the region.

Ultimately, the work of CMES historians is to improve our understanding of the societies and cultures of the region, past and present. At the same time, those same historians face the challenge of acting upon the growing awareness that "doing Middle East history" means "doing" much more than the Middle East, strictly defined, and "doing" much more than history, strictly defined. It is in its attempt to cope with that challenge, while continuing to generate original and innovative research according to exacting standards of scholarship, that the study of Middle East history at Harvard is poised to remain an intellectually vibrant and enjoyable field.

A discipline that must continue to be a major player in the symphony of approaches that are the raison d'être of CMES

Philology

Wolfhart P. Heinrichs

There was a time when almost anybody who dealt with the Middle East academically in the West was a philologist. The meaning of the term underwent substantial changes from post-medieval to modern times, but the common denominator was the study of texts, with the concomitant activities of producing grammars and dictionaries. For a long time "philology" was restricted to its classical variety (Latin and Greek), and this usage has not completely died out. But due to theological interest in the scriptural language Hebrew (and, to a lesser extent, Aramaic), "oriental philology" had an early start in Europe. One has to keep in mind, though, that well into the nineteenth century, "oriental" referred to all Asiatic regions, or even all non-Western cultural areas, including Africa and native America. This is how the famous "orientalist" societies, founded around the middle of the nineteenth century, and their respective journals understood their mission (*Journal of the America Oriental Society, Journal of the Royal Asiatic Society, Journal Asiatique, Zeitschrift der Deutschen Morgenländischen Gesellschaft, Wiener Zeitschrift für die Kunde des Morgenlandes*). It was only after the Sinologists, Indologists, and Africanists (to name but these) defined their disciplines as independent fields of study that "Oriental Studies" began to refer, by default, to sundry Near Eastern (Middle Eastern) languages and cultures. The notion of "philology" had been generalized in the meantime, beyond "classical" and "oriental" philology, to allow its application to all written documents of all times and places (after much controversy, the "new philologies"—i.e., those dealing with modern languages such as English, German, and French— were admitted into the universitas litterarum). Likewise, around the middle of the nineteenth century, the evolution of comparative and general linguistics posed a new problem for the philologists. Some suggested that linguistics was dealing with the "nature" side of language, while philology addressed the "culture" side of it.

Wolfhart P. Heinrichs is the James Richard Jewett Professor of Arabic in the Department of Near Eastern Languages and Civilizations, where he teaches classical Arabic language and literature. His main research interests are medieval Arabic poetics and Islamic legal theory, with Neo-Aramaic as a sideline. His recent publications in these three fields include "Naqd al-shi'r" [Criticism of Poetry], in *Encyclopaedia of Islam* (new ed., Supplement) (Brill, forthcoming, 2004); "Qawā'id as a Genre of Legal Literature," in Bernard Weiss (ed.), *Studies in Islamic Legal Theory* (Brill, 2002); and "Peculiarities of the Verbal System of Senâya within the Framework of North Eastern Neo-Aramaic (NENA)," in Werner Arnold and Hartmut Bobzin, (eds.), *Festschrift für Otto Jastrow zum 60. Geburtstag* (Harrassowitz, 2002). He received his doctorate at Giessen in 1967 and taught there until 1978, when he came to Harvard, first as Professor of Arabic, and since 1996 in the Jewett Chair.

Others considered language a product of the mind/intellect (Geist) and thus entirely within the purview of philology. Until the advent of modern structuralist, transformational, and other approaches to language, this position carried the day and comparative and general linguistics became part and parcel of philology (cf. Semitic Philology in the Department of Near Eastern Languages and Civilizations [NELC]). The modern paradigms of linguistics, however, which try to find algorithms for the internal workings of languages without paying much attention to their cultural context, have to be considered outside the compass of philology. A widening gap is noticeable here; philologists and linguists dealing with language problems hardly speak the same (meta-)language. Philology as an approach of study, or a paradigm, remains text-bound and develops into a method of interpretation, a hermeneutics. Here one might want to distinguish between "lower" and "higher" philology, the former being a technique of establishing critical texts based on grammatical, lexical, paleographical, and editorial expertise, while the latter, in its most ambitious formulation, is an interpretive approach to a corpus of texts in order to define the character of a literature, a discipline, or even an entire culture. The whole enterprise of philology in this "higher" sense is decidedly historicist.

An Enduring Paradigm

As an area studies center, the Center for Middle Eastern Studies is, of course, not beholden to any one method/approach/paradigm in its attempts to make sense of the Middle East. On the contrary, its raison d'être is the multiplicity of approaches. Philology was, is, and should continue to be a major player in this symphony of methods. One external reason for this is the close collaboration between the Center and the NELC. The latter is strongly philologically oriented. But even in non-philological disciplines philology may have a satellite existence (examples added in parentheses): archeology (epigraphy), fine arts (calligraphy, illustration of texts), anthropology (ethnopoetics), ethnomusicology (indigenous musical theory). It is thus important that the basis for all of this be provided: to wit, competent and intensive language instruction. This is offered by NELC, but in close cooperation with, and support from, CMES. The present situation with regard to the major Middle Eastern/Islamic languages (Arabic, Persian, Turkish,

Hebrew, and Urdu) is quite satisfactory, even though some growth in faculty and student numbers would not come amiss. Some less common languages are also being taught, either regularly or if there is an interest on the part of students (Levantine Arabic, Kurdish, several Turkic languages, Swahili, Turoyo [Neo-Aramaic], and Sindhi).

In view of the fact that CMES also houses a Moroccan Studies Program, it might be a good idea to initiate Berber studies at Harvard. Nationwide the study of Berber has practically died out (after the death of E. Abdelmasih and the retirement of Th. Penchoen). Since the language and culture of the Berber have been becoming more important in recent years (thanks to such developments as the lifting of the ban on writing it and the assertion of nationalist aspirations), this might be a good time to introduce it into the Moroccan Studies Program.

"Philology" is viewed by some, possibly many, experts on the Near/Middle East as a paradigm that has had its day. This holds true even if one separates the Modernists from the Medievalists. With regard to the sources of their data, the Modernists obviously have a number of options other than texts (fieldwork with interviews, audio and video recordings, statistics, and so on), while the Medievalists, if they do not make "dumb" cultural artifacts speak (as in art and architecture), are pretty much restricted to texts. But even here the wealth of new viewpoints and theories, developed in Western historical, legal, literary, anthropological, linguistic discourses and applied to the interpretation of premodern texts, has made "philology" look superannuated and dusty to certain eyes. Is it?

As far as "lower" philology is concerned, there is no doubt that it will be around for many years to come. The sheer amount of texts that exist only in manuscript and have not yet been made accessible in critical editions is staggering, even if we count only known manuscripts. (It is, however, common knowledge among the experts that many private libraries, especially in Iran and the subcontinent, have been jealously guarded—presumably against government intrusion—and kept inaccessible to scholars. Sensational manuscript discoveries are still possible.) Given the low-budget, low-frequency publication activity of the Center (as well as of NELC), one should consider a publication series of critical editions and translations. Another activity in the lower-philology category is the compilation of manuscript catalogues. It is a shame that Houghton's collection of Arabic manuscripts has not

"The fundamental question is: how do we study a differnt culture, how should cross-cultural epistemology work?"

yet been catalogued (apart from rather defective typewritten lists and a number of entries on HOLLIS). The collection is not as rich as some others (e.g., Princeton), but it does have some remarkable specimens, also from the point of view of illumination. I will soon embark on compiling a catalogue of the collection.

Turning now to "higher" philology, it should be said that some of the non-philological approaches alluded to above have indeed contributed to our deeper understanding of certain texts. For example, the "histoire des mentalités" approach and speech-act theory have produced highly illuminating studies in the field of classical Arabic literature. Other applications of recent theories have been far less successful and have not met with general approval. The underlying problem is this: modern theories tend to be abstracted from (or inspired by) Western sets of data, the assumption, nonetheless, being that they are of general validity. The more formal and less rich in content they are, the more likely is their applicability. The deeper imprinted they are with Western notions and data, the greater the danger of distorting the non-Western phenomenon to which they are applied. But this is a matter of degrees. The fundamental question is: how do we study a different culture, how should cross-cultural epistemology work? Edward Said, in his critical and polemical characterization of Western "Orientalism," has addressed the—in part wilful—distortions that the "Orient" undergoes in the Western imagination (of course, "Orientalism" is a much broader term than academic "Oriental" studies), but he has left the philosophical or hermeneutical problem of cross-cultural study pretty much alone. It is easy to show that the application, to a non-Western culture, of even vague and general Western notions such as "law" or "literature" (let alone specific theories) is liable to prevent a correct understanding of the phenomena they are used to designate. At this point a definition of "culture" would be in place, but this Pandora's box will be kept shut. Let's just say that "Islamic culture" is one member of this class. It is at this point also that philology, of the "higher" kind, will have a contribution to make. We owe to the Assyriologist Benno Landsberger the coinage of a beautiful, long German term, the *Eigenbegrifflichkeit* of a culture, perhaps best rendered by an English calque such as "auto-notionality." This means that the various worlds within a culture—that is, the natural, legal, political, spiritual, literary, and linguistic worlds (to name but these)—are structured by individual terminologies, taxonomies, hierarchies of disciplines, and similar word-webs,

> "[T]he application, to a non-Western culture, of even vague and general Western notions such as 'law' or 'literature' (let alone specific theories) is liable to prevent a correct understanding of the phenomena they are used to designate."

which are likely to be unique in cross-cultural comparison. How philology can elucidate a system of notions that is uniquely "other" cannot be set out here (constant semantic feedback would be one of the features of this process). But philology has had successes in this enterprise. It is hoped that it will continue to fertilize the content-defined disciplines that are grouped together at the Center for Middle Eastern Studies, and thus lead to a truer and more coherent understanding of Islamic culture and its present-day manifestations.

☉ "[P]hilology can elucidate a system of notions that is uniquely 'other.'"

Seeking ways to stimulate work in a vital but relatively neglected field

Economics

Roger Owen

E. Roger Owen is A.J. Meyer Professor of History. He was director of CMES from 1996 to 1999 and since 1995 he has directed the Center's Contemporary Arab Studies Program. The leading authority on Middle Eastern economic history in the nineteenth and twentieth centuries, for the last ten years he has been Harvard's principal figure in the teaching of the region's modern economic history. His publications include *Cotton and the Egyptian Economy, 1820–1914: A Study in Trade and Development* (Oxford University Press, 1969), *The Middle East in the World Economy, 1800–1914* (Methuen, 1981), *A History of Middle East Economies in the Twentieth Century* (with Şevket Pamuk, Harvard University Press, 1998), and *State, Power and Politics in the Making of the Modern Middle East* (2nd ed., Routledge, 2000). His most recent work, a biography, is *Lord Cromer: Victorian Imperialist, Edwardian Proconsul* (Oxford University Press, 2004). Before coming to Harvard, he was at Oxford, where he directed St. Antony's College Middle East Centre.

For half its life, CMES's main connection with the study of the Middle Eastern economies and their history was the role played by A.J. Meyer, who was its Associate Director from 1957 until his untimely death in 1983. Apart from his own work as both an oil and a development economist, A.J. attracted a number of academic economists to work with him, as well as using the AM in Middle Eastern Studies to attract a considerable number of talented students, many of whom went on to have distinguished university and business careers. Some, such as Yusif Sayigh and Edmund Asfour, had their research published under the auspices of the Center or in its Middle East Monograph series, which began in 1959.

A.J. also played a significant role in establishing relations with Middle Eastern governments and with the international oil companies working in the region, most notably through the assistance he provided by taking a high-level team to Saudi Arabia to assist with the preparation of the country's first five-year plan (1970–75). With A.J.'s death, the direction of the Center's economic activities passed successively to Professor Tosun Aricanli and then, from 1993 onward, to me, following my appointment as the first A. J. Meyer Professor of Middle East History.

Relations with Harvard's Economic Department have always remained something of a problem. Neither A.J. himself, nor Roger Owen, were/are members of the department. Although CMES has had a series of good working relationships with leading Harvard economists—most notably its previous Chair, Jeffrey Williamson—it was for only a short period of time under Tosun Aricanli that a joint PhD program in Economics and Middle East could be properly sustained.

Mention should also be made of important relations established by Tom Mullins, Associate Director from 1993 to 2002, with the Business School and the Islamic Legal Studies Program to produce an important study of Islamic banking, *Islamic Law and*

Finance (published in 1998), and with Professor Peter Rogers (Department of Engineering and Applied Sciences) to write a proposal for the better management of the Middle East's water (*Water in the Arab World: Perspectives and Prognoses*, 1994). Tom can also be regarded as the father of the Harvard Islamic Finance and Information Program, begun in 1995.

Given A.J.'s own interests, as well as what might be called the "spirit" of the times, it was inevitable that the intellectual agenda should be dominated by development studies. This agenda flourished in the 1960s and 1970s but was seemingly overtaken by the triumph of the neo-classical approach in the 1980s. It was revived in the 1990s by a renewed interest, in Washington and elsewhere, in problems concerning economic transition in the former Soviet Union and, more generally, in the forces that either encourage or inhibit long-term growth. From an area studies point of view, the notions of development and transition have the great advantage of combining economics and economic history in a single frame of reference in which political and social factors have also to play a leading role. The downside is that it also permits a great deal of what is little more than agenda-driven speculation concerning the reasons for the alleged economic backwardness of either the "Arab" or the "Muslim" economies, something that has become particularly troublesome since September 11, 2001.

The Last Decade

Given my own interest, I have concentrated most of my teaching since 1993 either on survey courses in nineteenth- and twentieth-century economic history of the region or on graduate seminars dealing with problems in writing the region's economic and social history. Although attracting some economics concentrators, the audience in these courses has mainly been graduate students with a general interest in the region but very little knowledge of economics itself. My own PhD students have followed very much the same line—for example, Said Saffari's PhD thesis study of banking in Iran, "On the Rollercoaster of Development" (1997); Jon Alterman's "Egypt and American Foreign Assistance: 1952–1956" (1997); Relli Shechter's work on the history of the Egyptian cigarette (1999); Misako Ikeda's study of "Sociopolitical Debates in Late Parliamentary Egypt: 1944–1952" (1998); and Amy Johnson's biography of the public life of one of Egypt's leading social activists, Ahmad Hussein (1999). Other students have gone on to do work on the pre-modern Middle East with a significant economic component under the supervision of my colleagues Roy Mottehedeh and Cemal Kafadar.

As far as my own research is concerned, I used my first years at Harvard to co-author (with Şevket Pamuk of Bogacizi University) the textbook *A History of the Middle East Economies in the Twentieth Century* (1998). My second large Harvard project, a biography of the first Lord Cromer (just published in the UK), though largely historical, also contains important chapters on Cromer's work as a member of the Public Debt Commission in Egypt, 1877–80; as Finance Member of the Viceroy's Council in India, 1880–83; and, finally, as the man in overall charge of the economic management of Egypt, 1883–1907. I now plan to use some of the ideas originating in this work as the basis for both a course on the Middle East in the first era of modern globalization, 1870–1920, and a book of essays on the same subject.

The study of the economic history of the Middle East has also benefited greatly from a number of local associates and visitors. Of great importance in the first category is Dr. Sara Roy with her work on the contemporary economic situation in the Palestinian West Bank and Gaza. In the second category, the French Middle Eastern demographer, Philippe Fargues, gave a course in the late 1990s that then became the basis of his *Générations Arabes: l'alchemie du nombre* (2000). Two other visitors, Amy Singer and Martin Bunton, assisted me in organizing two very successful workshops on the modern history of the concept of landed property in the Middle East, papers from which were then edited by me as *New Perspectives on Property and Land in the Middle East* (2000). I should also mention the course in Middle Eastern economics given by Dr. Julia Devlin of the World Bank during my sabbatical term, Fall 1999, and the useful teaching assistance I received from John Sfakianakis who came to Harvard to work with me on his London University PhD thesis, "Businessmen, Families and Oligarchs: The Political Economy of Crony Capitalism in Egypt" (2003).

The Future

I see two important new directions that the study of Middle East economics/economic history at CMES can take in the years to come. One concerns the history of business enterprises in the region. This has begun with the research planned by CMES student Mazen Jaideh on the family firm, for which he has created a committee consisting of myself, Sven Beckert (History), and members of the Harvard Business School, including the newly arrived Geoffrey Jones, the author of *The History of the British Bank of the Middle East* (1986). It has been continued recently by a small group consisting of myself, Robert Vitalis (University of Pennsylvania), Ellis Goldberg (University of Washington), and AbelAziz EzzeArab (Amerian University in Cairo). We organized a conference on Egyptian business history in Cairo in May 2004, which is to be followed by a series of workshops designed both to encourage interest in the field and to provide training for graduate students interested in research in this area. Among many other things, this initiative seems a good way to begin to try to bridge the great gap that has opened up between universities in the West and the major Arab states since the 1970s. To the same end I organized a workshop in Lebanese economic and social history in association with colleagues from two Lebanese universities in March 2004.

Second, it is important to use Harvard's expertise to make a contribution to the economic history/economic future of Iraq. I have already participated in the writing of a report on the future management of the Iraqi oil industry for the British government's Department of International Development. A second initiative will be to organize an international seminar that uses Hanna Batatu's great work on *The Old Social Classes and the Revolutionary Movements in Iraq*, which is based on his Harvard thesis of 1959, as the foundation for attempting to map out the main features of contemporary Iraqi economic and social structure. If we are able to secure the presence of some economists from the universities of Baghdad and elsewhere, so much the better. To this end it may be better to run such an initiative in association with the London Center for Middle Eastern Studies.

Initiatives of this type have a number of aims: they raise the Center's profile inside and outside the University, they allow CMES to create partnerships with colleagues in other parts of Harvard, they build bridges toward our colleagues in Middle Eastern universities, and they help to create an interest in an important and expanding field that has many ramifications for work in the United States, Europe, and the Middle East itself.

Harvard is not delivering on its potential for leadership in this field.

Eva Bellin is Associate Professor of Political Science at Hunter College/City University of New York. A specialist in the politics of the Middle East and North Africa, she was formerly Associate Professor in the Government Department at Harvard, where she taught courses on comparative politics of the Middle East and a broad range of related subjects, including the politics of Islamic resurgence and the struggle for Palestine-Israel. Her recent interests center on questions of authoritarian persistence, democratization, state-society relations, the political economy of development, and, most recently, the politics of cultural change. Her publications include *Stalled Democracy: Capital, Labor, and the Paradox of State-Sponsored Development* (Cornell University Press, 2002). She is currently working on a second book that explores the role of the supreme/constitutional court in arbitrating the religious identity of the state in Israel, Egypt, and Pakistan.

Politics

Eva Bellin

These are crucial times for the study of Middle East politics in the United States. Recent events have spelled massive demand for expert analysis of the dynamics of the region. Broad constituencies of students, government officials, and private sector actors are clamoring for guidance about topics as diverse as the ambitions of political Islam, the prospects for democratic contagion in the region, and the potential for institutional reform. Beyond the press of current affairs, the discipline is undergoing a seismic shift that stems from a generational change in the academy. Over the past five years, the first generation of Middle East politics professors, trained primarily during the post-war boom of the 1950s and 1960s, have nearly all retired and there is a crying need for new leadership to shape the profession, define the debate, and, most importantly, train the next generation of analysts, professors, and writers in this field.

As an intellectual powerhouse, Harvard is exquisitely well positioned to play the leading role in meeting both these challenges. Nationally, Harvard is one of the few institutions that command the multiple resources necessary to deliver comprehensive expertise on the region as well as to train the experts of tomorrow. The Government Department is the top-ranked political science department in the nation and as such attracts the very best and brightest students from around the world. The University boasts an unparalleled library; rich course offerings in Middle East history, languages, literature, and law; an active Middle East center, and access to extensive private and public funding, notably FLAS (Foreign Language and Areas Studies) grants. In short, Harvard boasts all the collateral resources necessary to train experts in Middle East politics. Across the United States, only Princeton rivals Harvard in its historic prominence in this field and in its capacity to pull this package of resources together.

Sadly, however, Harvard is not delivering on its potential for leadership in this field. And although the Center for Middle Eastern Studies is not responsible for Harvard's failure, it must marshal all its resources, political and persuasive, to press the University to recapture its leadership role and deliver on its institutional promise.

What Is Wrong?

The primary weakness in the study of Middle East politics at Harvard stems from the lack of academic appointments in this sub-field and, most importantly, the failure to make a senior appointment in Middle East politics. Ever since Nadav Safran retired from the Government Department nearly fifteen years ago, the department has gone without a tenured professor in this area. Instead, the department has preferred to hire a string of junior and visiting professors (myself included) to meet the consistent (and growing) student demand for courses on the region. Although I believe we stringers did a credible job serving the University, the truth is that junior and visiting faculty possess neither the security, stature, nor long-term time horizons that are necessary to launch Harvard into a leadership position in this discipline.

To play this leadership role, the University must have a faculty member who can afford to sacrifice precious research time to organize conferences and consortia, who has the stature to serve on committees of national prominence in the discipline, who has the clout to sign off on recommendations with impact, and who has the institutional foundation to define research agendas and directions. Ultimately, much of this capacity can stem only from commanding a tenured post at the University. Leadership requires investment in institution building—a venture that is priceless to the community but enormously costly to the individual. Focusing on this would spell death to the career of an untenured faculty member. Given the University's reliance on untenured faculty over the years, such institution building has gone lacking and Harvard's role in the discipline has dwindled.

Harvard's declining stature in the field would be alarming were it not for the fact that other universities are in similarly bad shape. To my knowledge, only one of the top ten research universities in the United States today has a senior professor in Middle East politics with an active research agenda. Prospective graduate

> "Leadership requires investment in institution building—a venture that is priceless to the community but enormously costly to the individual. Focusing on this would spell death to the career of an untenured faculty member. "

students looking for a university with the package of goods necessary for effective graduate training in the discipline (that combination of senior faculty, top-ranked department, library, and funding, as well as collateral courses in language, history, and culture) typically come up empty handed. Sometimes they end up at Harvard by default. Others leave the subdiscipline for better honed paths to academic success. The result is persistent anemia in this subfield.

To some degree the reluctance to appoint senior professors in Middle East politics is a consequence of a trend in the discipline of political science that increasingly disfavors regional specialization and prefers less historically and culturally grounded approaches to the study of politics. In this sense political science is going the way of economics and sociology, which no longer embrace regionally bound approaches to their subjects. Gone are the courses I so loved during my own undergraduate days on the economic experience of Africa or sociological developments in China. Social scientists have ceded this expertise to colleagues in business schools and law schools who often lack the grounding in the analytic tools that a PhD in the social sciences confers. The result is a great loss in national expertise on critical subjects.

> "[T]he Center ought to support workshops and conferences that are theoretically driven by major questions in the discipline."

This is the most pressing shortfall of Middle East politics at Harvard. Without senior leadership no progress on the institution-building front is likely. But there is also the problem of insufficient hiring at the junior level. May I point out that most other regions of the world (e.g., Latin America, Western Europe, Asia, and the former Soviet Union) are typically covered by a team of both a junior and a senior faculty member in the Government Department at Harvard. This ensures consistent coverage of the field in the face of periodic leaves and disciplinary specialization (comparative versus international relations). But team coverage has not been the norm for the Middle East, and this has meant spotty and inconsistent course offerings on the region despite consistently large student demand for them.

What Is to be Done?

What initiatives might the Center for Middle Eastern Studies pursue to enhance the study of Middle East politics at Harvard? In tandem with persuading the University to make a senior and junior hire in this subfield, the Center might consider three other initiatives.

First, the Center ought to support workshops and conferences that are theoretically driven by major questions in the discipline. Currently the Center boasts a host of speaker series and workshops that are focused on policy and current affairs. While these are often analytically rich, they should be complemented by colloquia that seize on the driving questions in comparative politics and international relations and that might capture the interest (and collaboration) of other centers and departments. A workshop on the dynamics of authoritarianism, the political impact of globalization, or the construction of national interest might draw insight from the experience of the region and provide important cross-fertilization with specialists from other regions of the world.

Second, the Center should pursue more cross-school collaboration at Harvard and aim for the creation of joint professional degrees. The University of Pennsylvania has started an innovative joint MBA/MA program between the Wharton School of Business (Lauder Institute) and the Middle East Center. CMES should follow this lead and propose joint MA degrees with the Business School, the Law School, and the Kennedy School of Government. There is a huge demand for experts in law, business, and public affairs who have familiarity with the politics, history, and languages of the region. By offering a joint MA program with these schools, the Center would answer a pressing national need.

Third, the Center should prioritize some specific funding to support undergraduate research. Almost every other regional center at Harvard funds some summer undergraduate thesis research. Some centers fund summer language training as well. There is strong student interest in such training and research. Supporting this even on a limited basis would fuel the pipeline of future specialists and bring CMES in line with other regional centers at Harvard.

Overall, there is a complaint abroad that the field of Middle East politics is anemic. The major research universities complain that there is no one of stature to appoint to senior positions in this subfield, but they are complicit in the field's lack of distinction. By failing to seize a leadership role and commit to the field's development, they are caught in a vicious circle that spells morass for the study of Middle East politics. Harvard must step out of this circle to promote vibrant research and expertise on the region. To foster this outcome CMES must lead the way.

"The major research universities complain that there is no one of stature to appoint to senior positions in this subfield, but they are complicit in the field's lack of distinction."

Capturing the centrality of the legal realm in the making of Muslim states and societies

Frank E. Vogel is Custodian of the Two Holy Mosques Adjunct Professor of Islamic Legal Studies and founding Director of the Islamic Legal Studies Program at Harvard Law School. His research and teaching concern the comparative study of Islamic law and legal institutions with an emphasis on the contemporary period. His recent course offerings have included an introduction to Islamic law and legal systems, both historical and modern, and a comparative inquiry into contemporary Islamic legal thought. His major publications include *Islamic Law and Legal System: Studies of Saudi Arabia* (Brill, 2000). He also is co-author of *Islamic Law and Finance: Religion, Risk, and Return* (Kluwer, 1998), and has contributed a 200-page entry on "The Contract Law of Islam and of the Arab Middle East" to the *International Encyclopaedia of Comparative Law* (Max Planck).

Islamic Law and Civilization

Frank E. Vogel

As I look to the future of the Center for Middle Eastern Studies, I do have a favored vision. It obviously arises from my interests in Islamic law, but I don't think my stance is too parochial when I consider how many of my colleagues at Harvard University, and in universities nearby, share many of the same interests. The proposal I put forward can also claim some urgency, from a world historical perspective, as demonstrated by transpiring events and by demands now being pressed on Middle Eastern studies by our students as well as by many outside our field.

I hope that explaining this particular vision will serve well enough as an indication of how I would like to see Middle Eastern studies at Harvard develop in general. Themes in that respect involve greater interdisciplinary and inter-faculty coordination, open recognition of Islam and Muslim civilization as the organizing principle for much of our work, emphasis on late medieval Islamic civilization worldwide, and enhanced capacity in modern Muslim history and politics and in Islamic societies outside the Middle East.

My proposal, my favored vision, projects as a major focus for the future the writing—for the first time ever from a critical perspective or objective stance—of a history of law in Islamic civilization after 1000 CE. I noted that the need for this is reflected in recent events and in recent demands on our field. No doubt these events and demands relate most explicitly to contemporary Islamic legal and religious doctrine. But it is my premise—hopefully obvious to all who enter into the subject more than a media moment, or who consider Islam not only as a matter of faith—that inquiry into Islamic doctrine cannot be divorced from the context, including the history, of the Muslims who today espouse it. Of the fourteen centuries of Islamic history, the more pertinent from this particular perspective are the more recent centuries, and for these we possess sufficient materials for writing a contextual history.

I know, as a student of law, that one cannot understand *fiqh* as law without awareness of the legal systems, including particularly systems of religious-legal and legal authority and jurisdiction, for which and in the context of which that *fiqh* was being produced. From a purely contemporary perspective, every word in debates today about Islamic law or related powerful ideas can be understood only in terms of the series of worldly systems, structures, relationships, events, and transformations from and through which such words have reached their users today. Attempts to weigh the significance of modern positions on Islamic law and related doctrines lead at once into such historical inquiries.

Neglects of History

For various reasons—perhaps the paucity of people trained in the necessary fields, past scholarly doubts as to the practicability of Islamic law or of its pertinence to Muslims' behavior, or an expectation that secularization would soon deprive Islamic law of any contemporary legal status—the role of Islamic law in historical societies and states has attracted little sustained attention from historians, even those in Muslim countries. Paradoxically, the same scholars often take for granted the immense significance, symbolically at least, of Islamic law for Muslim societies. Recent research has demonstrated the vital need to replace these two stances with a more meaningful account of how Islamic law shaped past societies and was shaped by them—how, by whom, by what institutions, through what channels, through what conflicts and compromises, did past Muslim societies reconcile themselves with Islamic law? Clearly, for societies as law-preoccupied as recent Islamic states appear to have been, such an account is a prerequisite to understanding them.

> "[I]nquiry into Islamic doctrine cannot be divorced from the context, including the history, of the Muslims who today espouse it."

Law also played a central role in the transformations of Islamic states into today's modern Muslim nation-states, and we have precious few accounts that capture how law—complexly Islamic, customary, dynastic, ideological, positivist and Westernizing—played that role.

If this much can be accepted, a further reason this vision of the future compels me is the fact that Harvard seems uniquely suited to pursue it. First, we have at CMES, the Faculty of Arts and Sciences (FAS), and nearby institutions an extraordinary group of faculty not only capable of but also interested in aspects of such a

"[H]ow, by whom, by what institutions, through what channels, through what conflicts and compromises, did past Muslim societies reconcile themselves with Islamic law?"

project. Through Professor Kafadar and his Ottoman court records project, Harvard enjoys unique access to the extraordinary historiographic advances springing from work being done worldwide on *qadi* records and other legal documents. Many of the discoveries coming to light from these researches reflect on, and are reflected upon by, law. Professor Kafadar has hosted, sometimes with the support of the Harvard Law School Islamic Legal Studies Program, a series of important related conferences. Professor Mottahedeh (History) and Professor Heinrichs (Near Eastern Languages and Civilizations, NELC) have both published on Islamic law and count it a major interest. Various departments besides History and NELC have other eminent faculty with strongly related interests, including Religion, Anthropology, and (intermittently) Government. We are strong in Islamic thought and history generally and in the most important languages. And surrounding Harvard are many faculty with immediate involvement in Islamic law, such as Engin Akarli, A. Richard Norton, Sohail Hashmi, Kevin Reinhart, Shahla Haeri, and others.

Second, among many other supporting strengths at Harvard, its libraries possess the best collection on Islamic law and modern Muslim laws after the Library of Congress. Third, Harvard Law School has an endowed chair in Islamic law. Fourth and last, the Law School has an endowed research program dedicated entirely to Islamic law, fully staffed, including, as Associate Director, Peri Bearman, and, as Research Associate, Aron Zysow. This program has at any time several scholars of Islamic law in residence. Besides the two courses on Islamic law that I teach annually at the Law School, the program has often sponsored courses in law by visitors at NELC. It organizes workshops and conferences and funds scholarships and research projects. It provides a link to the world of legal scholarship. It devotes endowed funds to building Harvard's collections in Islamic and modern Muslim law, including maintaining a full-time bibliographer (Lesley Wilkins) and other staff, and creating a dedicated reference collection in Islamic law.

A Productive Future

As to matters that I would to like to see us at CMES do differently, the first concern—again with specific relation to my preferred vision but also more generally—is to put the study of modern history, economics, and politics on a sound footing to cover as much of the Muslim world as is practicable. I would like to see greater strengths in late medieval and modern Central or South Asia or Iran as a means to compare and enrich Ottoman studies. But, most basically, I would like to see CMES find more techniques to surmount a problem pervasive at Harvard: the problem that coordinated work—particularly when it bridges different disciplines and departments, not to mention different faculties and schools, as work on Islamic civilization so demonstrably does—proves difficult to accomplish despite all good intentions. One way to achieve it, it seems to me, may be to identify certain broadly shared areas of interest among faculty and students—such as the one I suggest here—and then lend these areas special institutional emphasis and support.

As I hope is obvious from my statement, for me the opportunities and strengths of CMES far outweigh its challenges and weaknesses, which can be surmounted. In the great Harvard tradition, I expect for CMES a productive future confined not by institutional drawbacks or limitations but only by the natural human limits of creativity and energy of its assembled faculty and students.

> "[M]y preferred vision . . . is to put the study of modern history, economics, and politics on a sound footing to cover as much of the Muslim world as is practicable."

The growing intellectual domain of gender and sexuality in Middle Eastern research and pedagogy

Women's Studies

Afsaneh Najmabadi

Afsaneh Najmabadi holds a joint appointment as Professor of History and of Women's Studies. She also chairs the Committee on Degrees in Studies of Women, Gender, and Sexuality. She is author of *Women with Mustaches and Men without Beards: Gender and Sexual Anxieties of Iranian Modernity* (University of California Press, forthcoming), a study of cultural transformations in nineteenth-century Iran centered on reconfigurations of gender and sexuality. She is working on two new projects, "Sisters of a Kind: Women's Sexuality and Sociality in Qajar Iran," and "Genealogies of Iranian Feminism." Her previous publications include *The Story of Daughters of Quchan: Gender and National Memory in Iranian History* (Syracuse University Press, 1998). Iranian-born Najmabadi came to the United States in the mid-1960s, and after obtaining BA and MA degrees in physics from Radcliffe and Harvard, she took up social studies, along with an engagement in social activism, before completing a PhD in sociology at the University of Manchester (UK).

Women's studies is a relatively new field in academia. Initially spurred by the search for alternative ways of knowing on the part of activists of women's movement in the late 1960s, it soon developed into a vibrant sphere of interdisciplinary research and teaching. It played a critical role in the emergence of related fields, such as studies of gender and sexuality, and has intersected in intellectually productive ways with other academic endeavors. At Harvard, the concentration in Studies of Women, Gender, and Sexuality has elaborated this intellectual interaction in the following terms: "Cultural and historical differences in femininities and masculinities, transnational sexualities, women writers, gender and media studies, lesbian/gay/bisexual studies, transnational feminisms, gender and environmental movements, philosophies of embodiment, queer theory, women's history, transgender studies, gender and religion, the political economy of gender, feminist theory, race/class/gender politics, technology and gender, gender and science, and masculinity studies are just a few of the areas of study that fall within this concentration's purview."

This is a very tall order. The emergence of studies of women/gender/sexuality within area studies has been highly uneven. Within Middle Eastern studies, the discipline that emerged early as a privileged field for such work was anthropology. The placing of women in the home and within the family seemed to make a discipline dominated by studies of kinship the natural place to turn to for students and researchers who were interested in gender issues. History has attracted some interest in this area, and the heightened centrality of women's and gender issues in politics and visions of social movements in the Middle East in recent decades has produced gender-attentive research in sociology and political science as well.

Multidisciplinary Potentials

Unlike the field of women's studies more generally, studies of women, gender, and sexuality within area studies seem to have remained structured largely by existing disciplinary delineations rather than by movement in a more multidisciplinary, if not interdisciplinary, direction. It is here that CMES could begin to play a major role in changing the shape of the field. Middle Eastern studies in general has had a tendency to ignore many critical developments in academia. At one conference, a leading historian expressed this sentiment in terms that echo beyond his own proclivity: "This theory, too, shall pass." We are fortunate at Harvard to have a number of scholars whose primary field of research and teaching is focused on issues of gender and sexuality. They are located in many schools and departments. Bringing this critical mass of scholars and the students' growing interest in these fields into sustained conversations, conferences, and publications could begin to have an impact on the larger academic world.

The field of studies of gender and sexuality is also a prominent intellectual domain in which a growing number of scholars are learning to reach across the major religious traditions of the Middle East, in particular Judaism and Islam. Exciting work on these topics by scholars of Jewish and Islamic traditions and cultures has brought to our attention not only the historical cross-fertilization of the two but also its potential. The strength of scholarship in these fields at the University, in particular with the new appointments at Harvard Divinity School, makes it possible to imagine Harvard as a scholarly institution that would encourage this type of interculturally productive scholarship.

Building across area studies programs at Harvard, in particular the growing field of South Asian studies, offers another direction in which Middle Eastern gender and sexuality studies could benefit from the rich scholarship in these other areas and contribute to the formation of comparative inquiry.

The University has numerous other resources with which CMES could pursue and build this field and become nationally prominent in setting its intellectual agenda. The Radcliffe Institute for Advanced Study has a focused commitment to research on issues of gender and culture, and it supports Exploratory and Advanced Seminars that could provide an ideal setting for such pursuits. In May 2003, Professor Kathryn Babayan (University of

> ⊙ "[T]he heightened centrality of women's and gender issues in politics and visions of social movements in the Middle East in recent decades has produced gender-attentive research in sociology and political science."

Michigan, Ann Arbor) and I organized a Radcliffe Advanced Seminar, "Crossing Paths of Middle Eastern and Sexuality Studies: Challenges of Theory, History, and Comparative Methods." This brought together scholars from numerous national and international institutions for an exciting three-day exchange on this topic, the results of which will be published as an anthology.

This year CMES itself, as part of the 50th anniversary events for the Center, organized a day-long workshop on "Challenges in Sexuality Studies in and of the Middle East." The event was co-sponsored by the Harvard Committee on Degrees in Studies of Women, Gender, and Sexuality and was organized by Professors Steve Caton, Susan Kahn, and myself. Six papers were presented by young scholars in the field. The papers were pre-circulated and discussants were invited from close disciplines that are focused on areas outside the Middle East. The workshop attracted a diverse group of students and faculty at Harvard, and its success has produced enormous enthusiasm for similar undertakings in future years.

What Harvard Can Do

Clearly, the interdiscliplinary field of studies of gender and sexuality is an intellectually thriving field, and CMES could become a focal point for engaging researchers and students in this area. Much of this scholarship is being carried out by a younger generation of scholars and students who are now trained in modes of interdisciplinarity to which few earlier scholars have been exposed. To bring the teaching and scholarly contributions of this younger generation to Harvard, post-doctoral fellowships (with or without a teaching component) centered on this theme could lead to a sustained interest in our Center. Lectures, seminars, and workshops around these contributions could be regularly organized and the results published.

Other University-wide programs include the Harvard Islamic Studies Program at the Law School and the Human Rights Committee, both of which have strong gender components. In addition to numerous faculty at Harvard, many more scholars and students of this field are to be found within the array of educational institutions in the Greater Boston area. Again, CMES could take the initiative in bringing this community together. Here the

⊙ **"Clearly, the interdisciplinary field of studies of gender and sexuality is an intellectually thriving field, and CMES could become a focal point for engaging researchers and students in this area."**

Graduate Consortium in Women's Studies, of which Harvard is a member, could provide us with a model.

Much of the current public, and sometimes even the scholarly, interest in the United States centered on Muslim and Middle Eastern women may have been sparked by contemporary political events. The kind of interest that this orientation engenders may force us to occasionally and despairingly ask, as Lila Abu-Lughod has done, "Do Muslim Women Really Need Saving?" (*American Anthropologist*, v. 104, no. 3 [Sept. 2002], pp. 783–90.) Yet we cannot remain aloof from these cultural, political, and scholarly productions and contestations. To paraphrase the famous challenge of the Guerrilla Girls poster addressed to the New York Metropolitan Museum ("Do women have to be naked to get into the Met. Museum?"), Muslim and Middle Eastern women, it seems, have to be burqa'd or veiled to attract the attention of the West. CMES can position its resources and talents to bring a richer range of ideas and images about Middle Eastern women to public attention. The CMES Outreach Center has taken initiative in this direction in the past, and could perhaps more systematically and pointedly provide an informed public voice in these debates in the future.

In recent years, cinematic productions have proved to be yet another rich field for representations of women, gender, and sexuality. In conjunction with other University and area resources— such as the Department of Visual and Environmental Studies, the Harvard Film Archives, and the Boston Museum of Fine Arts—the Center could further explore this stimulating connection of film studies, Middle Eastern studies, and gender and sexuality studies. In March 2004, CMES cosponsored, along with the Committee on Degrees in Studies of Women, Gender, and Sexuality and the Harvard Film Archives, a conversation with the Tunisian filmmaker Moufida Tlalti, who was visiting Harvard to receive an award and attend the screening of her films. Encouraging this kind of event could provide us with another direction for moving CMES across disciplines and campus initiatives.

As this brief overview has demonstrated, the potential for CMES to move to the forefront of research and pedagogy on studies of women, gender, and sexuality is vast. As we plan beyond the first fifty years of the Center, this is clearly a field that could establish a challenging and unique profile for CMES that would attract the best scholars and students in the field to Harvard.

> "Muslim and Middle Eastern women, it seems, have to be burqa'd or veiled to attract the attention of the West."

The most essential tool in creating cultural literacy in Middle Eastern studies

William Granara is Gordon Gray Professor of the Practice of Arabic. He is director of the Arabic language program at the Department of Near Eastern Languages and Civilizations and teaches all levels of classical and modern Arabic. He specializes in the history and culture of Muslim Sicily and has written on cross-cultural encounters between Islam and Christendom throughout the Middle Ages, as well as on the poetry of Ibn Hamdis, Sicily's most celebrated Arab poet. In addition, he lectures on contemporary Arabic literature and has published a number of critical articles on modern Arabic fiction. He has also published several translations of Arabic novels and short stories. He studied Arabic at Georgetown University and the American University in Cairo and received his PhD in Arabic and Islamic Studies at the University of Pennsylvania. He is the former executive director of the Center for Arabic Study at the American University in Cairo and former director of the Arabic Field School of the US Department of State in Tunis, Tunisia.

Modern Arabic Language and Literature

William E. Granara

The establishment of the Center for Middle Eastern Studies at Harvard University in the 1950s created a new academic space and an expanded role for the teaching of Modern Standard Arabic, colloquial Arabic, and modern Arabic literature and culture.

In response to the emerging strategic, geopolitical, linguistic, religious, and cultural importance of the Arab world in the post–world war period, the newly established area studies centers began to take a new interest and active role in the teaching of Arabic. This interest resulted in three major shifts in language studies: (1) the expansion of Arabic beyond its classical, philological foundation; (2) a stronger emphasis on proficiency-based teaching and learning; and (3) a more meaningful integration of area studies content into the language curriculum.

Modern Arabic as a Medium of Instruction and Research

Harvard University, like its counterparts in other research-centered universities, had a long history of teaching Arabic that was rooted in a centuries-old tradition of biblical and oriental studies. Semitic philology was the premier discipline, and Arabic as the language of the Quran and classical Islamic studies, not to mention the language of the huge corpus of the classical literary production (*al-turath*), was the object of scholarly inquiry. The emphasis on Modern Standard Arabic and its role in the formation of area studies and Middle Eastern studies centers was underscored by the need to know and understand the history, politics, and national literatures of the newly emerging independent Arab states. As the official language of government, of the media (newspapers, journals, and TV broadcasts), of academia and scholarly research, and of the many strands of creative literature, poetry, essays, short stories, and novels, Modern Standard Arabic (MSA) has become the most essential tool in creating a cultural literacy for students pursuing both graduate and undergraduate degrees in Middle Eastern studies.

In response, Harvard's Center took a leading role in this new direction. The Center broke new academic ground within the University by encouraging students to study one or more of the Arabic dialects, the native language of everyday life, films, TV, and other media of popular culture. Over the years, Harvard has offered, on occasion, courses in Moroccan, Egyptian, and Levantine Arabic, giving our students the means to interact on a daily basis with native speakers of Arabic and to undertake new venues of research in the host countries. Alongside the classical track of Arabic offered by the Department of Near Eastern Languages and Civilizations (NELC), the track in modern Arabic was built on a four-year sequence, beginning with the teaching of phonology and script and culminating in more highly concentrated courses designed to help students read a wide variety of modern texts. Harvard's emphasis on research requiring the use of primary sources has had a heavy impact on the ways that modern Arabic has been and continues to be taught.

> "The Center broke new academic ground within the University by encouraging students to study one or more of the Arabic dialects, the native language of everyday life, films, TV, and other media of popular culture."

Toward a Proficiency-Based Classroom

In the 1970s, the proficiency movement forced its way into the teaching of foreign languages throughout American universities. Its proponents advocated an expansive and realistic approach for classroom instruction, one that took into account what students needed to do in the language and how best to reach those goals. The more traditional and prevalent grammar/translation approach no longer monopolized the language class; audio-visual materials were introduced, and the development of listening and reading comprehension, creative writing, and speaking skills were stressed along with grammar and translation.

CMES was instrumental in recruiting faculty and raising funds for state-of-the-art equipment, teacher training, curriculum development, proficiency evaluation, and intensive summer grants, all of which helped raise the level of teaching and learning both in and outside the classroom. Gradually, intermediate and advanced MSA began to be taught in the Arabic curriculum, and the

⟲ "The advanced Arabic
language class is the
forum in which the
historian, anthropologist,
art historian, linguist, and
student of comparative
religion and comparative
literature come
together."

classroom evolved from a teacher-centered to a student-centered one. The proficiency movement introduced a task-oriented pedagogy that helped students to perform more efficiently in the class. It emphasized real-life skills, such as skimming and scanning texts, engaging in debates, giving oral briefings, and writing summaries and response papers to texts. Harvard's modern Arabic language program continues to encourage students to take an active role and a higher degree of responsibility in language acquisition—to engage and interact in the language, not merely to be passive recipients.

Through the encouragement and support of CMES for Arabic language training, there has been a staggering increase in the number of students who pursue intensive summer and full-year language study throughout the Arab world. In the past ten years, Harvard students have participated in programs in Tangiers, Fez, Tunis, Cairo, Nablus, Jerusalem, Amman, Beirut, Damascus, and Sana'a.

Area Studies and Content-Based Curriculum

The close working relationship between CMES and the modern Arabic language program has allowed for a more meaningful integration between language-based courses and area studies content. In recent years, advanced Arabic courses have incorporated a wide variety of historical, archival, biographical, geographical, and literary texts representing periods as early as the reformist movements of the nineteenth century and issues as contemporary as those concerning Islam and politics. Three such "custom-designed" advanced Arabic courses include Readings in the Arabic Renaissance (*al-Nahda*), Maghribi Historical and Literary Texts, and Issues and Polemics in Contemporary Islam. In addition to helping students to develop advanced reading and research skills, these courses provide an opportunity to discuss and debate the content of readings as well as write critical essays. The reinforcement of grammatical structures, the mastery of stylistic devices, and the mastering of a wider range of registers of both technical and idiomatic language within the political, social, religious, artistic, cultural, and literary contexts form the basis of a modern philosophy of teaching Arabic.

The advanced Arabic language class is the forum in which the historian, anthropologist, art historian, linguist, and student of comparative religion and comparative literature come together and interact through a multidisciplinary, multi-discursive environment. The end product, the ultimate goal, is a wonderful combination of a full working proficiency in Arabic and a high level of Arabic "cultural literacy" that is the hallmark of the modern Arabic language program at Harvard.

Recent years have also seen a strengthening of contacts between Harvard and universities throughout the Arab world. In addition to student exchanges, there has been an increasing number of faculty exchanges, visiting scholars and researchers, conferences and lectures. Under the auspices of CMES and NELC, and with support by the Shawwaf Visiting Professorship, distinguished faculty continue to offer courses in Arabic language, literature, and culture. Abdelfettah Kilittio and Abdelsalaam Chedadi (Morocco), Gaber Asfour and Hoda Loutfi (Egypt), Ridwan El-Sayed and Mahir Jarrar (Lebanon), and Samar Attar and Abdelrazaq Moaz (Syria) have given courses ranging from Islamic legal texts to contemporary Arabic literary criticism. In addition to this rich roster of scholars, eminent novelists and poets have lectured at Harvard. Among them are Radwa Ashour (Egypt); Bensalim Himmish (Morocco); and Elias Khoury, Hasan Daoud, and Hanan Shayk (Lebanon).

A Look Toward the Future

Arabic at Harvard has grown steadily, particularly in the past ten years, as a reflection of the increasing importance of the Arab world in international relations and the global economy. The emergence of Islam as a world religion and a voice for political expression; the growing awareness of Arab culture and its interactions with other cultures through literature, film, music, and the arts—all these developments have intimately affected Arabic language teaching. In 1993, Arabic classes at Harvard witnessed a significant increase, from 70 to 100 students. In the academic year 2002–03 the number reached an all-time high of 175 students. Of particular interest in these statistics are two elements. First is the increase of undergraduates, most significantly freshmen, in Arabic. Second is the composition of classes, traditionally made up of concentrators in Near Eastern Languages and Civilizations and Middle East area studies, which now has widened to include students from other disciplines and schools. Hence, Comparative

> "Planning for the next ten years will continue to take into account the latest ideas on the pedagogy of second-language acquisition [and] the new directions, issues, and events that continue to shape and define modern Arab culture and society."

Literature, Anthropology, Art History, and Government, the Law School, the School of Education, the Kennedy School of Government, and the Divinity School have all figured in the growing numbers. The increase in students and the increase in faculty specializing in Middle Eastern and Islamic studies have been met with a corresponding expansion in the ranks of Arabic language faculty. Through generous donations from Khalid Alturki and Gordon Gray, two preceptorships in Arabic have recently been endowed.

Planning for the next ten years will continue to take into account the latest ideas on the pedagogy of second-language acquisition, the new directions, issues, and events that continue to shape and define modern Arab culture and society, and, above all, the multifaceted, multidisciplinary approach of our students in the pursuit of their studies. With a solidly based elementary and intermediate Modern Standard Arabic language program now in place, Arabic at Harvard will concentrate its efforts in expanding its offerings in advanced courses that cross disciplines.

We hope to embark upon a long-term project to design a custom-made curriculum that will draw on a wide range of historical, cultural, and literary texts to meet students' needs and interests. In addition, the Arabic language program, until now limited to literary Arabic, will strive to make available on a regular basis courses on regional dialects—Moroccan, Egyptian, and Gulf Arabic, for example. This will undoubtedly enable our students to develop the communicative skills, both cognitive and productive, needed to interact with native speakers of Arabic in more meaningful ways. We will emphasize in-country training, especially for undergraduates, by encouraging and assisting students to spend a semester or year at an Arab university. We have begun to work closely with Harvard's Office for Overseas Programs to help us with planning and advising. Our ultimate goal is to provide our students with the proper linguistic tools to achieve full working proficiency, and thereby enable them to position themselves for employment opportunities in and beyond academia.

The new and exciting uses of modern technology in the foreign language classroom in recent years will also play a major role in how we explore new ways to teach and learn Arabic in the future. The accessibility through the Internet of various printed and recorded media, dictionaries, charts, maps, current events, and directions of all kinds, as well as on-line aids and electronic journals, will allow us to think more creatively about how to develop and execute a new kind of syllabus for language classes that emphasizes all the basic language skills: listening, speaking, reading, and writing. From the elementary to the most advanced levels, locating and manipulating both language and content information quickly and accurately will constitute a daily classroom activity and will evolve into an essential research tool. Our objective will be to enable our students to assume greater responsibility for their own Arabic language learning and to acquire the basic training and confidence to use it well beyond the classroom walls.

> "Our ultimate goal is to provide our students with the proper linguistic tools to achieve full working proficiency."

Why the discipline needs the Middle East—and vice versa

Engseng Ho is Associate Professor of Anthropology and of Social Studies, and Academy Scholar at the Harvard Academy for International and Area Studies. He serves on the standing committees on Middle Eastern, South Asian, and Social Studies. He is interested in how issues of mobility challenge received theories of society and state. He pursues this interest through the study of diasporas and empires across the Indian Ocean, employing historical and ethnographic material from Yemen/Arabia, India, and the Malay archipelago. Recent publications include "Empire through Diasporic Eyes: A View from the Other Boat," in *Comparative Studies in Society and History* (2004), and "Names Beyond Nations: The Making of Local Cosmopolitans," in *Études rurales* (2002). His book, *The Graves of Tarim: Genealogy and Mobility across the Indian Ocean*, will be published by the University of California Press in 2005.

Anthropology

Engseng Ho

Cultures or Connections? Entanglements

When asked what anthropology is about, many anthropologists today will say something along the lines of: the study of cultural diversity through long-term ethnographic fieldwork of particular cultures in concrete places. As pioneered by Bronislaw Malinowski, ethnographic fieldwork is intensively local description of a culture derived from direct observation *in situ*. As in science experiments, participant observation is the secure basis of knowledge. In the mode of ethnography, anthropology was pioneered by a Pole stuck in Melanesia as a prisoner of war during the First World War: a side show of a side show of a side show. Anthropologist and native were both bystanders in a gigantic conflict among nations mobilized to manufacture death as an output of industrial production. Not being able to do very much about human folly on such a large scale, Malinowski directed his considerable powers of observation at life around him. He described a whole world unto itself far from Europe, a fascinating world he learned about not from books but direct participation. Following Malinowski, residence of a year or two in a field site has been a hallowed rite of passage in the making of anthropologists, and indeed a major source of disciplinary mystique as well as gossip. Such a method of gathering data in turn produced studies of cultures and communities that were characteristically presentist, aural, local, and internally cohesive but separated from others.

Although there were dissenters throughout, a consensus arose to repudiate the local and internalist aspects of the collective enterprise in the past dozen years. The word "globalization" seemed to sum up all that was wrong with the canon of venerable monographs on islands, tribes, and villages. Instead of isolation, transnationalism became the watchword, and anthropologists turned to the study of diasporas, migration, colonialism, borders, flows, hybridity, scientific networks, technology. Transnationalism meant that foreign relations were no longer the business only of states, but of people from all walks of life as well. In the 1990s, a sudden and remarkable consensus developed that the world had fundamentally changed: why exactly, it was not clear, but it had something to do with the Internet, the fall of the Berlin Wall, the rise of the stock market, the triumph of capitalism, the speeding up of space and time, the crush of migrants to the West, even the end of nation-states. All this seemed new, and few wanted to be caught napping. September 11, 2001, added to the feeling of newness a novel dark twist and a desperate urgency. There is today a palpable sense that one is seeing history in the making, and, paradoxically, this has intensified anthropology's long-standing focus on the present: to be a participant observer no longer of one foreign culture, but in the tortured plurality of international history. Still determined to celebrate separate but equal cultures, the international analogue to a liberal conception of the plural domestic state, anthropologists are now confronted with a series of events drawing together numerous entities variously spoken of as religions, civilizations, cultures, states, and worldviews in violent and knotty relations with one other. Within these international entanglements, the celebration of difference becomes fraught, as difference provides the basis for invidious targeting as well. The shine has come off the new, and as familiar specters reappear, newness itself becomes implausible.

The direction of current events adds irony to urgency. Even as the need to understand the contemporary Middle East grows, the possibility of conducting field research in it diminishes. This need not be an unmitigated disaster, for the problems of the Middle East are not problems internal to local culture or social structure. They are problems internal to relationships connected across the planet by airplanes, oil pipelines, wire transfers, and satellite TV; soured deals and partnerships in business and war; underemployed armies, mercenaries, militias, and military-industrial complexes; overemployed visuals coursing through electronic media; and steady streams of educational, technological, and arms transfers. While political scientists are scrambling to understand the entry of "non-state actors" into the clubby world of foreign affairs, anthropologists coming from the other direction are struggling to understand the leviathans impinging upon the lives

"There is today a palpable sense that one is seeing history in the making . . . [T]his has intensified anthropology's long-standing focus on the present: to be a participant observer no longer of one foreign culture, but in the tortured plurality of international history."

of peoples everywhere. This collapsing of disciplinary distances does not change, but rather intensifies the self-reinvention of anthropology of the past decade.

As professional amateurs inhabiting a discipline that never ceded its integrative ambitions in a world of specialists, anthropologists have been asking themselves such questions as: Does one keep the same ethnographic method but apply it to many more sites, or does the elusiveness of transnational phenomena require new approaches? Are symbolic, linguistic, and discursive analyses of collective representations, which transitioned so smoothly from tribal totems to ethnic and nationalist repertoires, helpful in understanding the images of terrorist acts and war crimes that shift and shape novel international constituencies and national voting blocs in continually evolving ways? Having hardly developed an anthropology of the state, how are we to chart its relations with ghostly "non-state actors," some of whom we've met on other occasions as "informants"? What are our units of analysis and geographical range? Should we seek greater levels of analytical abstraction to capture the global events that swamp every local place we touch? Or should we work through wide but concrete subregional relations? And, more recently, is post-colonial theory right in relegating colonialism to the past, or should we look beyond the present for hints of what an ethnography of empire might look like?

Old World Societies

Anthropologists need to study the Middle East because very little in the region can be adequately captured by the forms of methodological naiveté usually associated with ethnography's focus on the present, aural, particular, and internally cohesive. In the Middle East, as throughout the Old World, peoples from different places have long been in contact with one another, in ongoing relations of trade, tribute, raiding, warfare, intermarriage, conversion, enslavement, borrowing. The Silk Road, the Indian Ocean, the Mediterranean Sea, the Sahara—these are geographical labels for networks of routes that hosted such encounters. Numerous such routes met in the region designated by the military term "Middle East" today, formerly the "Near East" when the Ottomans were a problem for Europe. It is an old saw that the Middle East is a

⟳ **"This collapsing of disciplinary distances does not change, but rather intensifies the self-reinvention of anthropology of the past decade."**

space of transit across which mobile peoples, religions, states, and ideas travel and meet. In the Old World, no encounter is ever really new; there have not been diverse, separate cultures, religions, or languages come into fresh contact for a very, very long time. A host of European armies is assembled in the Middle East today as was another a millennium ago, and a number of times in between. The Gaugin model of a Pacific island anthropology both wide-eyed and jaded never worked here. As such, the old societies of the interconnected Old World, including the Middle East, provide a rich and instructive arena for developing new approaches to the study of encounters and connections on grand and miniature scales.

We can profit from such studies if we recognize that they provide starting points diametrically opposed to where anthropology began. Instead of simple, isolated cultures, they are complex, connected, and cosmopolitan fields of encounter. Instead of transpiring in a fictive and endless ethnographic present, they are constituted in an endless dialogue with pasts made real in archaeological sites, holy places and holy books, old buildings, sites of violence, tribal commons, historical chronicles, long-standing claims and counter-claims to truth as to territory. Instead of a founding unequal encounter between industrial colonizer and primitive native, we see a long and changing series of relations of domination, reversal, accommodation, assimilation, polarization, departure, return—a virtual kaleidoscope of social relations, if you will. Instead of the clear racial divides and broad parade grounds of late-colonial plural societies, we have here intimacies and distinctions rigged up at very close quarters. In the Middle East, connectedness, complexity, and cosmopolitanism are not products of modernity, but aspects of history.

Dialogues beyond Place: Complex Arts of Representation

So conceived, the anthropologist's Middle East is found not only seven thousand miles away in "the field," but here on campus as well. In language, literature, art, history, law, film, gender studies, music, history of science, philosophy, religion, government, and business, the Middle East is studied and taught on this campus in arenas beyond the confines of the aural and the present that still immure the new transnational anthropology. In all these spheres,

> "[CMES] can provide opportunities for shaping an anthroplogy that is cosmopolitan, unafraid of complexity, and eager to find out more than what exists in the present in aurally accessible media."

the Middle East has been in engagement with other regions. The products of these encounters studied by scholars are generated by complex arts of representation that are not simply expressions of a particular culture or set of collective self-representations. Rather, they are artifacts of continual dialogues beyond place, time, and culture. Musical scales, building proportions, conceptions of divinity, inter-textual quotations, legal codes, techniques of cooking and body hygiene are circulated, transformed, incorporated, rejected, discussed, and pronounced upon in numerous ways beyond a simple diffusion of cultural traits or exchange of economic goods. They enable us to imagine encounters of many sorts beyond the gross categories of peoples, states, cultures, and ethnic groups traditional to the social sciences, and challenge anthropologists to locate the peoples they study within such wider and more intricate fields of interaction. They push us to be more nimble in moving between scales of analysis and levels of abstraction. By providing a concourse in which anthropologists can mingle with scholars in other fields, the Center for Middle Eastern Studies can provide opportunities for shaping an anthropology that is cosmopolitan, unafraid of complexity, and eager to find out more than what exists in the present in aurally accessible media. The joint PhD in Anthropology and Middle Eastern Studies we already share provides an invaluable framework and support for this work. As well, it has given the Middle East a presence in the Anthropology Department as one of the largest research groupings, next to medical anthropology. This has allowed us to run a regular graduate anthropology workshop on the Middle East as a transnational arena for the past three years, joined by colleagues from area universities.

As we seek to develop anthropological attitudes beyond the local, I think the complex arts of representation provide platforms for joint explorations with other disciplines. Such arts are efforts at structuring encounters between different materials, styles, sensibilities, and genres of divergent provenance. As arts, their products are crafted with human purposes in mind, which can be understood by others. As representations, they involve the sorts of symbolic and communicable objects of human reflection with which anthropologists are already familiar. Even if in miniature, they may already be the kinds of complex, connected, and cosmopolitan fields of encounter with which anthropologists have to learn to recognize and work.

⟳ "Instead of a founding unequal encounter between industrial colonizer and primitive native, we see a long and changing series of relations of domination, reversal, accommodation, assimilation, polarization, departure, return—a virtual kaleidoscope of social relations."

To give one example, textuality is a medium in which such arts are pervasive, and their effects so profound that the space for an anthropology that begins and ends with only aural sources seems increasingly small in the Middle East. Not to put too fine a point on it, but it is probably no coincidence that the monotheisms originating in this region, which have traveled so far afield, are "religions of the book." Writing travels, and with it much else as well. Like empires, religions can be very mobile. What sustains that mobility is not sheer force of arms or conviction, but sophisticated means of communication. But this is not simply about diffusion, one place becoming more and more like another. As means of communication, writing serves as routes of encounter; as medium of representation, writing enables the articulation of complexities that accompany and amplify encounters. Such encounters can also subsist in time, as in intertextual relations that entangle the three literate monotheisms, sharing genealogies as they do prophets. We are not, of course, talking about transmission, but more difficult matters.

These difficult matters include the practice of anthropological writing itself, and here is perhaps something anthropology could offer colleagues in CMES. Beginning with Talal Asad's 1973 *Anthropology and the Colonial Encounter,* and with added force following upon Edward Said's 1978 *Orientalism,* anthropologists have unleashed upon themselves and their predecessors waves of criticism. The concern has been about representation, specifically the claim of anthropological writing to represent others. Asad's critique highlighted the power inequality straddling that representational divide. Said identified a tradition of representing others, evincing persistent tropes despite the experiences and efforts of different individuals. Middle East anthropologists were especially prominent in working out critical and adventurous responses to those challenges, as in the writings of Michael M. J. Fischer, Paul Rabinow, Kevin Dwyer, and Vincent Crapanzano through the following decade. I suspect that these ethnographers of Middle Eastern societies shared an underlying unease with anthropology as a project of translation from the aural world of their fieldwork encounters to the literate art of ethnographic representation. Clifford Geertz had taught them to think of cultural interpretation as textual hermeneutics, but this is to say that the cultures being represented in anthropological writing were being given honorary status as literature. Ethnography translated from an aural culture

> "[A]nthropologists have unleashed upon themselves and their predecessors waves of criticism. The concern has been about representation, specifically the claim of anthropological writing to represent others."

> "[A]nthropological attentiveness to issues of medium, genre, and translation can be our contribution to studying the encounters and entanglements that beset the connected, complex, and cosmopolitan Middle East."

to a written text: here perhaps was another inequality, another long-standing trope that might bear some relation to the gauntlets Asad and Said had thrown down. What if anthropology were about translation from one literate tradition to another? Or about the creation of a new canonical text (a classic ethnography) out of the canonically dominated texts of another tradition? Is that possible? Advisable? If complex arts of representation are where it is fruitful for anthropology to play with other disciplines, anthropological attentiveness to issues of medium, genre, and translation can be our contribution to studying the encounters and entanglements that beset the connected, complex, and cosmopolitan Middle East, in the Old World and the new era.

In all this, it is important to re-affirm that the university is sovereign in its own domain. Scholarship is a transnational enterprise that, though vulnerable within individual states, outdistances them in the long run. In a world of conflicting national interests saturated with propaganda, it is important that scholarship remain able to prosecute its own ways of adjudicating truths and values. While these may be propagated throughout the body politic, at a minimum they must be jealously guarded at the gates.

For CMES, and for Harvard at large, the interest and the opportunities are immense.

Music

Virginia Danielson

Virginia Danielson is the Richard F. French Librarian of the Loeb Music Library at Harvard University and Curator of the University's Archive of World Music. An ethnomusicologist by training, Danielson is author of the award-winning monograph *The Voice of Egypt: Umm Kulthūm: Arabic Song and Egyptian Society in the Twentieth Century* (University of Chicago Press, 1997) and co-editor of *The Middle East,* volume 6 of *The Garland Encyclopedia of World Music* (Routledge, 2002). She has authored numerous articles on musics of the Middle East, women in Middle Eastern music, and Muslim devotional music. She also has served as principal advisor to the film *A Voice Like Egypt,* one of two documentaries premiered at the New York Film Festival in 1996. She holds a PhD in ethnomusicology from the University of Illinois.

Over the past fifteen years, the study and performance of Middle Eastern music—or, better, musics, considering the rich diversity of traditions and practices in the region—have received increasing attention from the Center for Middle Eastern Studies. The Center has supported initiatives from both faculty and students admirably. Programs have engaged the musical traditions of North Africa, the Mashriq, Turkey, Israel and Palestine, Iran, Afghanistan, Iraq, and the Arabian Peninsula as well as issues related to music in Islamic devotional expression generally.

The types of programs offered have included public lectures on the scholarly aspects of Middle Eastern music, performances by major solo musicians, coaching and performance of student ensembles, musical films, and lecture-demonstrations on technical aspects of Middle Eastern musical styles. A few specific examples follow.

The major international virtuoso, Simon Shaheen, has given several concerts in Paine Hall and Sanders Theater, has offered dozens of master classes on musical technique, and has appeared a number of times in Harvard classes to discuss musical aesthetics and style. The Lalezar Turkish ensemble has visited the University for weeklong residencies, teaching classes and offering performances. Led by instrumental virtuoso Reha Sagbas and his wife Selma, an exquisitely accomplished and gifted singer, their last visit included a performance of Muslim devotional music introduced by three Harvard faculty members speaking about Islamic devotional expression, Turkish Sufism, and Islamic devotional music. This event, as our programs typically do, brought together numerous disciplines including musicology and music theory, ethnomusicology, composition, improvisation, gender studies, Middle Eastern history, and religious studies. Classes and lecture demonstrations have been offered by local musicians, including Kareem

Mohammed (percussion), Fred Stubbs (Turkish end-blown flute or ney), Jamal Sinno (Arab plucked zither, or qanun), and Feridun Ozgoren (Turkish music and musical instruments). A local classical Arab chorus, the Tarab Chorus, offered a concert in Paine Hall. Speakers have included Dr. Sherifa Zuhur, Professor Walter Armbrust, Professor Stephen Blum, Professor Steven Caton, Professor Deborah Kapchan, Professor John Baily, and Professor Anne Rasmussen. Respectively, they spoke on Farid al-Atrash, Egyptian film music, Kurdish song, Yemeni sung poetry, Moroccan gnawa performance in diasporic contexts, Afghani classical music, and the music of Arab Americans. The well-known Indonesian Quran reciter, Maria Ulfah, visited the University to speak about and demonstrate recitation.

A University-wide Appeal

These events have had wide appeal across the University. The Center has attracted many University partners, including the Music Department, the Eda Kuhn Loeb Music Library with its Archive of World Music, the Humanities Center, the Center for the Study of World Religions, the Near Eastern Languages and Civilizations Department, the Anthropology Department, the Islamic Legal Studies Program, and the Office for the Arts. These relationships have yielded fruitful cross-fertilizations.

Among all of these very good events, the Center has usually supported a performing ensemble consisting of students and local community members. This has been our most successful enterprise. Student interest in musical performance has increased dramatically over the years. It manifests itself by a more or less continuous interest in mashriqi Arab classical music and the spontaneous emergence of two or three Turkish ensembles as well as a Moroccan classical and devotional group. These groups have sprung up on their own with little faculty intervention, a fact that demonstrates the high degree of interest, even demand, for well-coached playing opportunities. The groups work best when professionally coached. We have been lucky, working with a number of donors and sister institutions, to have had the services of Dr. Nilgun Dogrusoz, William Nakhly, and, most recently, the international virtuoso Bassam Saba for periods of years. It is this particular activity around which we should plan our future.

"One of the beauties of placing ensemble coaching at the heart of the Center's music programming is the opportunity for the coach to offer ancillary lectures, classes, and lecture-demonstrations."

While, at first blush, concert sponsorship for programs by major musicians may seem the most attractive enterprise in a major university, in fact this is labor intensive (especially for faculty and administrators unaccustomed to the specialized needs of such work). In a major urban area such as Boston, such programming may be best left to local professional concert agencies and the like. Similarly, film series are difficult for non-professionals to do well. We are frequently presented with difficulties in finding good-quality copies of major films, the absence of subtitles to make films widely accessible, and a paucity of suitable available viewing spaces. On the other hand, the Harvard Film Archive and the Museum of Fine Arts in Boston both provide excellent film series that include the Middle East. We would probably do best to support these efforts rather than replicate them.

Most importantly, we are a teaching institution. Listening to the best concert does not seem to provide the real learning experience that hands-on playing under the supervision of an excellent coach does. In this context, students can work by themselves and with a superior musician, learning aesthetics, technique, and style over time as one would a language, for instance. The entire experience has the depth one would expect of a major university program.

Of course, few institutions would coach music without some way of expanding students' understanding of music in social, cultural, and historical context. The Music Department has consistently offered courses in musics of the Middle East, music in Islamic contexts, and musics of Israel and the Jewish diaspora. Additional courses, such as Professor Ali Asani's popular undergraduate class on Islam through the Arts, are offered through the departments of Anthropology and History and the Committee on Religious Studies. One of the beauties of placing ensemble coaching at the heart of the Center's music programming is the opportunity for the coach to offer ancillary lectures, classes, and lecture-demonstrations in support of the regular course curriculum.

Performance and teaching at Harvard are supported by what are probably the richest library collections in North America. The Judaica Collection is unparalleled in the world. The Archive of World Music offers nearly 20,000 audio recordings, with the Middle East as one of its primary strengths. The print collections of the University are legendary, including volumes of notations of Turkish classical music given to the library by the Sema Vakf

> "[R]ecordings of Center-sponsored demonstrations, classes, and performances will yield an archive of musical documentation that will be useful to future generations at Harvard."

Foundation and historic works such as al-Haik's collection of the 24 Moroccan classical suites or nawbat. These collections offer rich source materials for research and performance of Middle Eastern musics.

Given the proper support, recordings of Center-sponsored demonstrations, classes, and performances will yield an archive of musical documentation that will be useful to future generations at Harvard, to the CMES Outreach Center, and to the study of the history of Middle Eastern music itself. Certainly, every event will not require archival treatment. For those that do, additional support is needed here—not just for the costs of recording but also for preservation, using Harvard's emerging state-of-the-art facilities including its Audio Preservation Services and its Digital Repository.

Future Imperatives

Thus our experience to date suggests a number of imperatives for the future with attendant requirements for the deployment of resources. First, professional coaching is essential. Our students need the same excellent models of musicianship for Middle Eastern musics that abound in many contexts for Western music. Observing an excellent performer over the course of an evening or a daylong program has nowhere near the profound learning impact of working with an accomplished musician over a period of months. Ensuring excellent teaching implies adequate fees for the coach, lodging (since expert performers often come from outside of the immediate area), provision of rehearsal and performance space, and an archiving program for some, if not all, of the results of this program. A consistently funded visiting artists program sponsored by the Center would be an excellent and durable line of approach. Building from the strong partnerships already established by the Center, this could be integrated into multiple courses and programs, but its interests would need to expand beyond single-day events. To address the need for a visiting artist, the Office for the Arts seems an obvious partner, and relevant academic departments or other centers would be other helpful collaborators. Funding agencies for innovative teaching programs may also be good partners.

Concerning the critical issue of space, the Music Department

> "Our students need the same excellent models of musicianship for Middle Eastern musics that abound in many contexts for Western music."

has unanimously and continuously decried the lack of sufficient space for their own ensemble coaching and practice, not to mention for student ensembles such as the Middle East Music Study Group. In an interdisciplinary world where expressive culture plays a role in many areas of research and teaching, the lack of practice and performance space becomes everyone's problem. We need to make common cause to improve the opportunities for students to systematically learn from virtuosic performers.

To maximize the impact of sponsored events, we need to fund a recording program that will help build an archive of performances, lecture-demonstrations, and other events high in informational value. This collection will advance outreach programs in our communities as well as further teaching and research at Harvard.

The time is now to build arts programs that will acquaint our students and colleagues with Middle Eastern cultures in an informed, intelligent, historically contextualized manner. Furthering such a music program, already initiated by the Center, should be central to its mission in the future.

> "We need to make common cause to improve the opportunities for students to systematically learn from virtuosic performers."

Studying the distinctive development of cities in the Middle East and the Muslim world at large

Urban Design

Hashim Sarkis

Hashim Sarkis is the Aga Khan Professor of Landscape Architecture and Urbanism in Muslim Societies. He teaches design studios and courses in the history and theory of architecture. A practicing architect in both Cambridge and Lebanon, his projects include a housing complex for the fishermen of Tyre, a park in downtown Beirut, two schools in the North Lebanon region, and several urban and landscape projects. His publications include *Circa 1958: Lebanon in the Pictures and Plans of Constaninos Doxiadis* (Dar Annahar, 2003). He is also co-editor of *Projecting Beirut: Episodes in the Construction and Reconstruction of a Modern City* (Prestel, 1998). In addition to directing the Aga Khan program of activities at the Graduate School of Design associated with the Aga Khan Chair, he is director of the Master in Design Studies and the Doctorate of Design programs. He earned a PhD in architecture from Harvard and he has also taught at MIT, Yale, and the American University of Beirut.

Since the end of World War II, the environment of the Third World has been radically transformed by economic and social development: an ambitious modernist project that spanned continents and was considered by many to be a sign of progress, enlightenment, and emancipation. Muslim nation-states and societies have been part of this project, whether in countries guided by the development strategies of the Bretton Woods institutions, such as those of North Africa, the Middle East, and Southeast Asia, or in countries influenced by the planning models of the Soviet bloc, such as some Turkic states and Eastern European countries. This project was never without problems and contradictions, however. While it provided electricity, telephone connections, and roads in the territories of these states, it often destroyed local industrial plant and agricultural production and adversely affected land tenure and population distribution as well. Given the lack of resources, development policies were hardly ever fully or evenly implemented. In spite of these problems, development nevertheless provided the citizens of these countries with a collective identity and hope for the future. Indeed, the quest for economic improvement and social emancipation justifiably persists to this day, even though the policies and mechanisms of implementation have changed in the fifty years since their inception.

The metropolis (e.g., Cairo, Istanbul, Karachi, and Kuala Lumpur) and its rapid growth have consumed the energy of Muslim states' development policies, not to mention urban design and planning professions and academic disciplines concerned with urban design and development. With cities such as Cairo boasting a growth rate of three people every ten minutes, it is perfectly understandable that urbanization would receive so much attention, even though Muslim societies were, and continue to be, relatively rural. Official statements to the contrary, rural areas have in general been neglected, with the result that the gap between city and country has widened. For example, urban planners do not pay enough attention to land tenure patterns outside cities, even though these patterns are more influential in shaping urban growth than urban development master plans, which hardly get implemented anyway. Nor is much attention paid to secondary cities (e.g., Konya in Central Anatolia, Aleppo in agro-industrial northern Syria, and Tanta in the agricultural Nile delta) that have maintained strong links with their regional surroundings. Here, the side-effects of development have produced unusual physical features such as agro-landscapes extending into cities, industrial networks in desert areas, and advanced agro-industries catering to global niche markets from remote rural districts. None of these has received the serious and intense study they need. They challenge the urban/rural distinction and conventional disciplinary models of architecture/urban design/landscape.

Regional Challenges

At a time when we are being challenged to operate in a globalized building context, is it not outdated to propose regionally specific concerns? Are not Dubai and Beirut cosmopolitan centers? For example, the glitzy framing skills of *Wallpaper Magazine's* editors may make downtown Beirut look like downtown London, but even their reporters would have a hard time globalizing the tobacco-producing villages of South Lebanon, sixty kilometers away. I do not wish to extol the specifics of regions or to highlight their differences for their own sake; but I do wish to emphasize that the discussion about globalization tends to gloss over developmental differences between regions, defined in terms of stages, aims, and mechanisms. Furthermore, the encounter with colonialism is also important for understanding the emergence of regionally distinctive urbanism such as one finds in the Middle East. I have in mind not only European ideas about urbanism that have influenced the modernization of cities in developing countries, but also the ways in which urban planning and design ideas emanating from the Third World have contributed to the modernist project at large.

Clearly, the idea of a regional urban and landscape studies program that takes development into account in all the ways

"[T]he side effects of development have produced unusual physical features such as agro-landscapes extending into cities, industrial networks in desert areas, and advanced agro-industries catering to global niche markets from remote rural districts. None of these has received the serious and intense study they need."

suggested above has to be at the heart of the study of design in the Muslim world. The Graduate School of Design (GSD) at Harvard University, thanks to a generous grant from the Aga Khan Trust for Culture, extending for five years from 2003 to 2008, will be at the forefront of such study. The Aga Khan Trust supports cultural activities in the Muslim world, most notably architecture and the preservation of historic cities, and it has provided the GSD with funds to initiate and conduct various activities related to contemporary landscape and urban design in Muslim societies. These activities range from supporting courses and faculty research on the contemporary Muslim world to supporting universities in the Muslim world that are seeking to establish programs in landscape and urban design; they also include conferences, research, lectures and exhibitions. The fund will support qualified students from all departments within the GSD and the University at large. By looking at the shape of the land, land use and territorial settlement patterns, environmental issues, and the use of public space, the Aga Khan Program will address the historical development of cities in the Muslim world and the Middle East more specifically.

Cross-Fertilization

This initiative is uniquely situated both in the GSD and in Harvard at large. Until the Aga Khan Program was created three years ago, the GSD had no regional chairs. Its faculty was organized primarily by subdisciplinary interests rather than by geographic regions. The one exception was the school's focus on the region that lies between the Danube and the Mississippi (its capital shifting between Paris and Rome). Over the past decade, however, a real interest has expanded to include Asia and Latin America, and now the Middle East and Muslim societies more generally have been added to the list.

In light of this burgeoning interest within the GSD in Middle Eastern urban and landscape design problems, it stands to reason that the Aga Khan Program and the Center for Middle Eastern Studies would both benefit from collaborative intellectual exchanges. To begin with, building ties with CMES will help to strengthen the Aga Khan's Middle East and Muslim society focus within the GSD. Moreover, development is a topic

> "[T]he discussion about globalization tends to gloss over developmental differences between regions, defined in terms of stages, aims, and mechanisms."

that anthropologists, political scientists, sociologists, economists, and historians of the Middle East have tackled critically for some time, and their knowledge would be invaluable to design students. Conversely, even though the concept of the Muslim city is a relatively old one in Middle Eastern studies, it has never been given a precise architectural designation, which is what the Aga Khan Program at the GSD is attempting to provide. Insofar as the Muslim city has been studied at all, the emphasis has been on traditional and not contemporary urban spaces—not to mention their relations with each other—a lacuna in our understanding of the city that the GSD is trying to fill. And this is only the beginning of some of the exciting cross-fertilization that might take place in the future between CMES and the GSD.

"[E]ven though the concept of the Muslim city is a relatively old one in Middle Eastern studies, it has never been given a precise architectural designation."

A challenge at once profoundly intellectual and eminently practical

Health Care and Social Development

Salmaan Keshavjee

Salmaan Keshavjee is a Research
Associate at CMES, where he directs
the CMES Working Group on Health
and Social Change in the Middle East
and Central Asia. He has helped to run
the CMES Gender Seminar series, which
has focused on issues of gender and
health in the Middle East. In addition,
he has been a research fellow in the
Department of Social Medicine at the
Harvard Medical School. He is pursuing
research on a host of theoretical and
policy issues in health care and social
development while completing a clinical
residency at Harvard's Brigham and
Women's Hospital. He obtained a
degree in the CMES AM program in
1995 and a PhD in Anthropology in
Middle Eastern Studies in 1998, writing
a dissertation on the political economy
of health and social change in post-
Soviet Tajikistan. That same year he
went to medical school at Stanford,
where he completed an MD in 2001,
before returning to Harvard.

The region of the world that I refer to here as the Middle East and Central Asia spans from North Africa to the ancient Silk Road, and is home to almost half a billion inhabitants. It is well known that the majority of this population bears enormous burdens of poverty and disease, not unlike the poor parts of Africa, Asia, and Latin America. (World Health Organization, *The World Health Report, 2004.*) What is different about the Middle East and Central Asia is the type of colonial and post-colonial experiences, the fact that Islam has been the dominant religious and political force for fourteen centuries, and, in Central Asia, the legacy of seven decades of Soviet rule.

In terms of the daily reality faced by millions in the region, the basic human development indicators are revealing. The countries of the Middle East and Central Asia are disproportionately concentrated in the lower income and lower-middle income groups. (United Nations Development Program, *Human Development Report, 2000.*) Life expectancy at birth in Central Asia is 64 years and in the Middle East 68 years: fourteen years and ten years lower than in the high-income countries, respectively. In the Middle East the infant mortality rate is almost six times—and in Central Asia more than ten times—those of high-income countries. Likewise, compared with high-income countries, the under-five mortality rate is almost seven times those in the Middle East and more than fourteen times those in Central Asia. The great majority of premature deaths are due to treatable and often preventable diseases.

Closing these gaps will require both a strengthening of the region's capacity to deliver accessible, quality medical care, and a comprehensive understanding of the historical and social processes at the core of the regions' development and underdevelopment. In this enormous practical and analytic task, what role might there be for a research university such as ours—respected widely for its social science, humanities, and medical research and teaching—and for the Center for Middle Eastern Studies in particular? I propose here some challenges that present themselves immediately if we are to engage this task in its complexity.

Intellectual Challenges

The intellectual questions at the nexus of health care and social development in the Middle East and Central Asia are certainly vast. I venture here to identify only some areas of inquiry that seem intricately tied to the task of understanding and improving health care and health outcomes in the region.

It is critical to keep in mind that not only are the peoples of the Middle East and Central Asia considered to be a religious "other"; the majority are also poor and disenfranchised. It is at the juncture of these two discursive categories—Islam and global postcolonial development—that our understanding of and contribution to improvements in the delivery of health and social services in the region is located. Rigorous analysis of the contemporary situation will require what Farmer calls a "historically deep" and "geographically broad" analysis. (Paul E. Farmer, "On Suffering and Structural Violence: A View from Below," *Daedalus* [Fall 1999], pp. 261–83.)

Such an analysis would examine both the recent and remote historical processes around health and social development—and where appropriate the geographically distant ones—that are determinants of current health and social circumstances. This will require understanding both the antecedents to and the complex processes associated with the large burdens of infectious and chronic diseases, such as diarrheal and respiratory disease, tuberculosis, diabetes, and HIV/AIDS, and their associated morbidity and mortality.

Of course, one cannot study the contemporary Middle East and Central Asia without considering Islam. The second major intellectual challenge will be to understand the roles that Islam—politically, religiously, and socially—has played historically and currently in the area of health and medicine. Of salience too will be the modern search for Islamic authenticity in the face of post-colonial, neo-colonial, and globalizing forces. There is also a need

> ☯ "There is also a need to identify and delineate what may be called an Islamic ethic (or ethics) around health and social development."

to identify and delineate what may be called an Islamic ethic (or ethics) around health and social development, and to elucidate and describe how global and local political and economic orders interact with traditions and interpretations rooted in the Islamic tradition. Of particular interest are the local moral and ethical responses to long-term problems such as poverty, inequality, and underdevelopment, and also to newer issues such as communal violence, organ transplantation, and stem-cell research.

Finally, a third challenge will be to understand how institutions of civil society have addressed questions around health and social development in the Middle East and Central Asia. Since the early days of Islam, institutions of social development, such as *waqf* and Islamic charities, have formed a basis for civil society and have played a crucial role in local and regional development and social change. By understanding and studying the processes around these forms of organization, one can obtain a sound analytic purchase on how historical and contemporary institutions provide mechanisms for addressing current health and social problems. The diverging experience of those nations that experienced recent Soviet rule will be additionally informative.

Applied Challenges

The applied challenges inherent in the task of improving medical care and social services in the region are also enormous. Here I identify what I consider to be areas that could have an immediate tangible impact and may provide openings for larger collaborations.

First, accurate descriptive data are needed about the burden of infectious and chronic diseases and their impact on development. Poverty, urbanization and crowding, limited popular political participation, the reduction of the welfare state, the absence of tangible state social institutions, and the privatization of social services dominate the lives of the majority in the Middle East and Central Asia. Having information about these processes is essential for participating in the questioning of resource distribution and its effect on human survival and security. Rather than being limited by what local and international resources *are available* to the region, in the interest of global security, the opportunity for

> "Part of this investigation will be to identify local institutions—symbolic, structural, and material— that could play a role in the long-term promotion of health and development."

scholars and practitioners will be to outline the extent of the local health problems and define what resources *must be made available* in order to address the urgent basic needs of the populations.

Identifying effective mechanisms for the delivery of medical services is the other principal challenge for scholars and practitioners working in the region. Many chronic and infectious diseases require complicated, long-term and sometimes life-long treatments. Operations research will be needed to learn how best to deliver complex health interventions to address these diseases in poor urban and rural settings. Part of this investigation will be to identify local institutions—symbolic, structural, and material—that could play a role in the long-term promotion of health and development. The task for novel partnerships will be to identify program models that can be used in the Middle East and Central Asia regions specifically. This will require collaboration between scholars of the social sciences, humanities, and medicine.

Closely tied to this is the need for advocacy work to ensure that access to life-saving medications and treatment models are available to all who require them. Using local and international models, the aim of applied research would be to build national and international public and private partnerships to provide resources, technical assistance, and necessary training.

Plans for Research and Teaching

The challenges outlined briefly above point to exciting opportunities for research and teaching. The Center for Middle Eastern Studies already hosts a multidisciplinary Working Group on Health and Social Change in the Middle East and Central Asia, which was founded in 2001 by Professor Mary-Jo Good, Diana Abouali, and me. Our aim is to bring together scholars and practitioners engaged with all aspects of health and development in the region. Toward this aim, we will conduct and promote contemporary and historical scholarship addressing the challenges articulated above.

Today, as the University embarks on a major global health initiative, the Center is well placed to take the lead in the region by building the initiatives of the Working Group into a unique

"Today, as the University embarks on a major global health initiative, the Center is well placed to take the lead in the region."

interdisciplinary program. Through its support, the Center will help meet the Working Group's short- and long-term objectives:

1. To develop courses focused on health, development, and social change in the region.
These courses will form the basis of a curriculum to train new scholars and practitioners from a range of disciplines and faculties.

2. To support undergraduate and graduate research.
We aim to encourage and support both archival and field-based investigations of the historical, social, political, economic, ethical, and epidemiological determinants of current health conditions.

3. To host fellows and visiting faculty.
A visiting scholar program will build new relationships with scholars working on topics related to historical and contemporary aspects of health and social development.

4. To form linkages with research sites in the region.
These active collaborations will make possible mentored, long-term experiences for students and for the evaluation of our collective activities. A proactive set of field-based programs coupled to systematic historical and social analyses will both strengthen ongoing research and contribute to much-needed thinking on current problems in the region.

5. To convene workshops and conferences.
These fora will bring together scholars and practitioners engaged in the study of health and development in the region. The Working Group has already begun to draw in scholars from inside and outside our University. We hosted a two-year seminar series on gender and health in the region; in 2005 we will hold a conference on the historical role of waqf in social development.

6. To construct and manage a virtual database of students, scholars, and practitioners.
This resource will support a dynamic network of local and international actors linked by their common interest in health and development in the region. Working toward these objectives will permit us to build a lasting network of scholars that will both expand the current base of published scholarship and support research and educational programs devoted to the Middle East and Central Asia.

⟳ "[A] . . . challenge will be to understand how institutions of civil society have addressed questions around health and social development in the Middle East and Central Asia."

Conclusions

Tackling the enormous issues surrounding health and social change in the Middle East and Central Asia presents a major task for scholars and practitioners. The Working Group on Health and Social Change in the Middle East and Central Asia at CMES aims to tap the potential of our rich academic environment to make major contributions in these efforts through scholarship, teaching, and field-based research and programmatic work. Especially promising is the unique potential for collaboration across disciplines and faculties, and, through the Center, the international promotion and dissemination of this work so that it may inform global, regional, and national social policies affecting the health of millions living in poverty in the Middle East and Central Asia.

"Especially promising is the unique potential for collaboration across disciplines and faculties, and, through the Center, the international promotion and dissemination of this work."